a glossary of behavioral terminology

compiled & edited by

owen r. white, ph.d.

College of Education   University of Oregon   Eugene, Oregon

Research Press Company
2612 North Mattis Ave.
Champaign, Illinois 61820

To the children,
may we learn and grow
as readily as they.

ACKNOWLEDGEMENTS

I would like to acknowledge the support of Dr. James Crosson, without whom this work might never have been started; the numerous people throughout the United States and abroad who requested the original drafts and encouraged me to continue the work; my wife, Peggy, for her patience; and most importantly, Martin Waechter, for his invaluable assistance in compiling and proofing the final manuscript.

preface

The science of behavior, like all other sciences, is an attempt to systematize observable and empirically demonstrable relationships between natural phenomena, and to state those observations in the form of general "laws" which allow for the prediction and control of those phenomena. Observations of operations, processes, and functional relationships which are to lead to this end must be recorded and communicated in explicit, unambiguous terms. In compliance with this demand, a language of behaviorism has evolved and will continue to evolve.

As in the development of any language system, the majority of behavioral terms were derived or created to convey an explicit meaning. Unfortunately, however, it is often the case that the original meanings of the terms employed were never actually recorded, or lie hidden in the context of some lengthy research article. Without clear reference it is easy for the meaning of a term to alter over time as specific contexts change. The result of this "drifting" is a diversity of usages for terms which connote specificity.

This gradual redefinition makes communication between differing orientations difficult, and often renders the review of earlier works nearly impossible. This is not to say that a scientific language should not change. Indeed, with the development of new techniques, greater amounts of data, and the reformulation or addition of new behavioral principles, the language *should* change. The problem lies in the fact that often we are *unaware* of the change, or that the change may take more than one direction in the laboratories or classrooms of different schools. It is not the purpose of this text, therefore, to set once and for all the absolute meaning of a set of terms; but rather, to offer reference whereby changes may be more clearly noted and evaluated.

The terms in this glossary were compiled from glossaries, basic texts, reference volumes, and the current professional literature—as well as, of course, from direct communication with people currently working in the various behavioral areas. Because a list of contributing sources would fill a volume equal to if not greater than the text, one is not included.

Although some three years of research have already been invested in the compilation of this glossary, the work is far from finished. Indeed, the behavioral language will most likely change more in the next two years than it has in the past ten. In order to adequately document (and, thereby, facilitate) these changes, the Glossary will be updated and reprinted periodically as the circumstances warrant. Considering that the normal publication lag in the journals is close to or exceeding one year, the reader may be of great assistance to the continued process of revision if he communicates his comments and suggested revisions or additions to the Glossary directly to Owen R. White, c/o Research Press Company. If submitted terms or phrases are accompanied by references of use and contextual examples, the editorial staff will find it much easier to correlate the suggested revision or addition with other terms or uses of the same term. All communications will be gratefully acknowledged, and where possible, disposition of the suggestion explained.

Finally, if there are any questions regarding the terms defined in this glossary, or if the user wishes this editor to review and comment on any new term or system of analysis the user may construct, the editor would be more than happy to be of assistance. Whether recourse is through this editor or not, however, the purpose of language is to *communicate*, and any deviations from the usage denoted in this reference (the only one presently available) should either be *tested* for clarity on an unbiased audience, or clearly defined within the context of its use.

how to use the glossary

Generally speaking, a glossary is used like a dictionary. There are, however, some standard differences. First, a glossary will not usually break down its terms into syllables, and rarely will include an explanation of pronunciation. Perhaps the most significant difference, though, is the inclusion of several *phrases* in glossaries, while dictionaries are most frequently limited to *words*; and herein lies the problem. Should "conditioned reinforcer" be defined under "C" for "conditioned," or "R" for "reinforcer"? Since "reinforcer" is the basic term, and "conditioned" is the modifier, the reader will find it listed under "reinforcer, conditioned." Where the significance of various modifiers is less easily determined, however, confusion as to where a term should appear might obtain. To alleviate this problem, and to reduce the rate of "page-flipping" behavior, a word list has been constructed.

The word list contains all words and phrases defined in the glossary in every logical sequence. Words or phrases in bold type are those that are defined in the main body of the glossary. Other terms and phrases in the list are cross-referenced to the term under which their definitions are included. In addition to aiding the user in finding a *known* word or phrase, the word list may also be used to discover if a term exists which might fulfill some special purpose. Since all terms and phrases are grouped according to common roots and modifiers, one need only to scan the pages on which the root or potential modifiers are listed. What, for example, does one call a stimulus which is presented only after the previous response? Glancing down the list of "stimuli" in the word list we find "stimulation, response controlled"; and checking its cross-referenced definition, we find that it meets our requirements. The problem is resolved *without recourse to the invention of a new term*.

Where possible, the rationale for each term and its usage is cited, and a statement made as to the relative advisability of the specific definition which appears to best parallel the majority of current professional opinion. Since many terms in behaviorism have similar, but distinctly unique definitions, and since it has been the trend of late for certain schools to develop parallel languages for use with other disciplines or for communication with "lay" audiences, the reader will find this text heavily cross-referenced. To best understand the specific meaning or use of a term, the editor suggests that all cross-references be investigated when looking up any one definition.

Another advantage of the cross-referencing and word list may be explicated by an experience this editor had in a recent review of the literature. While trying to track down articles bearing on operant-to-operant rates in chained schedules, an assistant was able to find only three references in the past five years. After having determined the possible *misuses* of several related terms (e.g., IRT and IRAT) through the glossary, 213 articles were uncovered that were directly related to the issue at hand. The amount of information which is never effectively communicated to interested parties due to the lack of an appropriate term must be immense.

Several of the terms in this glossary could, and have, had books written about them. It would be foolish to assume, therefore, that all terms and phrases defined are treated completely and in full detail with respect to their many potential applications. Some breadth in the interpretations may be required. An inability to reconcile the reader's understanding of the term and the definition contained herein in *any* way, however, should prompt a careful review of source and rationale. In any event, the editor would appreciate learning of any discrepancies which may arise.

If it becomes necessary for the user to coin a term not contained in this glossary, he is urged to do so within the *logic* of the already established system. An investigation of basic modifiers and roots (e.g., "stimulus" vs. "event") will aid the writer, and several considerations are reviewed in the Appendix. The Editor, who may be contacted through Research Press Company, will be glad to offer any assistance he can. Remember, however, the purpose of language is to *communicate*, not merely to sound impressive, or to become more complex. Choose your words carefully.

behavioral terms

Words in **boldface** are defined in the main body of the Glossary. To find the definition of a word shown in regular type, see the word indented below it.

A
Abbreviation for "Arrangement." See **Arrangement.**

Abscissa
The horizontal, or *x* axis of a graph. In psychology the independent variable is usually plotted on the abscissa. See Figure 1.

Abulia
1. An organism which responds at a low rate (usually assumed to be due to a large amount of behavior required for reinforcement).
2. A low rate performance as a result of a strained schedule. An abulia may or may not be sustained (i.e., it could be momentary, as in the strained and lean first moments of a large FI schedule of reinforcement). See Figure 2.

Figure 1.   **X-Axis or Abscissa:** The independent variable is usually plotted in this dimension.

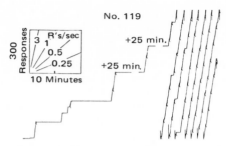

Figure 2. Abulia: Several abulias are evident in this cumulative record of a pigeon's performance under a large fixed-ratio schedule of reinforcement. Responding is recorded as vertical movement of the pen; and the passage of time as horizontal movement of the pen. Long periods of no responding may be noted, therefore, as long horizontal lines. Pauses following the delivery of reinforcement (noted as a short slash downward and to the right) under a fixed-ratio schedule are common, and would not usually be considered abulias for that reason. Several of the pauses in this record, however, occur *after* responding had already begun, but before reinforcement. As this is unusual in a fixed-ratio performance, those pauses *would* be called abulias, and taken to be indicative of a "strained schedule."[1]

Acceleration (Ac)

A change in the rate with which something is moving or occurring. In behaviorism, it is usually taken as the latter; and, more specifically, acceleration is usually taken as a change in the rate of responding of an organism. Literally, the change in rate may be either direction (i.e., a change to a slower rate or a change to a faster rate); but colloquially, acceleration is usually taken to connote an increase in rate. See also **Acceleration, Negative; Acceleration, Positive; Deceleration;** and **Plan Functions or Aims.**

Acceleration Analysis

In reference to any one of a number of possible procedures designed to analyze a set of sequentially dependent data (e.g., rate data collected on one subject over a period of several days) in which a consistent trend or progress may be expected to obtain. The purpose of analysis may be either simple *description* of that progress (e.g., describing how the subject in question progressed from day-to-day), *significance-testing* (i.e., determining the significance of any affect experimental conditions may have had on the progress or trend), or *prediction* (i.e., using the present data to estimate future performances of the same subject).

At present, no technique is available that has been designed

---

[1] Figure reprinted from "Fixed-ratio schedules of conditioned reinforcement with chimpanzees" by R. T. Kelleher, *Journal of the Experimental Analysis of Behavior,* 1958, *1*, 281—289. Copyright © 1958 by the Society for the Experimental Analysis of Behavior, Inc. Used by permission of the author and publisher.

and validated to perform *all* of the above functions simultaneously. Auto-correlation, for example, will define the nature of the sequential dependency, but may not be used (alone) in significance-testing or prediction. Auto-regression and the exponentially-weighted-moving-average may be useful in significance-testing, but since they remove the sequential dependency, they may not serve useful descriptive or predictive functions. The corrected-median-slope technique is presently used to describe progress and predict future performances, but has not been validated as a significance-testing design.

Acceleration analysis has also been called "trend analysis" or "time-series analysis"; but the latter in particular is more easily differentiated from the others in that it implies the *removal* of trend or dependency before analysis, rather than the specific *utilization* of that trend or dependency for descriptive and/or predictive purposes. See also **Line-of-Progress.**

Acceleration Finder

A device (usually transparent) used for determining the slopes of lines-of-progress. Each acceleration finder must be matched to the chart on which it will be used. Examples of two acceleration finders constructed for use on the standard Precision Teaching behavior chart are shown in Figures 3 and 4. See also **Line-of-Progress** and **Slope.**

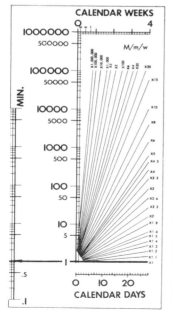

Figure 3. Acceleration Finder with Slopes: This acceleration finder, designed for use on the Standard Precision Teaching Behavior Chart, is used by matching the lines on the finder with the line on the chart for which the slope is desired. If necessary, interpolation between lines is performed. Care must be taken, of course, to keep the acceleration finder straight up and down on the chart. The lines on the finder are labeled in terms of "movements per minute per week," or, the factor by which the value of the line will be multiplied for each week it is extended.

To find the slope of a deceleration line, simple invert the finder so all the slopes point down and read the slope factors as "dividby" instead of "times."

3

Figure 4. Acceleration Finder with Expanded Scale: This acceleration finder, also designed for use on the Standard Precision Teaching Behavior Chart, represents a different approach to the determination of the slope of the line. The arrow on the left-hand scale is placed at some point on the line (keeping the finder vertical on the chart). The point at which the line in question crosses the right-hand scale indicates the slope of that line in terms of "movements per minute per week," or, the factor by which the value of the line is multiplied each week it is extended. If the line does not extend the full four weeks necessary to cross the right-hand scale, a straightedge may be placed beside it to indicate where it would go. By eliminating all of the actual lines indicating possible slopes (see Figure 3), the expanded right-hand scale may be considerably more detailed—thereby eliminating the need for most interpolation. The right-hand scale represents, simply, one highly detailed cycle of the standard chart expanded to four times its usual size and placed exactly four weeks to the right of the origin.

Deceleration slopes may be determined by inverting the finder so that the "x10" part of the right-hand scale is on the bottom (but still to the right). If slopes exceed an "x10" range, then a mark is placed by the 10, and the entire scale moved up so the "x1" is where the "x10" used to be. The new cycle is then from "x10" to "x100" (simply add a zero to every number on the scale). Movement may be continued, of course, to any range, adding a zero with each new cycle.

The lower part of this acceleration finder is marked off in two log scales corresponding to the scales directly above them. These, plus the notation of the fractional parts of a week, allow the analyst to convert the charted rates into logs and calculate the slopes or other statistics with greater accuracy.

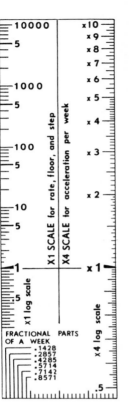

Acceleration, Negative

A change in the rate with which something is moving or occurring, where the change is to a *slower* rate of progress or occurrence. In behaviorism, usually taken as a point where rates of responding *de*crease. In colloquial usage, *negative* acceleration is sometimes called deceleration, but somewhat incorrectly. See Figure 5. See also **Acceleration; Acceleration, Positive**; and **Deceleration**.

Acceleration, Positive

A change in the rate with which something is moving or occurring, where the change is to a *more rapid* rate of progress or occurrence. In behaviorism, usually taken as a point where rates of responding *in*crease. See Figure 6. See also **Acceleration; Acceleration, Negative**; and **Deceleration**.

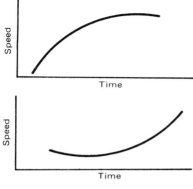

Figure 5. Negative Acceleration: This stylistic curve represents a body which is accelerating (changing speed) continually, but that change in speed is continually dropping off. Alternatively, this has been called "decelerating acceleration."

Figure 6. Positive Acceleration: This stylistic curve represents a body that is continually accelerating (changing speed), but where that change in speed is continually increasing. Alternatively, this has been called "accelerating acceleration."

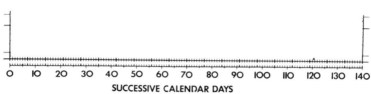

SUCCESSIVE CALENDAR DAYS

Figure 7. Across the Bottom on the Standard Chart—Successive Calendar Days: On the standard Precision Teaching chart the days are labeled by tens; but every seventh day is darkened to represent a Sunday. Charting follows the calendar, therefore, and days on which data were not collected are skipped on the chart. The analyst is able, by means of this convention, to readily determine the temporal distribution of observations.

Across the Bottom

A phrase, originating in Precision Teaching, in reference to the horizontal axis (abscissa, or x-axis) of a graph or chart. In Precision Teaching specifically, in reference to that scale of the standard 6-cycle, equal ratio (semilog) behavior chart which is divided into 140 successive calendar days. See Figure 7. See also **Chart**.

Across the Top

A phrase, originating in Precision Teaching, in reference to the scaling at the top of a graph or chart on the horizontal axis (abscissa, or x-axis). It is assumed that this scaling is somehow different than the scaling across the bottom. On the standard Precision Teaching behavior chart, for example, the scaling across the top is in terms of successive calendar weeks with spaces for the inclusion of specific dates once every four weeks; and the scale across the bottom is in terms of successive calendar days. See **Chart**.

Ad Libitum (Weight)

The average weight of a mature animal when it has had free access to food and water for a period of several days (and becomes stable). Ad libitum literally means "at liberty." In research with infrahuman subjects, for example, it is common to deprive the organism of food and/or water for a period until it reaches a certain percentage of its ad libitum weight (usually 80%) to insure a high probability that food and/or water will serve as an effective reinforcer.

Adaptation
1. As an operation: The repeated exposure of an organism to a stimulus.
2. As a process: A change in the extent to which the organism will react when presented with the stimulus. Repeated exposure to certain punishing stimuli, for example, will often lead to a reduction in the effectiveness of the stimuli in reducing rates of responding. See also **Adaptation, Decelerating**; and **Adaptation, Accelerating**.

Adaptation, Accelerating
Any process of adaptation which results in an increase in the rate or probability of responding. Sometimes called "positive adaptation," but somewhat confusingly since the general denotation of "positive" in behaviorism is "presentation" or "addition." See also **Adaptation**; and **Adaptation, Decelerating**.

Adaptation, Decelerating
Any process of adaptation which involves a reduction in the rate or probability of responding. Sometimes called "negative adaptation," but somewhat confusingly since "negative" has the general behavioral denotation of "removal" or "termination." See also **Adaptation**; and **Adaptation, Accelerating**.

ADJ
Abbreviation for "adjusting schedule." See **Schedule, Adjusting**.

AE
An abbreviation for "arranged event," and sometimes for "antecedent event." The latter, to avoid confusion, should more properly be abbreviated "AnE." Alternatively, the former may be abbreviated "ArE" to reduce the possibility of misinterpretation. See **Event, Arranged** and **Event, Antecedent**.

ALT
Abbreviation for "alternative schedule." See **Schedule, Alternative**.

Analysis, Differential Approach
Undertaking to analyze inter-organismic differences, that is, differences between two or more individuals. See **Analysis, Idiographic Approach**; and **Data, Interactive**.

Analysis, Idiographic Approach

Any analysis undertaking to describe intra-organismic differences, that is, differences *within* a single individual (usually across time or situations). See also **Data, Ipsative**; and **Analysis, Differential Approach.**

Analysis,Normative Approach

A special case of the "differential approach" to analysis, where the individual organism is analyzed in terms of the differences between it and some previously established "norm"—usually taken as the average in some greater number of similar organisms. See **Analysis, Differential Approach.**

Analysis of Behavior, Descriptive

That operation of listing all environmental events subsequent and antecedent to or during a recurring behavioral event or the general setting in which that behavior occurs, with the purpose of attempting to identify possible discriminative and reinforcing stimuli. Events identified may not be assumed to serve a particular function, however, until they have been removed or altered and characteristic behavioral processes observed. See also **Analysis of Behavior, Experimental.**

Analysis of Behavior, Experimental

A special case of the "functional analysis of behavior" in which previously identified environmental events are systematically manipulated for the purpose of determining (experimentally) their functional relationship to the behavior in question. "Teacher praise," for example, cannot be called a "reinforcer" until its contingency or non-contingency (or presence or absence) has been demonstrated to affect rates of responding. See also **Analysis of Behavior, Functional**; and **Analysis of Behavior, Descriptive.**

Analysis of Behavior, Functional

The identification and statement of the functional relationships which obtain between an organism and its environment. Such statements require that a high degree of covariance of incidents has been observed in a particular temporal sequence (e.g., when a specified event fails to follow a response, that response decreases in frequency). A functional analysis need *not* be obtained experimentally, but the power of an experimental analysis is considerably greater. See **Analysis of Behavior, Experimental**; and **Analysis of Behavior, Descriptive.**

Anxiety

An emotional response, usually taken to be demonstrated by changes in the frequency of broad classes of behaviors in the organism's repertoire as the result of an aversive or pre-aversive stimulus; but not necessarily so. Changes usually include a decrease in on-going operants, and an increase in operants which have in the past terminated or reduced the magnitude of the aversive stimulus.

In behavioral therapy anxiety is often taken as characterized by "subjective feelings of apprehension and tension." Anxiety is often differentiated from "fear" as being characterized by an increase in respiratory and cardiod functions, while fear produces the opposite result.

Anxiety, due to the range of effected performances, is often called a "state of the organism." See also **Emotion**.

Arithmetic Average (Mean)

The mean of any two or more numerical values. To calculate the arithmetic average:

1. Add all the numerical values (e.g., *rates*) together;
2. Count the number of values (e.g., the number of rate values that were added together);
3. Divide the sum of the values (the first number obtained above) by the number of values (the second number obtained above).

$$\text{The formula is: } \frac{\text{The sum of the numbers}}{\text{The number of values}}$$

EXAMPLE: If there are an even number of data points in a phase, then to find the middle rate one might take the arithmetic average of the two data points closest to the middle of the range. If those data points were 6 and 8.4, then: the sum of the values would be = 14.4; the number of the values would be = 2; the arithmetic average would be = $\frac{14.4}{2}$, = 7.2.

NOTE: In the case of two middles, if one is clearly more representative than another, then it is convention (in Precision Teaching) to choose it to report (as opposed to the average). See also **Middle**.

Arranged Event

An element of the "Is" Equation in Precision Teaching. See **"Is" Equation** and **Event, Arranged**.

Arrangement

An element of the "Is" Equation in Precision Teaching. See **"Is" Equation**.

Asymptote

A value (which may be graphically represented by a line) which a mathematical function or relationship continually approaches, but never reaches. Usually equated to the maximum possible value a function may achieve under "perfect" conditions, or if the function is continued into "infinity."

For example: If a cumulative record is being kept of the percentage of correct answers a child gives to the problem "2 + 2," then the only way in which the child will be able to get 100% correct is if he *never* gives the wrong answer. In the situation where he gives the answer wrong the first time, the first percentage is (0 correct/1 try =) 0%. On the second try, if the right answer is given, the percentage would be (1 correct/2 trys =) 50%. If the child never again gave the wrong answer, then the chart of his cumulative percentages would look like that in Figure 8.

No matter how far out the function is taken, since there will always be a count of one more "try" than "correct answer" (i.e., % correct = N−1/N), the function will never quite reach 100%. This function would then be called "asymptotic" with the asymptote set at 100%.

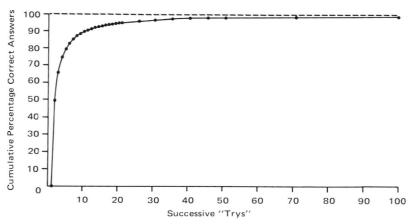

Figure 8. Asymptote: This figure represents the total percentage correct answers given to the problem "2+2 =" where only the first answer is wrong.

Attention, Intermediate

Attention which is periodic or interrupted with or without the control of the attending organism.

The specification of intermediate *attention* (as opposed to intermediate *responding*) implies that the organism is capable of the response, but is simply incapable of receiving or decoding the stimuli which would permit the processes of discrimination or differentiation (i.e., the organism is *able* to respond, but simply cannot determine *when* or in *what way* to respond). For example, a child with a severe visual handicap may be capable of emitting the verbal behavior in oral reading, but simply unable to focus his eyes properly from time to time to discriminate the written words to be read. See also **Responding, Intermediate.**

Auto-Correlation

The operation of correlating pairs of observations taken (sequentially in time) on the same variables for the purpose of determining the degree of sequential dependency. Pairs are described as being "t" units "lagged" (e.g., a "lag-2" where t=2 would pair observation 1, [1+2=3]; 2, [2+2=4], 3, [3+2=5]; etc.). A lag-1 autocorrelation states the dependency between any one observation and the one immediately preceding it; lag-2 states the dependency between any one observation of the one 2 units of time back; etc.

Auto-Correlation Function

The correlation of a time series (e.g., a set of sequential rate data) with itself, obtaining the paired observations as $(X, X+t)$ where $t=$ a set number of units. In $t=1$, for example, observation would be paired as:

$$1,2 \quad 2,3 \quad 3,4 \quad \text{etc.}$$

In $t=3$, observations would be paired as:

$$1,4 \quad 2,5 \quad 3,6 \quad \text{etc.}$$

This results in an estimate of the dependency between the successive observations. Also called "lagged correlations."

Auto-Shaping

A procedure for generating a response with a particular locus or discrimination in which a "noticeable" stimulus denoting the appropriate locus or discriminative stimulus cue is presented just prior to the presentation of (non-contingent) reinforcement; and in which the stimulus has a high probability of being the locus of some high probability behavior already in the repertoire of the organism. For example: A bright green light at "beak-level" is repeatedly illuminated in an otherwise dimly illuminated pigeon-experimental box just prior to the presentation of the grain-feeder. After several pairings of the stimulus and the feeder, the probability that the pigeon will peck the stimulus light (key) is found to increase—at which point feeder presentation is made contingent upon key-pecking. Note that (1) the stimulus was designed to be highly "noticeable," (2) that the response of pecking already had a high probability in the repertoire of the organism, (3) that the high probability response (pecking) has a very definite history of reinforcement with respect to the reinforcer used in auto-shaping (food), and (4) that the stimulus (the green light) also gains an association with that reinforcer by virtue of repeated pairings. Which parameters govern the efficiency of auto-shaping has not yet been fully investigated; but the general result supports previous research in the implication that any given S^D-S^{R+} relationship is generalizable to (may generate or control) a variety of possible responses—in this case, that response which has had the greatest association with that reinforcer in the past. See also **Shaping**.

Autor's Law

An hypothesis set forth by S. M. Autor in his doctoral thesis (1960) in which it is asserted that the selective response rate in the initial link of a chain matches the relative frequency of primary reinforcement in the terminal link. E.g., if a high response rate is required to obtain S^{R+} in the final link of a chain, then low rates of responding will obtain in the first component of that chain.

There appear to be many qualifications to this "law," however, and the evidences are as yet not conclusive as to their support or refutation of the basic hypothesis.

Baseline

A condition in which data collected during a specified period reflect stability and/or predictability to a degree which allows differences between that data and other data (collected on other organisms or at different points in time) to be discriminated. Not directly equatable with "steady-state" responding, since the data *may* still be reflecting change in performance characteristics, but the change must be highly consistent and predictable.

In use, it is common to confuse a "baseline" with a "reference phase." A reference phase is simply a period of time during which data are collected for the *purpose* of comparison with data collected under different conditions. Whether the data *will* be, in fact, stable enough to make such a comparison (meaningfully) is an empirical question. In fact, it is possible to ascribe "baseline" conditions to *any* phase which displays stability or predictability; but "baseline" is usually in reference to a "pre-experimental," "second reference," or "post-experimental" phase.

To avoid any confusion, it would probably be wise to use "baseline" as an adjective, as opposed to a noun. E.g., "one achieved baseline conditions in the first reference phase, but failed to do so in the second reference phase." See also **Phase, Reference**.

Behavior

The dependent variable in the science of behavior. Any activity of an organism. In the experimental analysis of behavior, "activity" is usually limited to any movement of the organism or part thereof through space. Other branches of behaviorism, however, allow the inclusion of "internal" activity *not* expressly involving movement or transposition through space.

In all areas of behaviorism it is necessary that the behavior be readily and reliably identified by at least one person. In the case of "internal" behaviors, of course, it is the behaving organism itself that must make the identification, otherwise "response externalization" procedures must be undertaken.

The term "behavior" is sometimes differentiated from "performance"—the former in reference to any *single* emission of activity; and the latter in reference to the sequential and temporal characteristics of any *collection* of those activities. One would speak, therefore, of a "key-pecking *behavior*" and "*performance* under a ratio schedule of reinforcement."

A specific behavior may be defined in terms of its physical and temporal properties, or in terms of the "critical effect" it has on the environment. For example, "key-pecking" could be defined as a certain sequence of muscle movements in the pigeon, or simply as any set of movements that cause an electro-mechanical device to register "closure." Definition by "critical effect" is most common.

See also **Response; Operant; Respondent;** and **Critical Effect.**

Behavior, Avoidance

Behavior which postpones an aversive event and thus provides temporary escape from conditioned aversive stimuli. Avoidance behavior cannot be generated in an organism unless a discriminative stimulus reliably precedes the presentation of the aversive stimulus, or unless the aversive stimulus is presented after regular intervals of time (i.e., allowing the passage of time to become the discriminative stimulus). The generation of this type of behavior is often concomitant with the frequent administration of punishment by a single agent or in a particular environment (i.e., where a teacher, a particular peer, the parent, or the school or home environment becomes the discriminative stimulus correlated with punishment, and therefore, the discriminative stimulus for avoidance behavior).

Behavior, Basic Procedures Which Decrease the Strength (Probability) of

See:
1. **Conditioning, Operant:**
   (of) **Response, Alternative Performance, Incompatible Reciprocal Inhibition;**
2. **Cost Contingency;**
3. **Stimulus, Discriminative** (for punishment);
4. **Drugs;**
5. **Extinction, Operant;**
6. **Extinction, Respondent;**
7. **Punishment;**
8. **Reinforcement, Delayed;**
9. **Restraint;**
10. **Satiation;**
11. **Time Out** (from positive reinforcement)

Behavior, Basic Procedures Which Increase the Strength (Probability) of

1. Training (See **Modeling, Molding, Task Analysis, Task Reformulation,** and **Training Program.**
2. Modification (i.e., reduction or elimination) of conditions which suppress or prevent desired behavior (See **Behavior, Basic Procedures Which Decrease the Strength of**)
3. **Behavior, Avoidance**
4. **Behavior, Escape**
5. **Conditioning, Operant**
6. **Conditioning, Respondent**
7. **Stimulus, Discriminative** (for positive reinforcement)
8. **Drugs**
9. **Reinforcement, Negative**
10. **Reinforcement, Positive**
11. **Shaping**
12. **Behavior, Superstitious**
13. **Reinforcement, Schedules of**

Behavior, Collateral

Behavior which is generated and maintained by reinforcement which is programmed for another behavior. A form of superstitious behavior where the reinforcement was in fact programmed, but for another behavior. For example: A speaker who is well-informed in an interesting subject matter may be well-received by an audience on those points alone. Should the speaker engage in a series of trite jokes, however, there is a good possibility that "joke-telling behavior" will be maintained at a high rate by the reinforcement delivered for the content of the speech *per se*—simply because the two behaviors (speaking and joking) occur in close temporal proximity.

Collateral superstitious behavior is likely to be more strongly reinforced than other forms of superstitious behavior due to the relative consistency with which it and the reinforcement programmed for other behavior are paired.

Behavior, Covert

Any behavior which is not directly observable, usually intraorganismic in nature. It is necessary to externalize covert behavior before it may be effectively measured by anyone other than the organism emitting that behavior. See **Response Externalization.**

Behavior, Escape

Behavior which terminates an aversive stimulus. The type of responding generated and maintained by negative reinforcement. This type of behavior is often generated by punishing situations. For example, if a father frequently punishes a child, then there is a high probability that the father will become (in himself) an aversive stimulus, and that the child will emit behaviors for the purpose of "escaping" from the father's presence—even in a "non-punishing" situation. See also **Behavior, Avoidance.**

Behavior, Mediating

Behavior occurring between two instances of the response being studied (or between some other event and such an instance) which is used by the organism as a controlling stimulus in subsequent behavior. (E.g., under drl the necessary delay in responding is often produced by the incidental reinforcement of mediating behavior which might be called "marking time"). Also, a time-out between response and reinforcement may not greatly reduce the effectiveness of the reinforcement if mediating behavior has been acquired during the TO.

Behavior, Overt

Any behavior which is directly observable by at least one person other than the responding organism. Also called "outer" or "public" behavior. See also **Behavior, Covert.**

Behavior, Superstitious

Behavior which has accidentally or coincidentally preceded the presentation or removal of reinforcing stimuli, and which as a result of this temporal relationship, has increased or decreased in probability or rate.

It is sometimes difficult to determine whether or not a particular behavior is superstitious, for while it may appear to serve no real function, it may be maintained by social consequences (e.g., smiling, joking, etc.) or serve to avoid aversive stimuli (warnings by the parents, shouts not to "walk under a ladder," "break a mirror," etc.). These latter cases might be called "pseudo-superstitions" since they are, in fact, controlled by real consequences; but not the consequences that are normally *believed* to be associated with those behaviors. Other superstitions may have had basis in fact at one time and have just carried over (failed to extinguish). (E.g., the third person on a match in wartime may have been the frequent target for snipers, but in New York City this is highly unlikely).

Generally speaking superstitions may be said to arise as a function of repeated coincidence, strong coincidence (e.g., where one particular and unique act was coincidentally followed by strong reinforcement), or failure to understand the true contingencies which did at one time exist, but no longer do. The majority of superstitions are maintained on a type of pseudo-avoidance schedule (i.e., "If I throw salt over my shoulder nothing bad will happen," and sure enough, nothing bad *does* happen), or under a system of delayed (but still coincidental) reinforcement (e.g., "I broke a mirror and three months later my sister took very ill").

To treat superstitious behavior one must understand the true contingencies (snipers and three on a match), or experimentally manipulate the variables and keep accurate records of the results (break mirrors on alternating seven year periods and keep track of "disastrous events").

Behavior, Target

That behavior which, while not presently in the organism's repertoire, the therapist or experimenter wishes to establish. Also called the "behavioral goal" or "aim." See also **Behavior, Terminal**.

Behavior, Terminal

That behavior which obtains at the close of a distinct interval of time (e.g., an experimental or therapeutic session), or at the end of a distinct chain of behaviors. The *terminal* behavior is distinguished from the *target* behavior in that it is *not* necessarily the behavior which the experimenter or therapist *wished* to establish. For example: One may wish to teach a child to tie a shoe. After the first session, however, perhaps the child has only progressed to the point where the shoe is put on and the bow only begun. The "terminal behavior," therefore, is "putting the shoe on and beginning the bow," while the "target behavior" remains "tying the shoe."

Some confusion also exists between "terminal behavior" and "steady-state performance or responding." The latter is in reference to the characteristics of responding after it has ceased to change from observation to observation. See also **Behavior, Target;** and **Performance, Steady-State**.

Behavioral Contrast

A temporary increase in the rate of responding of an organism under the S^D condition (during discrimination training) while responding is extinguishing in the presence of an S-delta. Recently this term has been generalized to apply to any situation in which a decrease in performance under one stimulus is associated with an increase in performance under another (e.g., if the behavioral requirements of a terminal link in a chain of behaviors is increased, thereby reducing the behavioral rates in that section of the chain, the performance may increase in the initial links of the chain).

Behavioral Homeostasis

Any set of behaviors which adjust and change to maintain a certain specific relationship between the organism and its environment. Braking and acceleration behaviors while driving a car, for example, may be considered homeostastic if they are emitted in order to maintain a certain distance between the organism's vehicle and the vehicle in front.

BIC

An abbreviation for "behaviorally independent contingency." See **Contingency, Behaviorally Independent.**

Block Counter

A counting device or visual display which is activated by the completion of pre-determined "blocks" or fractions of the total required performance under a ratio schedule of reinforcement. For example, a block counter may be incorporated in an FR 1000 schedule to illuminate a light panel whenever 100 responses had been completed. Ten illuminations, then, would occur for each delivery of the terminal reinforcer. Studies indicate that the effect of a block counter is to divide the ratio into discrete units which then function as individual components of a chain with, on a sufficiently large ratio, a brief pause following each block counted. See also **Chain; Schedule, Fixed-ratio;** and **Block Timer.**

Block Timer

A device which causes some sort of visual or auditory display following certain preset intervals of time (usually during a fixed or variable interval schedule of reinforcement). For example, a block timer might be set to illuminate a panel whenever 75% of the programmed time of a particular interval in a VI schedule had elapsed. This would allow the organism to form a discrimination with respect to the probability of reinforcement for responding. See also **Block Counter; FI;** and **VI.**

Brief-Stimulus Procedure
A procedure in which a stimulus is presented briefly in accordance with some specified condition in the environment—presumably with the intent that the organism is then able to discriminate that condition. For example: In a second-order schedule of reinforcement, the change in conditions of terminating one component and instating the schedule of the next could be noted by the presentation of a brief stimulus. Stimuli used in this manner may be similar or different in nature (i.e., specific to the change from one particular component to another, or the same—noting only a change, and not necessarily to which of several possible components). In the brief-stimulus procedure, responses in the presence of the stimulus *per se* have no scheduled consequences. The stimulus only denotes the completion of one set of responding and the beginning of another. See also **Schedules, Higher-Order**.

C
An abbreviation for "consequence." An element of the "does" equation in Precision Teaching. See **"Does" Equation**.

Cafeteria Method
A method for determining preferences or "subhungers" in which potential reinforcers are presented simultaneously, and the organism selects from among them. Relative preference may be determined by the frequency with which each is selected, or by the amount of each selected. See also **Preference**.

Calendar Synchronization
The convention of having all charts in one project location (e.g., school, day-care center) with the same labeling across the bottom regardless of when they were started. Example: Having all the charts in a particular school district labeled so that the first week on every chart corresponds with the first week of school for that term or semester (even if the project did not start until the middle of the term or semester). This will mean

that some charts will not have any data points at the beginning of the chart, but it allows any chart in the project location to be overlayed and easily compared with any other chart, even as to when the projects started. Sometimes called "calendar coordination."

'Celeration Line
A term, used in Precision Teaching, denoting a line-of-progress or best-fit-line. "Celeration" is the root of "*ac*celeration" and "*de*celeration"—the directions in which trend or progress may occur. See **Line-of-Progress**.

Chain
Abbreviation for "chained schedule." See **Schedule, Chained**.

Chaining
The operation of conditioning an organism to procure reinforcements under a chain schedule. Usually involves the conditioning of each **S-R** component, and then the combination of those components into the chain. See **Schedule, Chained** and **Chaining, Reverse**.

Chaining, Forward
A training or teaching tactic in which the first component in a chain of responses is established in the repertoire first, then the next is added, etc., until the entire chain has been acquired. For example: A child is taught to put a lace in a shoe (in the bottom two holes), then to lace, then to tie. While this sequence is common, it has been found to be generally less effective than reverse chaining. See **Chaining** and **Chaining, Reverse**.

Chaining, Reverse
A specific operation for the conditioning of an organism to operate under a chain schedule in which the last **S-R** component in the chain sequence is trained first, and the discriminative stimulus allowed to acquire reinforcing properties; and then the second to the last element is trained, using the discriminative stimulus for the last response as the reinforcer; etc., until all elements of the chain are acquired and are being performed in sequence. This method has the advantage of always reinforcing the organism for completing the chain as opposed to shifting the training reinforcer from element to element. In this sequence the discriminative stimulus of the next element in sequence is the reinforcer for the element being trained, since that stimulus has already been

associated with the ultimate reinforcer at the end of the chain. See Figure 9.

Change, Amount of

The relative (or ratio) change in rate or rate of change that has occurred between any two points in a project (e.g., between any two data points, middles, between the first and last rated days in any one phase, or between two lines-of-progress).

The manner in which the amount of change is noted in any single instance of data analysis is dependent upon the manner in which the data are presented (in tabular or graphic form). If the data are presented in tabular form, or on a chart with linear scales, then the amount of change is given as the absolute difference between the two values in question. If, on the other hand, the data are charted on a semilog chart, then noting the amount of change in terms of the ratio between the two numbers is more in keeping with the way in which the data will appear on the chart. Figure 10 demonstrates these relationships.

See **Change Finder** for the convention (in Precision Teaching) of determining and noting the amount of change.

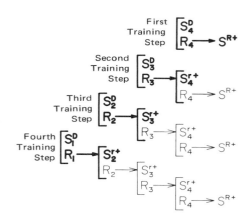

Figure 9. Reverse Chaining: In each of the successive steps in the chaining of this hypothetical four component chain, the step actually being trained is indicated by the darker lettering and lines. Subsequent components, already learned by the subject, are indicated by light lettering and lines. In Step One the fourth and last component in the chain is trained first. The stimulus in the presence of which it will produce the primary reinforcer (S_4^D and S^{R+} respectively) is presented and that response trained until a specified criteria is obtained. The stimulus for the third component is then presented (S_3^D) and the third response is trained (R_3). Notice, however, that the completion of R_3 does *not* produce the primary reinforcer (S^{R+}), but rather the stimulus associated with the fourth component (S_4). Note also that S_4 has been relabeled a conditioned reinforcer (S^{r+}) instead of a discriminative stimulus (S^D). Although S_4 will still retain its discriminative ability and "cue" the subject to emit the fourth response (which will result in the primary reinforcer), it has also gained secondary reinforcing ability via its association with the primary reinforcer during the first step. The "reinforcer" for learning the third component of the chain, therefore, is the opportunity to emit the fourth component and thereby receive the primary reinforcer. In the third training step the stimulus associated with the third component is relabeled a conditioned reinforcer and the reinforcement for learning that component is the opportunity to complete the chain. In the fourth and last step the same conditions apply.

19

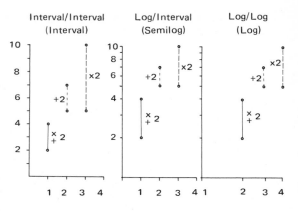

Figure 10. Change on Various Grids: There are basically three common grids in use for the graphic representation of data—the interval/interval (or simply "interval"), the log/interval (or simply "semilog"), and the log/log (or simply "log"). Each grid combination alters the visual picture created by the data in its own particular way. In each of the examples shown, three pairs of data are drawn. In the first set of data the highest data point may be considered either a "times" or "plus" two of the lowest data point (i.e., one would achieve the highest data point by either adding or multiplying two to the lowest data point). The second pair of data represents a "plus two" relationship, and the third pair of data represents a "times two" relationship. On the interval grid the two "plus" (interval) changes appear to be the same, and on the other two grids the two "times" (ratio or log) changes appear to be equal. Notice also that on the first two charts (with interval scales on the abscissa) the sets of data appear equally (intervally) spaced, but that on the third grid (with logs on the abscissa) the data sets appear "ratio" spaced.

Choice of how to describe the difference (change) between data is based on whichever system (times or plus) makes equal changes appear equal on the grid used. "Plus" would, therefore, be chosen for the interval chart, and "times" for either the semilog or log chart.

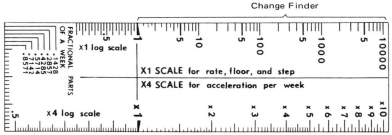

Figure 11. Change Finder: The "times one" scale on either acceleration finder may be used as a change finder. Place the (1) next to the lowest of the two data points between which the change factor is desired; and read the difference between them as that point on the scale which falls at the same height as the highest data point. In this case, since the scales are logarithmic, the answer is read as a "times" or "divide" factor by which the first data point must be treated to obtain the second data point. In the case of a change factor devised for a linear scale, however, the answer would be "plus" or "minus" something to obtain the second data point from the first.

Change Finder

A device (usually made of transparent materials) for determining the ratio of (or relative) amount of change in rate that has occurred between one point on a chart and another point on the chart.

Regardless of the chart on which it is to be used, the change finder is always comprised of a scale identical to the vertical axis of *that* chart. Placement of the "origin" on the change finder (i.e., "zero" if an interval scale; "one" if a log scale) next to the lowest data point then allows the relative difference between the two data points to be determined as that point on the change finder scale which falls at the same level as the second data point. Where log scales (and charts) are used it is particularly easy to note the similarity between the use of a change finder and a slide rule. See Figure 11.

Change-Over (CO)
A change from one form of response, stimulus condition, or schedule of reinforcement to another form of response, stimulus, or schedule of reinforcement. Change-over time, delay, or frequency is sometimes used as a measure of the "preference" an organism has for one form of response, stimulus, or schedule of reinforcement over another.

Change Over Delay (COD)
A period following the change from one form of responding to another, or from one schedule to another during which reinforcement is *not* available. Such a delay lowers the probability that reinforcement delivered in the second case (new response form or schedule *to* which the change is made) will follow closely enough to reinforce responses in the first case (old response form or schedule *from* which the change is made).

Chart
A term, originating in Precision Teaching, as an alternative for the word "graph." In Precision Teaching the chart is a standardized semilogarithmic grid for the presentation of daily rate data. "Across the bottom" (the x-axis or abscissa) the scale is marked off in 140 successive calendar days (i.e., Monday, Tuesday, etc.). "Up the left" (the y-axis or ordinate) the scale is marked off logarithmically (i.e., in a "ratio" scale) and labeled "movements per minute."

Two versions of the chart are available. One chart (produced by Behavior Research Co., Kansas City, Kansas) has six cycles "up the left" ranging from .001 (i.e., a rate of one movement-cycle in 1000 minutes) to 1000 (i.e., a rate of 1000 movement-cycles in one minute). The second chart (produced by Graphics for Behavioral Measurement, Eugene, Oregon) has 6.16 cycles "up the left," ranging from .00069 (i.e., a rate of one movement every 1440 minutes, or one per 24-hour day) to 1000 (i.e., a rate of 1000 movements in one minute). The

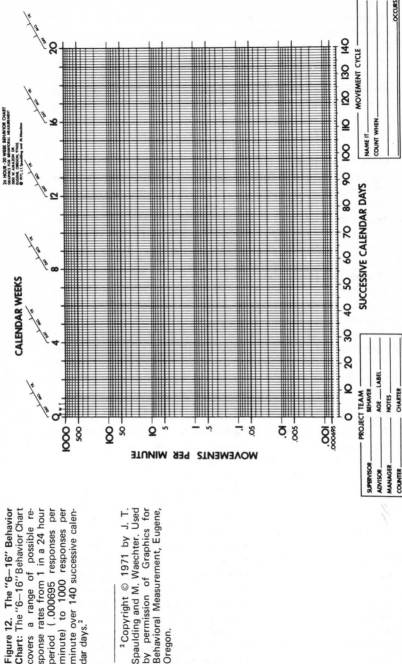

Figure 12. The "6–16" Behavior Chart: The "6–16" Behavior Chart covers a range of possible response rates from 1 in a 24 hour period (.000695 responses per minute) to 1000 responses per minute over 140 successive calendar days.[2]

---

[2] Copyright © 1971 by J. T. Spaulding and M. Waechter. Used by permission of Graphics for Behavioral Measurement, Eugene, Oregon.

"6-16" chart also has an emphasized "five-line" in each cycle to increase the facility with which rates in the middle of each cycle may be found.

Other than these differences, however, the "6-cycle" and "6-16" charts are identical in size and nature of grid, and are, therefore, completely compatible analytically (i.e., data charted on one will look the same when charted on the other, and all appropriate rate and acceleration finders will work on either chart). See Figure 12.

See also **Days, Successive Calendar; Up the Left; Across the Bottom**; and **Movements Per Minute**.

CO
An abbreviation for "change-over." See **Change-Over**.

COD
An abbreviation for "change over delay." See **Change Over Delay**.

Coercion
A type of dyadic interaction (i.e., an interaction between two and only two organisms) in which one organism is reinforced for interacting with the other via the positive reinforcement paradigm and the other through the negative reinforcement paradigm. Example: "A" screams to demand that "B" watch. When "B" watches (complies) the screaming stops. "A" 's behavior (screaming) is consequated by the production of a positively reinforcing stimulus event (watching—compliance); "B" 's behavior (watching) is consequated by the termination of a negatively reinforcing stimulus event (screaming).

COLAB
Abbreviation for "*CO*mmon *L*anguage *A*nalysis of *B*ehavior." See **Lindslian System**.

Complex Event
Synonym for "integral event"; see **Event, Integral**.

Complex Stimulus
Synonym for "integral stimulus"; see **Stimulus, Integral**.

CONC.
Abbreviation for "concurrent schedule." See **Schedules, Concurrent**.

Concept
An organism is said to exhibit a concept when he responds differentially to any member of a set of related situations, or any stimulus of a class of stimuli, to the exclusion of all other

stimuli or situations not in that class (e.g., when a child can identify all cars as being "cars" and not "trucks"). Demonstration is further defined as the identification of appropriate stimuli (e.g., "cars") which were never before introduced to the organism; but which, due to properties in common with previously identified members of the concept set (e.g., "cars") are included in that set by the organism. See also **Concept Formation.**

Concept, Conjunctive

Where the S^D class of a concept is made up by the intersection or conjunction of two or more other S^D classes. E.g., the concept of "round pegs" is comprised of the conjunction of the concepts of "round" and "pegs." Concepts based on the conjunction of two or more concepts *already* in the repertoire of the organism are more easily learned than concepts based on S^D classes *not* currently controlling the behavior of that organism. See Figure 13.

Concept, Disjunctive

A concept in which a particular response is under the control of a broad class of stimuli, but in which there is no integral, necessary link between those stimuli. In such a class the discriminative stimuli are arbitrarily included in the class, and generalization is limited if not impossible. See **S^D Class, Arbitrary** for an example. See Figure 14.

Concept Formation

An organism acquires a concept through an explicit history of differential reinforcement (or through the verbal mediation of the concept, that mediation being dependent upon a history of differential reinforcement) in the presence of a subset of those cases which are the concept. E.g., a child acquires a concept of "cars" by being reinforced for saying "cars" in the presence of cars, and not being reinforced for saying "cars" in the presence of trucks, bicycles, trolley cars, etc. Concept formation is most usually facilitated by presenting a wide variety of the stimuli in question (the common elements between which define the basis for the classification of the concept) in conjunction with other stimuli *not* in the concept set (e.g., trucks as opposed to cars—the common elements between which not being the basis for classification). Repeated presentation of the same stimuli, on the other hand, all of which may be included in the concept, usually results in a more limited type of stimulus control and little or no generalization to other members of the concept set.

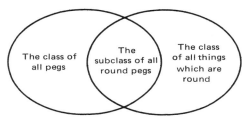

Figure 13. Conjunctive Concept: Each ellipse represents a class of stimuli—the class of all "pegs" and the class of all things "round." The overlapping area of the two ellipses represents the subset in each class of all "round pegs."

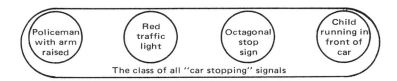

Figure 14. Disjunctive Concept: Each of the smaller circles represents a class of stimuli—the class of all policemen raising their arms and signaling "stop"; the class of all "stop signs"; the class of all red traffic lights; and the class of all children running out in front of a moving car. All of these stimuli should be discriminative with respect to "car stopping" behavior, and yet they are included in that class arbitrarily with no necessary physical characteristics in common. Those circles are not, therefore, shown as overlapping; but they are all contained in a larger figure denoting the class of all "car stopping signals."

Conditioning, Operant

1. As an operation: The reinforcement of a response, or more specifically, the presentation or removal of a reinforcing stimulus or stimulus event subsequent to the emission of a response. Generally speaking it is connoted that the reinforcement is contingent upon the response, and that the operation is repeated more than once to affect conditioning, but neither of these conditions are strictly necessary.

2. As a process: The resultant increase in the probability or rate of that conditioned response in the presence of the stimulus conditions under which conditioning took place.

Also called "Type R," "Thorndikian," "instrumental," or "law of effect conditioning."

Conditioning, Respondent

1. As an operation: Pairing (temporarily) an unconditioned eliciting stimulus (UCS) with a neutral or conditioned stimulus (CS). See also **Respondent Conditioning, Temporal Relationships Between CS and UCS During Conditioning**.

2. As a process: The resulting capacity (or maintenance of that capacity) of the neutral or conditioned stimulus (CS) to

elicit the same respondent behavior as the unconditioned stimulus (UCS).

CONJ
Abbreviation for "conjunctive schedule." See **Schedule, Conjunctive**.

Consequence (C)
A term whose use is most formalized in Precision Teaching as a reinforcer that bears a definite arrangement (if not an actual contingency) to the emission or repeated emission of a specified response. In Precision Teaching the function of a consequence (i.e., its effect on rates of responding) is assumed known. Usage in the general literature, however, is often in reference to an event which *may* be reinforcing, but the actual function of which is as yet *un*determined. This confusion of usages demands that the reader attend to the specific context in which the term appears in order that its particular meaning may be determined. See also **Event, Arranged**; **"Is" Equation**; and **"Does" Equation**.

Contingencies, Branching
A set of contingencies, a subset of which are enacted sequentially; and in which each contingency is determined (in part) by the nature of the responding or consequences which obtained under the preceding contingency.

Example: If, under an FR 10, responding is at or above a rate of 3.8 per minute, then the organism will be placed under CRF food reinforcement for a period of one minute. If responding under the FR 10 is less than 3.8 per minute, then the organism will be placed under time out for a period of one minute. After the one minute of CRF or time out, the FR 10 will be reinstated, and the same contingencies will hold.

Contingencies, Nested
Any set of two or more contingencies which mutually determine the delivery of one or more consequences contingent upon responding. In particular reference to conjunctive, interlocking, or interpolated schedules of reinforcement, but sometimes in reference to alternating, complex, or concurrent schedules as well. See one or more of the schedules given above for examples.

Contingency
1. In operant conditioning: The temporal and/or physical conditions under which a response is followed by a positive or negative reinforcing stimulus or the removal of either.

2. In respondent conditioning: The conditions under which unconditioned and conditioned or neutral stimuli are paired.

In both definitions the dependency of one event upon the other is explicit. When a response occurs with the specified characteristics the "dependent" or "contingent" reinforcement is delivered.

Contingency is also an element of the "does" equation in Precision Teaching, and is equivalent to "schedule" in that context. See **"Does" Equation**.

Contingency, Behaviorally Independent (BIC)
A contingency defining the conditions which must be met prior to the occurrence of some environmental event (usually reinforcement) that is in no way affected or altered by the emission of any behavior by the subject in question. Sometimes called non-contingent (i.e., with respect to the organism in question) reinforcement.

Contingency Building
The operation of increasing the temporal or physical requirements for reinforcement until the intermittency of reinforcement is far greater than that which would have originally maintained the performance.

Contingency Control
Any instance in which the rate with which an operant is emitted has been demonstrated to be altered by the presence or absence of the particular conditions of consequation defined by a schedule of reinforcement.

Any instance in which a schedule of reinforcement has demonstrated an effect on the rate with which an operant is emitted.

Note that the *schedule* of reinforcement, in this case, is divorced from the reinforcer itself, implying that the reinforcer delivered or obtained remains the same; and only the conditions under which it will be delivered are altered in a demonstration of contingency control. See also **Reinforcement, Schedules of**; and **Contingency**.

Contingency, Irreversible
Any contingency which results in or relies upon a set of circumstances such that it may not be repeated. The irreversible nature of the contingency may be due to the stimuli employed, the consequence delivered, or the schedule of the contingency. Examples: A contingency which is initiated by the birth of the first child to a particular set of parents may not be repeated for those parents; a contingency which has as its consequence the death of the organism may not be

repeated on that organism; and a schedule that adds 1 to a ratio with the delivery of each reinforcement with an upper limit for the ratio of infinity may never be repeated on that organism. Sometimes confused with a terminating contingency. See **Contingency, Terminating.**

Contingency, Null

The lack of any special or programmed consequences for the emission of a response. Not entirely equivalent to total extinction since accidental or random environmental events may occur subsequent to the emission of the response, whereas extinction implies that the environment is controlled to prevent such occurrences.

Contingency, Probabilistic

Any contingency in which the probability of a specific response being consequated by a specific reinforcer or event is less than (1.00). All intermittent schedules are a form of probabilistic schedule, but the notation of a probabilistic contingency implies that *some* consequence will occur for every response, but the type of consequence may vary according to the stated probabilities. Whenever feasible all the possible outcomes for each response should be listed and the associated probabilities of their occurrence stated. The notation of a probabilistic contingency also implies that the schedules by which the different consequences are delivered are random or probabilistic in nature (i.e., any single instance is indeterminable, but the overall frequency of occurrence over several opportunities to occur is estimable).

Contingency, Prosthetic

A reinforcement contingency which will generate and maintain a performance only as long as it is in effect. The discontinuance of the contingency results in the discontinuance of the performance. See **Prosthetic** and **Therapeutic.**

Contingency, Repetitive

Contingencies which reinstate the original conditions of the contingency by the fact of their completion, and thereby set up the circumstances by which they may be repeated.

A fixed ratio schedule, for example, may be set up so that the delivery of reinforcement resets the counting mechanism and reinstates the conditions necessary for completing the ratio again to obtain another reinforcer. See also **Contingency, Terminating.**

Contingency, Terminating
Any contingency which results in the termination of the experimental session or the circumstances under which the contingency may exist. Terminating contingencies may be reinstated at some later time, however, as opposed to irreversible contingencies which may not be reinstated.

Contingency, Therapeutic
Contingencies which will generate behaviors that will still maintain when the contingency is discontinued. See also **Therapeutic** and **Prosthetic**.

Contrasting Interaction
A change in rate in one set of conditions which is *opposite* the direction of the change in rate in *another* set of conditions. See **Interaction, Discriminated Operant**.

Control
A functional relationship between a performance and the variable of which it is (at least in part) a function. E.g., a performance is controlled by deprivation to the extent that deprivation determines the nature of the performance.

Control, Aversive
Any reinforcement paradigm which utilizes aversive stimuli. The most common are punishment and negative reinforcement.

Control, Environmental
Changes in the frequency of operant performances produced by the presence or absence of discriminative, setting, or reinforcing stimuli. See also **Stimulus Control**.

Control, Positive
Any reinforcement paradigm which controls behavior without the use of aversive stimuli. The most common is positive reinforcement.

Corrected Median Slope
A median slope, generally used in lines-of-progress, calculated from a corrected data set. The correction is usually performed to remove any trend in deviations which may exist in the data, and which may affect the estimate of trend or progress. The corrected data set is formed by taking the average of each successive pair of data (1&2; 2&3; 3&4; etc.). Procedures thereafter are identical to finding the median slope (see **Median Slope**). After the slope has been determined, the line is drawn over the *original* data in a position which divides that data into two equal parts (see **Median**).

Since the corrected and original data sets are by definition different, the corrected median slope will *not* minimize the sum of the unsigned deviations about it when placed over the original data. It is not, therefore, an actual "median slope" with respect to that data set. Usually the corrected median slope will represent a compromise between the least-squares and median solutions to the same problem. See Figure 15.

Cost-Contingency

The procedure whereby an organism loses a reinforcer (conditioned or primary) already in its possession contingent upon the emission of a particular behavior. E.g., the emission of "running-through-a-red-light" behavior will result in the removal of $5.00 (a generalized reinforcer previously earned, and presently in the organism's possession). This procedure is not to be confused with Time Out which is the removal of the organism from the environment in which it may *obtain* reinforcers *not* presently in its possession. E.g., when a workman fails to meet the production quota for one full week, he may be laid off for one week. No money was *taken* from him that he had already earned, but he was prevented from earning any more for the duration of the Time Out.

The cost-contingency procedure will result in the reduction of the rate or probability of the behavior that produced it (assuming it was an effective reinforcer that was removed). Strictly speaking, losing "privileges" not presently being enjoyed (used) is *not* an example of cost contingency (e.g., a "bad" student is told he will have no recess). In fact, this *prevention* of obtaining a "regular" reinforcer may result in the overall reduction of performances usually associated with it (e.g., now the student has "nothing to lose," so . . .). Similar results may obtain in a situation in which the organism, as a result of cost-contingencies, is found to be in a "negative-total" reinforcer situation. In a class, for example, where points are given for appropriate work and points removed for inappropriate work, it would generally be unwise to set the contingencies in a manner that would allow a student to "go in the hole" with respect to points (i.e., lose so many that he has lost more than he has earned—thus "owing" the teacher or going into "debt").

Counter-Conditioning

Any of several specific behavioral therapies in which new conditioning procedures are instituted for the express purpose of counteracting previous conditioning.

A technique often used in behavioral therapy to reduce or eliminate anxieties by pairing the anxiety-producing stimuli

Figure 15. Corrected Median Slope: This figure demonstrates the effect of the correction factor applied to data prior to calculation of a median or middle slope. The solid dots represent the original data. Although the data as a set has no trend up or down, it *is* becoming variable—with each successive data point further from the "center" than the one preceding it. The circles represent the corrected data—derived by taking the middle of each line connecting successive data points. Note that the trend in deviations is removed (i.e., that the corrected data do not get progressively further away from the "center"). While the line-of-progress calculated on the original data is a function entirely of the trend in deviations, the corrected data—with the trend in deviations removed—defines the true trend (or lack thereof) in rate.

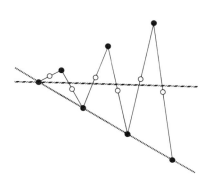

with states of relaxation. Via the process of respondent conditioning, it is hoped, the previously aversive stimuli will acquire "relaxation-producing" properties. See **Systematic Desensitization.**

Count When _____ Occurs

A phrase, originating in Precision Teaching, and found on one of the two Precision Teaching Charts, in reference to the specification of that part of a movement-cycle which should "cue" the counter to register one emission of that behavior. With behaviors of short duration there is little need for such a specification, but frequently it may take several seconds or minutes for one complete cycle to be made; and if two or more observers are counting the movement when different portions of the cycle are completed, then varying counts could result. For example: In a workshop situation one of the tasks may be to repaint wooden pop-bottle carriers. The movement-cycle of "Pop-bottle carriers painted" may take, in each instance, several minutes to complete. If one observer is counting the cycle as completed when the last coat of paint has been applied, and another is counting only those finished and dried carriers stacked on a platform for return to the bottle company, then it would be quite possible for the counts on any given day to be different. The statement "count when stacking for return shipment occurs" on the bottom of the chart will minimize those differences. To some extent this problem may exist in the counting of all movement-cycles, but becomes more apparent as the duration of any single movement-cycle increases.

CR
Abbreviation for "conditioned response." See **Response, Conditioned.**

CRF
Abbreviation for "continuous reinforcement." See **Schedule, Continuous Reinforcement.**

Critical Effect
Any change produced in the environment by behavior. Generally speaking, however, only changes considered "important" with respect to some criteria are defined as "critical" effects. It may not be important, for example, that a child write with his left or right hand, start at the top or bottom of a digit, or write with heavy or light pressure on a math-fact quiz—only that the correct digit be written. The "critical effect" on a math-fact quiz, then, would be defined as "correct digits written legibly."

The definition of a behavior in terms of critical effect (i.e., what the behavior *does*) is generally considered a more efficient and practical method than the description of all specific physical, topographical, and temporal characteristics (i.e., what the behavior *is*).

Critical Incidents Techniques
A polling of behaving organisms to determine what specific behaviors in what specific situations they believe would be most effective or ineffective in procuring reinforcement or punishment. Usually analyzed by a type of factor analysis.

It should be noted that in the critical incidents technique one is not measuring what the organisms would *in fact* do in the proposed situations; only what they *say* they would do. In the strictest sense, therefore, the study is one of verbal or written behavior only, and any correlation between that behavior and the behavior described (i.e., what they say they would do) must be established independently.

CS
Abbreviation for "conditioned stimulus." See **Stimulus, Conditioned.**

Cue Set
The class of all related stimuli which function as S^Ds for a specific operant response or class of related operant responses. To be differentiated from a stimulus set which are normally taken to elicit a reflex.

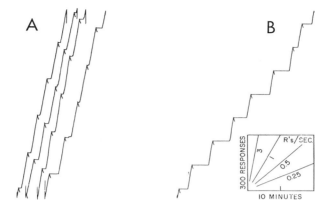

Figure 16. Cumulative Curve: A cumulative curve representing responding of a pigeon under two fixed-ratio schedules of reinforcement. The small grid in the lower right-hand corner denotes the amount of pen movement in the vertical for 300 responses; and in the horizontal for 10 minutes. Sample slopes for the determination of rate are also included. From this record it may be easily determined that response rates under condition A (FR200) are considerably greater than those which obtain under condition B (FR120).[3]

Cumulative Curve

A curve showing the total (cumulative) number of responses emitted along the ordinate (Y-axis, or vertical axis), and the passage of time along the abscissa (X-axis, or horizontal axis). Rate of responding may be read as the slope of the line. The steeper the slope, the faster the rate of responding. Cumulative records are usually made electro-mechanically at the same time that the subject is being run. See Figure 16.

Cumulative Recorder

A device designed to automatically draw a cumulative record of responding concurrent with the emission of these responses. See **Cumulative Curve**.

Curve Fitting

A method of summarizing (for purposes of analysis) time series data. The purpose of the line is to describe the general change in data over time (i.e., what the data would look like if all "random" or "error" variances were removed). Comparisons between the slope and intercepts of the lines for differing experimental phases is taken to indicate the effect of the differing "treatments." See also **Slope**; and **Line-of-Progress**.

---

[3] Figure from Ferster, C. B. and Skinner, B. F., *Schedules of reinforcement*. New York: Appleton-Century-Crofts, p. 52. Copyright © 1957. Used by permission of Appleton-Century-Crofts, Educational Division, Meredith Corporation.

Cycle

Literally a process or action that is capable of repeating itself in the same order or sequence. A complete sequence of steps in which the last is identical (or similar) to the first.

The major uses of the word cycle in behaviorism are found in the term movement-*cycle* (Precision Teaching), and in reference to logarithmic-*cycles*, the basis for several types of behavior charts. See Figure 17.

Daily Chart

A chart with successive calendar days marked off across the bottom. See **Chart**.

Data, Interactive

Any data which may be collected on more than one organism without procedural interdependence of the individual data points either within or between subjects of measurement, that is, the value of any single data point does not (procedurally) constrain the possible value of another data point. Free-operant rate is an example of such data. The rate of responding at one point in time does not affect the *possible* values of rate at another time within or between subjects being studied. Percentage, on the other hand, *is* interdependent—if a certain percentage of the responses are emitted at one time, then the percentage of responses that can be measured at another time is limited (e.g., if 40% of the total number of responses occur in the first half of a multiple schedule, then no more than 60% can occur in the last half). Percentages, then, could *not* be called interactive data. Interactive data is, generally, the most desirable type of data to have when cross-subject analysis is desired. See also **Data, Ipsative**.

Data, Ipsative

Any form of data characterized by the following:
1. Relates to intra-organismic changes (i.e., changes within a single individual—usually across the time or situations).
2. Constrained scales so that the sum of all measures taken together will be a constant (e.g., as in the case with percentages summing to 100).

Figure 17. "Cycles" on the "6–16" Behavior Chart: The standard "6–16" Behavior Chart comprises 6.16 log cycles ranging from .000695 (equivalent to the rate per minute of one behavior in a 24 hour day) to 1000. Notice that the value of a line in any one cycle is exactly 10 times less than the same point in the next cycle up, and 10 times greater than the same point in the next cycle down. Because of this consistent relationship, log charts are often called "ratio scales."

3. Measures are methodologically interdependent (i.e., the results of one measurement will, at least in part, determine the results of another measurement—as in the case with percentages, once a value has been determined, say "x-%," then no other measurement can exceed 100-x%).

Ipsative data may only be interpreted in a relative sense (since the original information has been transformed to hold to a constant base, as in the case of percentages), and only within the context of that "organism" to which the base refers (i.e., if percentage of a particular organism's behavior is the base, then analysis may be made only with respect to that organism and no other). Between-subject or between-group analysis is, therefore, impossible unless all measurement bases are directly equatable. Also called "idiographic data." See also **Data, Interactive**.

Data, Normative

A special case of interactive data in which comparisons will be made between individual organism data and some set of normative data—usually compiled as the average of some set of other, similar organisms. See **Data, Interactive**.

Data Point

Any point on a chart which represents the value of a dependent variable for a single observation or group of observations. While "data" may be in reference to any part or all of a set of information, "data point" definitely implies the visual representation of that information.

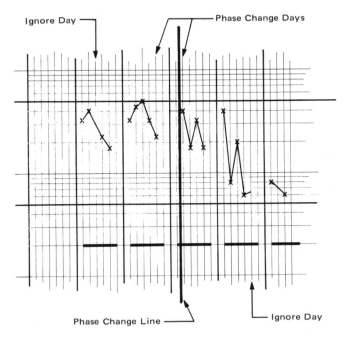

Figure 18. Day Types: This blow-up of a section of actual classroom data demonstrates the various types of days which might occur during the course of a project, and the manner in which they are noted on the chart. *Rated days* are days on which data were collected and charted. On this chart they are noted by placing an "x" on the chart at the appropriate rate, and on the appropriate day. Except as noted below, lines are drawn to connect all successive rated days. The "x" denotes a project designed to *dec*elerate rates of responding; the use of a "dot" would denote a project designed to *ac*celerate rates of responding. *Ignore days* are days on which the behavior occurred and *could* have been rated, but for some reason was *not*. Obviously no data point may be placed on an ignore day; but a line *is* drawn across such a day connecting the preceding and succeeding rated days on either side (except as noted below). *No-chance days* are days on which the behavior could not have occurred; or at least could not have occurred in the usual project location (e.g., classroom). No data point is placed on such a day, and no line is drawn across such a day. If an ignore day precedes or succeeds a no-chance day, then the line is drawn from the nearest rated day to the ignore day "pointing at" (i.e., in the direction of) the next rated day—but not crossing the no-chance day. An example is shown and noted in this figure. *Phase change days* are the last data point before a change and the first data point after a change. Note that the phase change line is drawn ½ day before the first data point in the second phase—*not* half-way between the two phase change days. Essentially this denotes when one would expect the change to be noticed in the data—as opposed to when the change was planned.

Day, Ignored

A term, originating in Precision Teaching, in reference to any day on which the behavior being charted *may* have occurred, but for some reason was not counted or charted.

In Precision Teaching such days are noted on the chart by drawing a line across them (from the last data point to the next), but (of course) not placing a data point on that day. If an ignored day is preceded or succeeded by a no-chance day, then a line is drawn from the nearest data point across the ignored day and "pointing" to the next data point, but not crossing the no-chance day.

Such a convention allows the analyst to differentiate between days when data were simply not collected (ignored days) and days when data *could not* have been collected (no-chance days)—each of which may have different affects on responding.

Although in Precision Teaching reference is always to "days," it would certainly be possible to ascribe the same label to other time-bases (e.g., weeks, hours, months). See Figure 18 for examples. See also **Day, No-Chance**; and **Day, Rated**.

Day, No-Chance

A term, originating in Precision Teaching, in reference to a day on which the response (or in Precision Teaching, the movement-cycle) had no opportunity to occur. No-chance days in a school project, for example, would include weekends, sick days, and vacations.

In Precision Teaching, no-chance days are differentiated on the chart by *not* crossing those days with rate-lines (i.e., not connecting a line from the last rated day to the next rated day). These "breaks" or "gaps" in the data facilitate the analysis of whatever affects "absences" may have on responding. Although in Precision Teaching reference is always to "days," it would certainly be possible to ascribe the same label to other time-bases (e.g., hours, weeks, months). See Figure 18 for examples. See also **Day, Ignored**; and **Day, Rated**.

Day, Rated

A term, originating in Precision Teaching, in reference to any day on which data were collected and charted. The term "rated," of course, explicates the type of data in question; but the terms "observed," "charted," or "data" may be employed as alternatives if other forms of data are used.

In Precision Teaching the type of project to which the data apply is noted as an "acceleration target" or "deceleration target" by the use of "dots" and "x's." A rated day noted on the chart with an "x" indicates that the purpose of the project is to decelerate (reduce) the rate of responding, and the use of a "dot" indicates that the purpose of the project is to accelerate (increase) the rate of responding.

In Precision Teaching reference is always to "days"; but it would certainly be possible to ascribe the same label to other time-bases (e.g., hour, week, month). See Figure 18 for examples. See also **Day, No-Chance**; and **Day, Ignored**.

Days, Successive Calendar
A term, originating in Precision Teaching, in reference to the horizontal axis of the standard 6-cycle behavior chart. All days of the week are represented on this scale, and may not be altered—even if data does not exist for every day. The purpose of standardizing by calendar days instead of by session or observation period is to allow the analyst to easily determine the temporal relationship between successive observations (e.g., are there observations on every day, or just certain days; regularly spaced, or irregular in occurrence) and note if any pattern in responding or progress occurs as a result of that distribution of observations. See Figure 7 under **Across the Bottom**.

Dead Man's Test
In Precision Teaching, a guideline to the identification of movement-cycles (i.e., responses). If the behavior in question may be emitted or demonstrated by a "dead man" (e.g., sitting, staring, lying, being quiet), then it is not a movement-cycle, and not, therefore, an appropriate choice of behavior to rate. If a "dead man" can engage in the "behavior" then it may be more properly called the *absence* of behavior (or movement). In such a case it is the behavior which the behaver *should* be emitting (or which *is* being emitted and should *not* be) which *does* involve movement that is (in Precision Teaching) identified and rated.

Deceleration
To decrease the rate of responding (or the value of some other dependent variable) as opposed to acceleration. See also **Deceleration** under Plan Functions or Aims.

Deficiency-Produced Specific Superiority
An instance in which a handicapped organism demonstrates superiority over a nonhandicapped organism in one or more specific behaviors, and where that superiority is directly or indirectly related to the existence of that handicap. For example, it is certainly the case that blind persons are able to

negotiate in dimly lit areas with greater ease and confidence than are sighted people, and that this ability is directly related to the fact of their handicap.

Definition, Functional
A statement of the effect the object or event being defined will produce in a specified dependent variable. E.g., see the definition of a **Reinforcer, Positive.**

Definition, Operational
A statement of what must be done, including the measurements that must be taken, for someone to observe the phenomenon being defined. Observe, in this sense, means to see, hear, smell, or otherwise discriminate. For example, see the definition of **Multiple Baseline** for an operational definition of one type of experimental procedure.

Dependency, Sequential
A series of events (some or all of which may be behavioral events—responses) in which the occurrence of one event is dependent upon the occurrence of one or more other events in sequence. For example: To walk across the threshold of a locked door one must first unlock the door and then open it. The events "unlock door" and "open door" must occur *in that sequence* before the event "step-over-threshold" can occur.

Behavioral data are often called sequentially dependent inasmuch as the value of any given data point is frequently "predictable" (within limits) given knowledge about preceding data. If the data were totally *in*dependent, then knowledge about previous data would in no way aid in the prediction of future data. Since behavioral data are usually collected in sequence (i.e., over days, minutes, or some other unit of time) they would be, then, sequentially dependent. See also **Independence.**

Deprivation
1. As an operation: Withholding a reinforcer such as food, water, sexual contact, etc. Any program establishes a "level" of deprivation which must be stated in quantifiable terms (e.g., 22 hours water deprivation, food deprivation until the organism reaches 80% of his free feeding weight, etc.).
2. As a process: Resulting changes in the functional value of the reinforcer, usually greater with increased deprivation, and correlated changes in the behaviors of the deprived organism which produce those reinforcers.

Descriptive Statistics

Statistical manipulations, values, etc. which are used to summarize or describe data (a group of numerical values such as would be obtained in the course of an experiment, study or observation) as opposed to drawing inferences from those data to describe their representativeness of a larger (untested) population. Examples: mean, median, mode, range, standard deviation, and variance. NOTE: Each of these terms *may be used* in inferential statistics, but by themselves are purely descriptive.

Deviation

The difference between any two values. Usually one of the values is an "expected" or "predicted" value and the other the "real," "actual," or "obtained" value. The deviation, then, would be between what one *expected* and what actually *happened*.

For any given set of data the mean will minimize the sum of the *signed* deviations ("+" deviations are values *above* the mean; and "-" deviations are *below* the mean), and the median will be that point from which the sum of the *un*signed deviation will be the least. See **Mean** and **Median**.

Deviations are usually analyzed in the "static" sense (i.e., the difference between all data and a single point) to estimate how "variable" the data are. "Variance" is, literally, the sum of the deviations-squared divided by the number of data points (or, in other words, the average squared deviation):

capital Greek letter "sigma" meaning "to sum all of the following"

$$\sigma^2 = \frac{\Sigma (X_i - \overline{X})^2}{N}$$

lower-case Greek letter "sigma"-squared, meaning "variance"

Where X_i = any score and $\overline{X}$ = the mean of all scores.

Deviations may also be analyzed in the "dynamic" case, however, as the difference between each data point and a *line* that passes through them (e.g., a regression line or line-of-progress). Each deviation is then compared to a *different* value (i.e., the value of the line at that point). Analysis of dynamic deviations can be useful in determining if: a) the line adequately describes the data; and b) there is any trend in variability in the data (perhaps reflecting "adaptation" or some other behavioral process). See Figures 19 and 20. See also **Mean**; **Median**; **Line-of-Progress**; **Static Analysis**; and **Dynamic Analysis**.

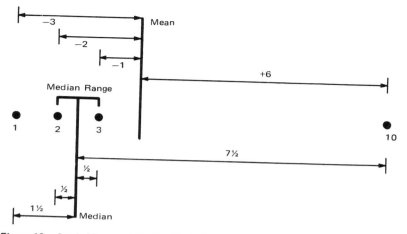

Figure 19. Static Mean and Median Deviations: In the figure above four data points are represented with the values of 1, 2, 3, and 10. The mean and median for that distribution of data points are noted along with the deviations (differences) between those values and each of the datum. By summing those deviations one will be able to determine that the median will yield the least sum of *un*signed deviations (forget the side on which the data point falls); and the mean will yield the least sum of *signed* deviations (subtract the total of the deviations on one side from the sum of the deviations on the other side). Note also that the median may vary within a *range* defined by the two "middle-most" data points (when, of course, there are an even number of data points) because movement in one direction adds exactly the same to the deviations on that side that it subtracts from the other side (there are the same number of deviations on either side). Since sign is important in the case of the mean, however, moving in either direction *must* alter the sum of the deviations.

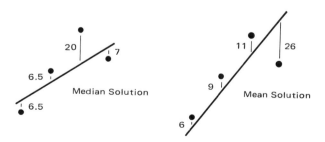

Figure 20. Dynamic Mean and Median Deviations: In this figure two identical sets of data are summarized by a line passing through the points to describe the "average" change over time those data represent. The data on the right are summarized by the *mean* line of progress (regression line); and those on the left by the *median* line of progress. By summing the deviations in both cases, counting the signs in the case of the mean, and discounting the signs in the case of the median, one is able to see the differences in the manner with which the data are treated by the two methods. The mean will minimize the sum of the *signed* deviations; and the median will minimize the sum of the *un*signed deviations. In general the median slope will be a more "conservative" estimate of progress than the mean.

41

Differential Reinforcement of High Rates (DRH)
A contingency in which reinforcement is delivered for rates of responding which exceed some minimal value. Rates may be calculated as "averages," or on an operant-to-operant basis. The latter is far more effective in generating the desired high rates, but considerably more difficult to manage (i.e., calculate and use to decide if the criteria for reinforcement has been met in time to actually deliver reinforcement before the next response has been emitted).

Differential Reinforcement of Low Rates (DRL)
A type of contingency in which the delivery of reinforcement is made dependent upon rates of responding which fall below a certain predetermined value. The rates upon which the decision as to reinforce or not is made may be "averaged rates" taken as the average rate of responding over a specified interval, or "operant-to-operant" rates, in which each interval between the initiation of one response and the next is measured and analyzed for the low-rate property. The latter of these two methods, while considerably harder to measure and analyze in time to actually deliver reinforcement, is by far the most effective in rapidly obtaining low rates of responding.

Differential Reinforcement of Other Behaviors (DRO)
A schedule of reinforcement in which the organism is reinforced for abstaining from the emission of a particular response for a specified period of time. Since a reinforcer reinforces that instance of behavior which just preceded it in time, and since the specified behavior *cannot* precede the reinforcer, one speaks of this paradigm as reinforcing "other" behaviors. The result is a decrease in the probability or rate of responding for the specified behavior. NOTE: If any single behavior or class of behavior accidentally precedes the delivery of reinforcement repeatedly, then it may be expected that it will increase in probability or rate. Since it is common for classes of behavior to be associated with any one particular reinforcer in the history of the organism, and since these classes of behavior are frequently of a similar nature, one may simply be replacing one form of (presumably "undesirable") response for the one being differentially "non-reinforced." Care should be taken, therefore, when this procedure is employed. It is frequently better, for example, to specify *which* behaviors may be reinforced to the exclusion of the one for which reduction is desired.

Differential Reinforcement of Paced Responding (DRP)
A schedule of reinforcement in which the organism is reinforced for emitting a specified behavior or class of

behaviors at rates of responding which fall within two arbitrary limits. Rates may be calculated as "averages" taken over some specified unit of time ; or as operant-to-operant rates—the latter method, while more difficult to employ, is by far the most effective in generating the desired pacing.

Differentiation
1. As an operation: The differential reinforcement of responses which satisfy some formal specification with respect to intensity, duration, or topography.
2. As a process: The resulting change in relative frequency of responses showing the specified property. An organism which has learned to differentiate is able to determine which of a number of responses in his repertoire will have a higher probability of being reinforced.
(or)

1. As an operation: The differential reinforcement of one response or class of responses (as opposed to another response or class of responses) in the presence of specific stimulus conditions.
2. As a process: The resultant increase in rate or probability of responding in that stimulus condition for that reinforced response or class of responses, where the rate or probability of responding for the unreinforced responses in that stimulus condition decreases or remains the same. We speak of differentiation as determining *which* of a number of responses will be reinforced, and discrimination as the process of determining *when* (in the presence of what stimulus conditions) that response will be reinforced. In order for the process of differentiation to occur some discrimination must also occur.

Discrimination
The control of an operant performance by a discriminative stimulus. Discrimination is said to have occurred when the discriminative stimulus predictably affects the rate of probability of those responses which will produce a reinforcing event or punishing event in its presence.

Discrimination, Operant
1. As an operation: The differential reinforcement of responses emitted in the presence of a stimulus with specific properties (e.g., responses to a red key are reinforced, responses to a green key are not).
2. As a process: The resulting change in rate as a function of the properties of the stimuli, observed either concurrently or under later conditions. The organism "shows a discrimination" by responding more rapidly in the presence of the property

correlated with reinforcement, and less rapidly or not at all in the presence of the property correlated with nonreinforcement or punishment.

Discrimination, Respondent
1. As an operation: Arranging a third stimulus in respondent conditioning in the presence of which unconditioned and conditioned stimuli are paired; and in the absence of which the pairing of the two stimuli is unknown.

2. As a process: A change in the behavior so that the probability that the conditioned response is elicited increases or remains the same in the presence of the discriminative stimulus; and decreases or remains the same in the absence of that stimulus (dependent upon whether the conditioned and unconditioned stimulus were never paired or sometimes paired when the discriminative stimulus was *not* present).

Discrimination, Temporal
The phenomena of discriminated responding to the stimulus of the passage of time (e.g., the low rates of responding at the beginning of a fixed-interval schedule, and high rates at the end). If there is any external stimulus which changes as a function of the passage of time (e.g., a clock or the position of the sun) of which the organism may be aware, then the discrimination may not be considered solely temporal. Some experimenters maintain that no discrimination based totally upon temporal stimuli is possible; but rather, that the nature of responding is dependent upon the emission of similar and/or dissimilar responses previously emitted. E.g., as the number of responses previously emitted since the last reinforcement increases, the probability of the next reinforcement also increases and results in higher rates of responding; or, a chain of "mediating" responses is learned to "mark time" until the next reinforcement is available. The completion of the mediating chain would be, therefore, the discriminative stimulus for the reinforced response.

Disposition (D)
A synonym for "setting," and a component of the "does" equation in Precision Teaching. See **"Does" Equation**.

Dividby (÷)
A statement of change, originated in Precision Teaching, in reference to the difference between any two points or lines in a data set where the second point or line represents a lower value than the first. The statement is in terms of that factor by which the first must be divided to obtain the second. For example: If the first data point represents a rate of 8.0

responses per minute, and the second data point represents a rate of 2.0 responses per minute, then the amount of change between the two is expressed as 8/2 = 4, or "dividby 4."

The use of dividby statements is limited to statements of change represented on semilog or ratio charts. On such charts changes are always represented in proportions or ratios; and regardless of the position of the numbers yielding that ratio on an absolute scale, equal ratios will always appear to occupy equal portions of the chart. The change from 200 to 100 (a dividby 2), for example, will look exactly the same as a change from .02 to .01 (also a dividby 2). See also **Times** and **Chart**.

"Does" Analysis
A term originated in Precision Teaching to denote the operation of altering components of the "is" equation to determine their effects on rate of responding; and then rewriting those components which demonstrate an effect into the "does" equation. See **"Is" Equation** and **"Does" Equation**.

"Does" Equation
A type of analytic paradigm originated in Precision Teaching which is comprised of a list of environmental events and behaver movement-cycles which have been demonstrated to affect or be affected by each other (i.e., to be functionally related). The "does" equation describes what *does* work in an effort to change rates of responding. Before any event may be described in "does" equation form it must be demonstrated that by altering or changing that event (in form, frequency, or by adding or removing it from the plan) the rates of responding also change. Each component of the "does" equation has a corollary in the "is" equation. The only difference between the two is the demonstration of the effect that the components have on rates of responding. The advantage of "translating" the equation from the "is" to the "does" as the components are found to be effective is to keep it clear as to what was *tried* and what was actually found to *work,* aiding in the formulation of future plans. See Figure 21. See also **"Is" Equation**.

Double Equation
A term, originating in Precision Teaching, in reference to a plan which includes equations for both the acceleration of one movement-cycle or response, and the deceleration of another movement-cycle or response. The rationale for using a double equation lies in the fact that often times a particular movement-cycle or response may be accelerated more quickly if another (presumably competitive) movement-cycle or

Figure 21. "Does" Equation:

Disposition (D): The equivalent of program in the "is" equation, except that by altering the program it has been demonstrated that it does effect rates of responding. What was called the program can now be said to "dispose" the behaver to respond in a particular manner; hence, the program is now called a disposition. See **Program** in the **"Is" Equation**.

Stimulus (S): The equivalent of program event in the "is" equation, except that by altering the program event it has been demonstrated that it does effect rates of responding. The program event, therefore, can be said to "stimulate" responding, and is now called a stimulus. See **Program Event** in the **"Is" Equation**.

Response (R): The equivalent of movement-cycle in the "is" equation, except that it has been demonstrated to be controlled by one or more elements in the equation. Since the movement-cycle can then be said to be "responsive" to changes in the equation, it is now called a response. See **Movement-Cycle** in the **"Is" Equation**.

Contingency (K): The equivalent of arrangement in the "is" equation, except that it has been demonstrated by alteration to control rates of responding. NOTE: To demonstrate that an arrangement *per se* has an effect on the rate of responding, the consequence must remain the same and *only* the arrangement altered. See **Arrangement** in the **"Is" Equation**.

Consequence (C): The equivalent of arranged event in the "is" equation, except that it has been demonstrated to effect rates of responding. The arranged event may then be said to effectively "consequate" the response; hence, it is now called a consequence. See **Arranged Event** in the **"Is" Equation**.

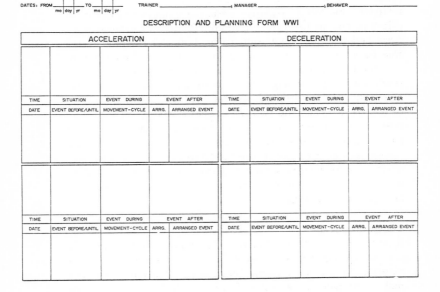

Figure 22. Double Equation: This form, borrowed from Waechter's descriptive analysis (see Appendix), is only one of several possible designed to explicate the dual planning of corresponding acceleration and deceleration projects. For a full description of the specific equations employed, see Appendix.

response is decelerated at the same time (or vice versa).
Example: When trying to accelerate "problem-solving" behavior on a math-fact sheet, it might be wise to attempt the deceleration of "out of seat" or "incorrect solution" behavior at the same time. See Figure 22.

Drive

The hypothetical organismic variable which is responsible for the probability that an organism will engage in a set of responses that will or have in the past led to the procurement of a specific reinforcer or class of reinforcers. Also called "motivation."

Reference to such a hypothetical variable is considered unnecessary as the simple statement of the probability of certain behaviors in the context of certain stimuli or stimulus events is sufficient for the investigation of the observable phenomena.

Drive, Acquired

A drive which governs the emission of a set of responses which have in the past led to the procurement of *conditioned* reinforcers. See **Drive** and **Reinforcer, Conditioned**.

Drive Level

The probability that an organism will engage in the class of responses (which will procure or have in the past procured a specific reinforcer or class of reinforcers). Reference to "drive level" is generally less preferred than a simple statement of probability. NOTE: These probabilities will generally change as a function of certain stimuli or stimulus events (i.e., the conditions under which the data relevant to the estimation of the probabilities were obtained), and it is most advisable that these conditions be clearly specified. Generalization of probability estimates beyond the conditions under which the estimates were derived is generally tenuous.

DRH

An abbreviation for "differential reinforcement of high rates." See **Differential Reinforcement of High Rates**.

DRL

An abbreviation for "differential reinforcement of low rates." See **Differential Reinforcement of Low Rates**.

DRO

Abbreviation for "differential reinforcement of other behaviors." See **Differential Reinforcement of Other Behaviors**.

DRP
An abbreviation for "differential reinforcement of paced responding." See **Differential Reinforcement of Paced Responding.**

Drugs (as used in behavioral therapy)
Any chemical compound which may be used to alter the type or form of an organism's behavior. It is important to realize that drugs are basically prosthetic in nature (i.e., they will have affect on the nature of the organism's behavior only for the duration of their use; discontinuance of the drug will usually result in discontinuance of the behavior instituted by their use). Drugs may be used (effectively) to control behavior, but without concomitant changes in the environment (reinforcement contingencies, discriminative stimuli, programs, etc.) there is no reason to assume that any permanent behavioral alterations will obtain beyond the discontinuance of the drug. For example: The use of drugs to affect immediate suppression of "hyperactive" behavior in a child might be necessary to prevent injury or destruction of personal property. Once the behavior has been thusly controlled, however, measures should be instituted to bring the appropriate behavior under *operant* control (i.e., reinforcement of moderate rates of responding, establishment of adequate stimulus control, etc.) so that there will be some basis for the *maintenance* of appropriate behaviors when drugs are discontinued.

Dynamic Analysis
Any analysis of data in which changes in one variable are predicted as a function of changes in another; and taken into account when an analysis of the data is performed. For example: If, when following a child through his math-fact curriculum, it is discovered that he increases his rates of responding at a rate of approximately x1.2 per week of practice; then when analyzing the effect of a change in the educational plan, that trend should be taken into account. The analysis would *not*, therefore be made as a comparison between his rates of responding *before* the change and *after* the change; but rather between the rates we would have *predicted* him to have (if no change were made) and the rates that actually obtained during the new condition. Dynamic analyses are the most appropriate forms of analysis for sequentially-dependent behavioral data (i.e., data taken over a period of several days). See also **Static Analysis,** and **Median Slope.**

E^D (E-Dee)

1. In operant terminology: An event in the presence of which the emission of a specified operant, class of operants, or chain of operants will (eventually) be followed by either a positive reinforcer or a punisher, or the removal of either and in the absence of which the contingency and occurrence of these subsequent events is indeterminable (except as noted below). Changes in rates or probabilities of responding as a function of the presence or absence of the E^D are unknown, but the *potential* function is that of an S^D—increases or decreases in the rates or probabilities. Once these functions *are* known, then the E^D is more properly called an S^D. In the special case where the E^D is present during *all* instances of consequation, one may speak of its absence as an E[△], and there will be a *potential* for complete stimulus control. This special case is *not*, however, inherent in the definition of an E^D. See also **Event; Stimulus; S^D**; and **E[△]**.

2. In respondent discrimination: An event in the presence of which the occurrence of a conditioned stimulus will always be followed by the occurrence of the unconditioned stimulus, and in the absence of which the occurrence of the unconditioned stimulus following the occurrence of the correlated conditioned stimulus is indeterminable. The use of the term "event" denotes the fact that the actual affect of the event on the probability of the elicited response is unknown. Because of its known correlation with environmental conditions, however, it may be considered to be a "potential" discriminative stimulus; and once the affect of the event is known, the use of the term S^D would be more appropriate. In the special case in which the E^D is present during all instances of conditioned and unconditioned stimulus pairings, then one may speak of its absence as an E[△], and there will be a *potential* for complete stimulus control. This special case is *not*, however, inherent in the definition of an E^D. See also **Event; Stimulus; S^D**; and **E[△]**.

E[△] ("E-Delta")

1. In operant discrimination: An event in the presence of which the emission of an operant, class of operants, or chain of operants will never be reinforced or punished (i.e., never consequated in any way); and in the absence of which the availability of consequences is indeterminable (except as noted

below). The affect that the presence of an E^Δ will have on rates or probabilities is unknown, but the *potential* function is the same as that of an S^Δ. Once the functions *are* known, then the E^Δ is more properly called an S^Δ. In the special case where the E^Δ is present during *all* situations *in* which consequation is *not* available, then one may speak of its absence as an E^D, and there is a *potential* for complete stimulus control. This special case is not, however, inherent in the basic definition of an E^Δ. See also **Event; Stimulus; S^Δ;** and **E^D**.

2. In respondent discrimination: An event in the presence of which the occurrence of a conditioned stimulus will never be followed by the occurrence of the correlated unconditioned stimulus; and in the absence of which the probability of the occurrence of the unconditioned stimulus is indeterminable (except as noted below). The affect of the E^Δ on the probability of the elicited conditioned response is unknown. Once this function *has* been determined, then the E^Δ is more properly called an S^Δ. In the special case in which the E^Δ is present during all situations in which the unconditioned stimulus will not occur, then one may speak of its absence as being an E^D, and there is a potential for complete stimulus control. This special case is not, however, inherent in the basic definition of an E^Δ. See also **Event; Stimulus; S^Δ;** and **E^D**.

Efficiency, Performance
The relationship that exists between the amount or type of performance presently being emitted by an organism for a given amount of consequation, and the minimum amount or type of performance *necessary* for the same or greater amount of consequation (NOTE: Either the amount and type of performance *or* the amount of consequation should be held constant when making the comparison—if both are changed then the result is a combination of the several variables, and difficult to interpret). E.g., if John changes body position seven times in the completion of a bath, and the same task could be accomplished with only three body position changes, then the ratio 3/7 (.43) reflects his efficiency relative to the "optimal" efficiency. Similarly, if by making motions in one direction Billy obtains six instances of teacher interactions, but *could* receive eight interactions if he were to make the same motions in a different direction, then he is operating at 6/8 (or .75) performance efficiency. Performance efficiency is an excellent way in which to note the ability of an organism to "analyze" contingencies, and maximize potential consequations.

Efficiency, Program

The relationship that exists between the performances achieved in a subject under one program and the performances achieved under another (or hypothetically "perfect") program. E.g., if one reading program results in reading rates of 300 words per minute, and another in rates in excess of 1000 words per minute, then the relative program efficiency of one to the other is 300/1000 (or .30). Frequently, there are several factors to analyze, however, like cost in time and money in addition to performance results. All factors are ratioed as above, and then presented individually. NOTE: Some people prefer to weight the importance of factors and then combine all ratios into one figure. The amount of information lost in this procedure, however, makes it somewhat less desirable.

EIR

An abbreviation for "extinction inflection ratio." See **Extinction Inflection Ratio**.

Electroconvulsive Shock (ECS)

An electric shock delivered to an organism resulting in convulsive responses (momentary paralysis or involuntary movement of some or all muscles). The affect of the shock on the movement of the organism may or may not be terminated at the moment the shock is discontinued, and can result in restricted responding in the organism for some time following. Because of this continuance of affect, the use of shock can sometimes result in confounded data. For example: The use of shock as a "punisher" may, in fact, reduce the probability of responding, but the suppression may be physiological as opposed to being due to "punishing properties" of the stimulus.

Elicit

A verb of action in reference to respondent behavior where the unconditioned response bears a one-to-one relationship to the occurrence of the unconditioned stimulus. Because the unconditioned stimulus determines both the form and frequency of the unconditioned responses (or conditioned response), we speak of the unconditioned response (or conditioned response) as being "elicited" rather than "emitted" as in the operant case. NOTE: This does not mean that the behavior elicited *cannot* occur independently of the eliciting stimulus; only that when the eliciting stimulus occurs, the response in question *must* occur. For example: An eye-blink may be elicited by a puff of air on the eye. Each puff of air will elicit (force to happen) the eye-blink. Eye-blinks *may*, however, occur in the *absence* of the puff of air.

51

Emit

A verb to describe the occurrence of an operant behavior. We speak of the operant as being emitted to emphasize the fact that ultimately the form and frequency of the operant are determined by stimulus events occurring *subsequent* to the emission of the operant (i.e., reinforcing events)—as opposed to antecedent "eliciting" events as in the case of the respondent. NOTE: While it is true that the rate and/or probability of operants may be (in part) determined by antecedents (stimuli) the ability of those stimuli to control responding is due to their association with reinforcing events occurring *after* the operant. "Control" may still, therefore, be attributed to subsequent events.

Emotion

A state of the organism in which the form and frequency of several behaviors in the ongoing repertoire are altered without expressed contingencies of conditioning or extinction. I.e., several responses are emitted which are not directly under the control of the contingencies presently in force. Distinction between emotional responses and mediating and collateral responses are vague and may differ in usage. Generally emotional responses are equatable with regressive "escape" behaviors—which may have served a function in the history of the organism, but no longer do; and collateral or mediating responses are equatable with responses recently, but superstitiously reinforced. See **State of the Organism**; **Behavior, Collateral**; and **Behavior, Mediating**.

Environment, Prosthetic

An environment especially designed and constructed to maintain behaviors which the organism would otherwise fail to or be unable to emit. Discontinuance of the prosthetic environment will result in discontinuance of the behaviors supported by it. See **Prosthesis**.

Environment, Therapeutic

An environment designed and constructed to generate behaviors which will still maintain when the environment is restored to its original state. See also **Therapy**.

Event

A change from one set of conditions to another set of conditions. In order to completely define an event the conditions present in the environment both *before* and *after* the change must be described. In some cases it is also necessary to describe the *agent* of change and/or conditions *during* the change (i.e., who or what causes the change; and what happens during the transition from the conditions "before" to the conditions "after."

Frequently "events" are defined in the literature solely by the conditions they create (e.g., a reinforcing event might be defined as "presentation of food" or simply "food"). In fact, however, the nature of the event *per se* (and, in turn, its affect) may change considerably with different antecedents. For example, the events defined below both result in "food," but would certainly have differing affects on rates of responding when employed as arranged-events.

	Event I	Event II
change from:	no food available	food available equal to the body weight of the organism
change to:	food available equal to 1/100th the body weight of the organism	food available equal to 1/100th the body weight of the organism.

In Event One the change results in an *increased* amount of food available; but in Event Two there is a significant *reduction* in food. The first event could conceivably result in positive reinforcement, and the latter in punishment; and yet both have the same "condition after." It *is* true that the majority of events described in the literature are a little more explicit than simply "food." "Delivery of one food pellet," or "presentation of the food magazine for a period of 6 seconds," for example, *do* explicate the fact that there is a necessary *in*crease in the food available; and the problem implied in Events One and Two above are eliminated—but not entirely. The descriptions of Events Three and Four below point out another potential difference.

	Event III	Event IV
change from:	100 food pellets available	no food pellets available
change to:	one more food pellet available	one more food pellet available

Now, even though the affect of both events is to increase the food available, there is a significant difference in the *relative* magnitudes of the increase involved. Still another potential difference is explicated in Events Five and Six.

	Event V	Event VI
change from:	no food pellets	no food pellets
change by:	experimenter's hand	mechanical mechanism
change to:	one food pellet available	one food pellet available

While the conditions before and after the event are now the same, the "agent" causing the event (and, therefore, the conditions during the transition from the "before" to the "after") are different. Again, there is a potential difference in the affects of the two events.

It should be clear that the description of *both* sets of conditions will result in more specific and informative communication. In fact, however, there are some additional advantages. The difference between "negative" and "positive" reinforcement, for example, ceases to exist. They are *both* events entailing a change from one set of conditions to another. Instead, then, of having to defend the assumption that one stimulus is "aversive" and the other "neutral" one needs only to demonstrate that changing from one to the other is "reinforcing" (i.e., increases the rate or probability of responding). In some situations this is quite important. A blast of air at $30°$ F, for example, would usually constitute an aversive stimulus. If, on the other hand, the organism is in *minus* $30°$ weather, then the same stimulus might prove quite reinforcing. Rather than attempting to determine if "heat" is being "removed," or "cold" is being "presented," both situations can be adequately and fully defined by simply describing the conditions before and after the change, and then ascribing the appropriate functional label (e.g., "reinforcing" or "punishing").

"Event" is basically a descriptive term (i.e., its use does not imply that the *function* of the event is known, only that it exists). Once the function of an event *has* been determined (i.e., it *is* known what affect it has on responding), then it is more correctly called a *"stimulus* event" (i.e., it "stimulates" the organism in some way). Frequently, however, this is shortened to simply "stimulus." See also **Stimulus**.

Event After
A descriptive term used to denote an event (i.e., a change in the environment) which (with some consistency) occurs after the emission of a specified behavior. The use of the term "after" instead of "arranged" implies that the event after is not (believed to be) *caused* by the behavior (or contingent upon it). For example: If after dinner a man has a habit of sitting down and watching the news broadcast on television (which may, in turn, upset him and have an adverse affect on eating behavior), the news broadcast may be called an event after (it certainly was not *caused* by the behavior of eating dinner, but it does *follow* it). The use of the term "event" is advisable whenever it is not known whether or not the change actually affects the rate or probability of the behavior it precedes. When function *has* been determined, the use of the term "stimulus" (or "reinforcer") is more appro-

priate. See also **Event Before**; **Event During**; **Event Until**; **Event Anytime**; **Event, Arranged**; **Stimulus**; and **Reinforcer**.

Event Always

A descriptive term to denote an event (i.e., a change in the environment) which occurs continuously (i.e., repeatedly) before, during, and after the behavior with a regular or semi-regular pattern. For example: A clock's ticking or the sound of machinery in a factory are steady, rhythmic events that would tend to occur often enough to occur before, during, and after each emission of a response. An event always is differentiated from an event anytime in that it tends to be more regular and more frequent (i.e., an event anytime *can* occur before, during, and after a behavior but tends, with any single emission of the behavior, to occupy only *one* of those positions); and is differentiated from the situation or situation-elements by virtue of the fact that it *is* an event (i.e., a change—repeated change) whereas situations or situation-elements are constants—things which do *not* change in the environment. The use of the term "event" is advisable whenever it is not known whether or not the change actually affects the rate or probability of the behavior in question. When a function *has* been determined, the use of the term "stimulus" is more appropriate. See also **Event Before**; **Event Until**; **Event During**; **Event After**; **Event, Arranged**; **Event Anytime**; **Event**; and **Stimulus**.

Event, Antecedent (AnE)

A term which combines the categories of event before and event until. Since the use of the term antecedent event is less specific, it should only be used if the distinction between event before and event until is not possible. See **Event Before** and **Event Until**.

Event Anytime

A descriptive term to denote an event (i.e., a change in the environment) which occurs in close temporal relationship to a specified behavior, but which can and does occur *anytime* (i.e., before, during, or after that response; and does not occur in any of those positions any more frequently than any other position). The use of the term "event" is advisable whenever it is not known whether or not the change actually affects the rate or probability of the behavior with which it occurs. When function *has* been determined, the use of the term "stimulus" is more appropriate. See also **Event Before**; **Event Until**; **Event During**; **Event After**; **Event, Arranged**; **Event Always**; and **Stimulus**.

Event, Arranged (ArE) or (AE)

Any environmental event which occurs just following the emission of a behavior, and which is *caused* by that behavior. The use of the term "event" denotes the fact that *function* is unknown (i.e., what affect this arranged condition has on the rate or probability of responding). When function *has* been determined, then the arranged event is more properly called a positive reinforcer or punisher (dependent upon its affect). Arranged events are a subclass of "events after." Although in Precision Teaching the abbreviation for the term "arranged event" is AE, this may be confused with the term "antecedent event"; which, while no longer used in Precision Teaching, still may be found in the literature. To avoid confusion the abbreviation ArE is recommended. See **"Is" Equation** for a detailed explanation of the use of this term in Precision Teaching. See also **Event** and **Event After**.

Event Before

A descriptive term used to denote an event (i.e., a change in the environment) that occurs (with some consistency) before the emission of a specified behavior. The use of the term "event" is advisable whenever it is not known whether or not the change actually affects the rate or probability of the behavior it precedes. When function *has* been determined, the use of the term "stimulus" is more appropriate. See also **Event Until**; **Event During**; **Event After**; **Event, Arranged**; **Event Anytime**; and **Stimulus**.

Event, Complex

Synonym for "integral event." See **Event, Integral**.

Event, Concurrent (CE)

A synonym for "event during." See **Event During**.

Event, Discriminative

An event (i.e., a change in the environment) which is correlated with the presence or absence of certain contingencies and consequences (positive or aversive). The use of the term "event" denotes the fact that the actual affect of the event on rates or probabilities of responding is unknown. Because of its known correlation with environmental conditions, however, it may be considered a "potential" discriminative stimulus. See also **Stimulus, Discriminative**; **Event**; E^D; and E^Δ.

Event During

A descriptive term denoting an event (i.e., a change in the environment) which occurs concurrently (i.e., at the same time as) the emission of a specified behavior. For example: If a teacher repeatedly tells a child to return to his seat while he is out of his seat (and, of course, *stops* telling him to return to his seat when, in fact, he has), then "telling" is an event during "out of seat" behavior. The use of the term "event" is advisable whenever it is not known whether or not the change actually affects the rate or probability of the behavior with which it occurs. When the function *has* been determined, the use of the term "stimulus" is more appropriate. See also **Event Before**; **Event Until**; **Event After**; **Event, Arranged**; **Event Anytime**; and **Stimulus**.

Event, Integral
A complex event in which there are many components which, although they could be separated *physically*, occur in conjunction (and perhaps in a particular sequence). Analysis of integral events should be made with event sampling techniques as well as time sampling techniques. NOTE: The designation of "event" as opposed to "stimulus" denotes the fact that no experimental evidence is available to assign definite function to these events, although one may be hypothesized. See also **Stimulus, Integral**.

Event Sampling
A technique of descriptive analysis in which all events (simple or integral) are described either in order of occurrence or, if only one event is described, in repeated detail (i.e., each time the event occurs, the description is altered and revised to achieve greater detail). In event sampling, one describes *what* the events are (or is), as opposed to describing their temporal distribution. No attempt is made during the event sampling operation to ascribe *function* to the event. This is done later by manipulating the content and occurrence of the event and noting any change in responding—after which the event in question is called a stimulus. See also **Time Sampling**.

Event, Subsequent (SE)
A synonym for "event after"; first used by the advocates of Precision Teaching, but since replaced with the terms arranged event and program event—which are not interchangeable (one denotes contingency, the other non-contingency). See **Event After**.

Event, Uncorrelated
A synonym for either "event anytime" or "event always." Since the use of the terms "event anytime" and "event always" are more specific, the term "uncorrelated event" should be reserved for those situations in which the specific

nature of the event is unknown (i.e., whether it is an event anytime or an event always). See **Event Anytime** and **Event Always**.

Event Until
A descriptive term used to denote an event (i.e., a change in the environment) which (with some consistency) occurs prior to the emission of a specified behavior, and continues to occur (either continuously or repeatedly) *until* the behavior occurs. Differentiated from an event before in that the event before does not (usually) occur more than once before the emission of the behavior. For example: If a teacher reads through a spelling list rapidly (and the children write the last word they hear), then each word is a potential event before; but if the teacher reads one word and then waits until all children have written it, repeating the word every so often, then the words are more properly called events until. The use of the term "event" is advisable whenever it is not known whether or not the change actually affects the rate or probability of the behavior it precedes. When function *has* been determined, the use of the term "stimulus" is more appropriate. See also **Event Before**; **Event During**; **Event After**; **Event, Arranged**; **Stimulus**; and **Event Anytime**.

Experimental Design, Multiple Time-Series
Like that of the time-series, with the exception that the time series of the experimental subject(s) is compared with a time series of non-experimental (control) subject(s). The multiple baseline is a special case of the multiple-time-series design. See also **Experimental Design, Time-Series**; and **Methods of Confirmation (Multiple Baseline)**.

Experimental Design, Pretest-Posttest
An experimental design in which comparisons are made between the value of a dependent variable before an experimental variable is employed and the value of the same dependent variable after the experimental variable is employed.

An experimental design of this nature, although common in behavioral research, is not able to define and analyze process (i.e., *how* the dependent variable changed), only *whether* it changed. See also **Experimental Design, Time Series**; **Experimental Design, Multiple Time Series**; and **Methods of Confirmation**.

Experimental Design, Time-Series
An experimental design in which several observations are taken on the dependent variable in temporal sequence over minutes,

hours, days, or some other unit of time before, during, and after the experimental manipulation. The only type of design that will allow the investigation of *process*, that is, the characteristics of the moment-to-moment or session-to-session changes in performance. Alternative approaches (e.g., the pretest-posttest design) rely instead on overall magnitude of change between conditions; and analysis is, therefore, reflective only of end result—with little or no attention to the process through which that result evolved. See also **Experimental Design, Pretest-Posttest; Experimental Design, Multiple Time-Series; Process;** and **Methods of Confirmation.**

Experimental Space
The enclosure in which an experiment is carried out; and in which all relevant independent and dependent variables may be controlled and/or observed. Also called a "Skinner box" when in reference to infrahuman studies.

EXT
Abbreviation for "extinction" (operant or respondent). See **Extinction, Operant** and **Extinction, Respondent.**

Extinction Inflection Ratio (EIR)
An index designed to indicate changes in rate between periods of conditioning and periods of extinction. Obtained by determining the relative difference between the rates of responding before and after the institution of extinction conditions.

$$EIR = \text{rate of responding before/rate of responding after}$$

More detailed investigations may be performed by dividing the extinction condition into smaller segments (e.g., dividing a 20-minute extinction condition into 2-minute segments) and then comparing each segment with the pre-extinction rates separately. Normally the pre-extinction condition is still treated as a whole, however, assuming that rates in that condition are reasonably stable.

Usually the range of possible EIR values is unlimited—determined solely by the respective response rate values. Some experimenters, in an effort to provide a common base to all EIR statements, prefer to employ the following formula:

$$EIR = \frac{(\text{average rate after}) - (\text{average rate before})}{(\text{average rate before})}$$

In this formula it can be seen that if the rates are identical, the EIR will always equal zero; if the rates before extinction are greater than those during extinction, then the EIR will equal some negative value (indicating rates went down); and if the rates after extinction has begun are greater, then the EIR will equal some positive value (indicating that the rates have increased).

Another adaptation of the EIR is based on the formula:

$$EIR = \frac{(\text{average rate after}) - (\text{average rate before})}{(\text{average rate after}) + (\text{average rate before})}$$

In this case it may be seen that the EIR will still equal zero when the before and after rates are the same; but now the limits of the EIR are plus and minus one—when the "rate-after" is zero, then the EIR will equal −1; and when the "rate-before" is zero, the EIR will equal +1.

While this last ratio is more clearly defined and unilaterally interpreted than either of the others, it does impose artificial limitations on essentially unrestricted measures, and, therefore, is not without drawbacks.

Extinction Interval
The average length of time taken to complete a ratio in a variable or fixed ratio schedule of reinforcement. Taken as that time which must elapse before the organism is able to discriminate the condition of extinction. No decrement in responding would be expected to occur prior to the passage of this interval since the last reinforcement. If a change is to be made from a ratio to an interval schedule, setting the interval's initial value equal or less than the extinction interval will maximize the probability of the transition without decrement in rate or probability of responding. See also **Extinction Ratio**.

Extinction, Operant
1. As an operation: The prevention of all reinforcement following a specified behavior or chain of behaviors.
2. As a process: The resultant decrease in rate or probability of responding to "zero" or operant level for that response.
NOTE: It has been observed in many cases where programmed reinforcement has been discontinued that response rates do not always return to operant level. Cases have even been noted where rates *in*crease. This maintenance may be attributed to stimuli which became strongly conditioned reinforcers during the duration of the programmed reinforcement; or, to the fact that certain behaviors, once shaped by programmed contingencies, enable the organism to procure reinforcers already existent in the environment which are beyond the control of the experimenter or therapist. For example: A particular child may have no inclination to learn

to read until certain specific reinforcement contingencies are set up for that purpose. It is unlikely, however, that once the child has learned, and the reinforcement contingencies removed, that the child will then cease to read. The reinforcements for this type of behavior are many and varied in the environment (e.g., the ability to determine which movie is playing, the opportunity to obtain better employment, etc.). It is most proper, therefore, that one speak of the *operation* of extinction as being applied to specified reinforcers, and then note the behavioral process as it occurs. In the above example, one may speak of placing the reading behavior on extinction with respect to social praise, and that the behavior maintained—presumably due to reinforcement procured from the "natural" environment.

Extinction has also been called "unlearning," but somewhat incorrectly, since it has been demonstrated that "recondition-, ing" an extinguished response is usually easier than original conditioning—thereby intimating that some "residual" learning from original conditioning remains.

The process of extinction is usually modified by the contingencies under which the response was emitted prior to extinction. After conditioning under an FR schedule of reinforcement, for example, the "extinction curve" is usually broken between "runs" of high-rate responding and intervals of no responding at all; whereas extinction following FI conditioning is usually represented by a gradual and smooth reduction in rates of responding over time. See Figure 23.

Extinction Ratio
The average number of responses emitted per reinforcement on a fixed-interval schedule after a steady-state of responding has been established. Supposedly this figure represents the approximate number of responses that the organism can be expected to emit before it becomes "aware" of the fact that reinforcement is no longer available (during extinction). Initial reduction in rates of responding may not, therefore, be expected before this time. NOTE: The extinction ratio will decrease with continued time under a fixed-interval schedule. Therefore, if transition to a ratio schedule is desired, it is best accomplished relatively early in FI conditioning. See also **Extinction Interval**.

Extinction, Resistance to
In operant behavior, the number of responses emitted by the organism, and often the time taken to reach some criterion of extinction (e.g., the organism emitted 700 responses in 63 minutes before reaching the beginning of a 20-minute period of no responding; in this case the criterion of extinction is 20

minutes without responding). Often it is not practical to undertake the extinction of a particular behavior just to determine its resistance to extinction. In fact, after a behavior has undergone *one* instance of extinction, its resistance to extinction *changes* (assuming, of course, that it has been reconditioned)—usually it is less resistant to further extinction operations. We know, however, on the basis of previous experimentation that certain procedures generate behaviors which are less prone to extinction. For example: High levels of deprivation, gradual contingency building, and variable schedules as opposed to fixed schedules (so that the organism does not know exactly when the next reinforcement is due) all lead to the maintenance of behaviors which are highly resistant to the process of extinction. On the basis of these and other general "laws" of behavior we can often estimate resistance to extinction, at least in a relative sense (i.e., behavior X is probably more resistant to extinction than behavior Y).

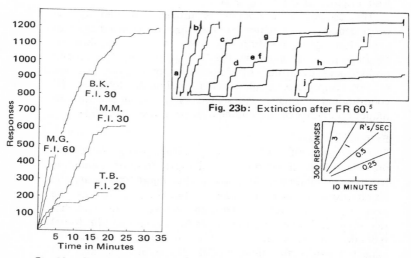

Fig. 23b: Extinction after FR 60.[5]

Fig. 23a: Extinction after fixed-interval schedules of 60, 30, and 20 seconds.[4]

Figure 23. Extinction Following Conditioning Under Fixed-Ratio and Fixed-Interval Schedules of Reinforcement.

[4] From "Operant extinction after fixed-interval schedules with young children," by S. Bijou, *Journal of the Experimental Analysis of Behavior*, 1958, *1*, 25—29. Copyright © 1958 by the Society for the Experimental Analysis of Behavior, Inc. Used by permission of the author and publisher.

[5] From Ferster, C. B. and Skinner, B. F. *Schedules of reinforcement*. New York: Appleton-Century-Crofts, page 58. Copyright © 1957. Used by permission of Appleton-Century-Crofts, Educational Division, Meredith Corporation.

Extinction, Respondent
1. As an operation: presenting the conditioned stimulus without pairing it with the unconditioned stimulus.
2. As a process: the resulting reduction in the magnitude of the response elicited by the conditioned stimulus; and usually the ultimate cessation of elicitation.

Fading
The operation of gradually changing a stimulus, reinforcer, or contingency controlling an organism's performance to another stimulus, reinforcer, or contingency usually with the intent of maintaining the performance without loss or alteration, but under the new conditions. Quite frequently in reference to the operation of removing (gradually) stimuli, reinforcers, or contingencies which have been artificially imposed in an environment, to bring the behavior under the control of the stimuli, reinforcers, and contingencies which existed in that environment prior to experimental or therapeutic manipulation.

FI
Abbreviation for "fixed-interval schedule of reinforcement." See **Schedule, Fixed-Interval**.

Findley Diagrams
A system of diagrams devised explicitly for the purpose of describing complex sequences of behaviors (e.g., chains, concurrent behavior, collateral behavior). Findley diagrams bear a striking resemblance to electrical drawings, but with some major differences. All diagrams are to be read from left-to-right unless otherwise noted. The various symbols indicate what must occur (or fail to occur) in order for the "circuit" to be completed, and progress made through the sequence of events. Following is a brief listing of the various diagrammatic elements and their meanings.

Response Notations: The notation of response types is essentially the same as the notation of switches—normally open, or normally closed.

Positive Operant: An operant which must be emitted before the events noted to the right of that operant may occur. (Figure 24.)

Negative Operant: An operant whose emission will *stop* progress along the circuit; that is, which will *prevent* the events noted to the right from occurring. (Figure 25.)

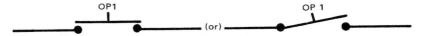

Figure 24. Positive Operant: The name or number of the operant is specified just above the symbol.

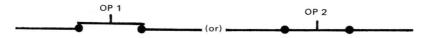

Figure 25. Negative Operant: The name or the number of the operant is specified just above the symbol.

Reinforcement Notations: The specification of primary or secondary reinforcer is the same as that in other notational systems (i.e., S^R and S^r); but the conditions *following* the occurrence of the reinforcing event are noted as "recycling" or "progressing" as follows:

Recycling: Following the occurrence of the reinforcing event the conditions just prior to that event are reinstated. (Figure 26.)

Progressing: Following the occurrence of the reinforcing event, the conditions noted to the right of that event are instated (i.e., the conditions which occurred prior to the reinforcing event are *not* reinstated). (Figure 27.)

Figure 26. Recycling: In this case the program would recycle to Operant #3.

Figure 27. Progressing: In this case the program would progress to Operant #22.

Combination: Figures 28, 29, and 30 indicate, respectively, a reinforcing event which may be followed by either a reinstatement of some previous set of conditions, *or* the instatement of a new set of conditions noted to the right; a reinforcing event which may be followed by the reinstatement of either of two possible conditions which occurred prior to the reinforcing event; a reinforcing event which may be followed by the instatement of either of two new sets of conditions noted to the right of that event.

OP 1; OP 13

Figure 28. Recycling or Progressing: In this case the program would either progress to Operant #13 or recycle to Operant #1.

OP 1; OP 2

Figure 29. Recycle to Either of Two Points: In this case the program would either recycle to Operant #1 or recycle to Operant #2.

OP 11; OP 12

Figure 30. Progress to Either of Two Points: In this case the program would progress to either Operant #11 or Operant #12.

Stimulus Conditions: The stimulus conditions which correlate with certain sections of the diagram (i.e., which are present when the sequence of events indicated by the diagram will or can occur) are noted in parentheses above the section to which they apply. If a single stimulus applies to a rather large section of the diagram, then that section may be "blocked off" with dotted lines. See Figure 31.

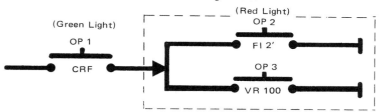

Figure 31. Stimulus Notation: The green light stimulus is associated with Operant #1 and the CRF schedule of reinforcement; and the red light is associated with both Operants #2 and #3 and those schedules.

Scheduling: The type of schedule under which an operant is emitted (i.e., the definition of how much and what type of responding will allow the sequence to progress in the case of a positive operant; or prevent progression in the case of a negative operant) is noted in "traditional" operant terms (e.g.,

FR, FI) and placed just below the symbol for the operant in question. Figure 32 shows one operant governed by an FR schedule, and another by a VR schedule.

Options: When one or more behaviors may be emitted at the same time, or when a choice is available to the organism as to which of several responses to emit, then the point of decision is noted by joining the lines prior to the operants in question. Options may be of several types:

> *Reversible*: An option in which the organism is able to emit the two or more operants in question in rapid alternation or at the same time. Responding on one operant does not, then, prohibit the organism from changing and emitting one of the other operants. The numbers listed below the notations of recycling reinforcing events indicate the part of the diagram which is reinstated. In this case the conditions surrounding Operants 1 and 2 are reinstated. See Figure 33.

> *Irreversible*: An option in which, after the organism has begun to emit one operant, it is no longer possible to emit any of the other operants—until, that is, recycling is specified later in the diagram. Notice that the symbol for "irreversibility" is similar, but not identical, to the symbol for a diode in electrical diagrams. In this case the arrow points in the direction in which the sequence of events *may* proceed; and once the organism has passed this point, he cannot "back-up" and go "against" the arrow. See Figure 34.

Figure 32. Schedule Notation: In this case Operant #1 is governed by a fixed-ratio 10 schedule of reinforcement.

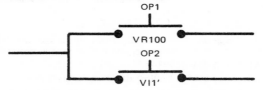

Figure 33. Reversible Option: In this case the subject may respond via Operant #1 under a VR100 schedule of reinforcement, or Operant #2 under a VI 1' schedule of reinforcement. At any time the subject may switch from responding under one operant to responding under the other.

Combination: An option which has one or more "reversible" operants, and one or more "irreversible" operants; that is, some behaviors may be emitted and dropped in favor of another, and other operants, once begun, prohibit any other operant from being emitted until such time as recycling occurs. See Figure 35.

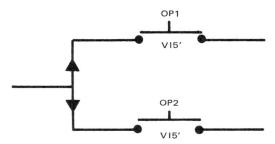

Figure 34. Irreversible Option: In this case the subject may respond via Operant #1 or Operant #2. Both are controlled by variable interval schedules of reinforcement. After responding has begun under one operant or the other, however, the subject can no longer emit the other operant until reinforcement has been delivered.

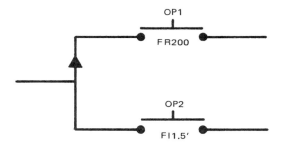

Figure 35. Combination Option: The subject may choose to emit either Operant #1 or Operant #2. If Operant #2 is chosen, then the subject may switch to Operant #1, at any time. If Operant #1 is chosen, on the other hand, the subject will no longer be able to switch to Operant #2.

Special Contingencies: There are basically two "special" contingencies listed in Findley diagrams—the *Behaviorally Independent Contingency* (BIC) in which circumstances entirely beyond the control of the organism can cause the diagram to progress; and the *Time Contingency* (T.C.) which specifies that if some other event does *not* occur (e.g., a negative operant is not emitted) the diagram will progress to the next listed event. Figures 36 and 37 show both contingencies.

Trees and Groves: A single branch-point in the diagram (i.e., a point at which the organism has an option as to which of several behaviors to emit) is called an option, as noted above. If an option occurs at some point in a larger sequence (e.g., a chain), then the entire diagram is called a *tree*. See Figure 38.

If several trees are linked in succession, then the resultant diagram is called a *grove*. See Figure 39.

Figure 36. The Behaviorally Independent Contingency: In this case the program will procede from left-to-right after five minutes has passed—regardless of the behavior the subject may emit.

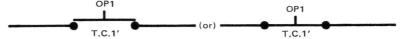

Figure 37. The Time Contingency: In each of these two cases the diagram will proceed from left-to-right in one minute *unless* the negative operants are emitted in that time.

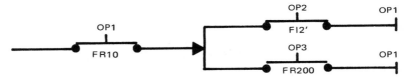

Figure 38. A Tree: Responding with Operant #1 under an FR10 schedule of reinforcement will result in a choice between responding with Operant #2 or Operant #3. Since the branch is reversible, however, the subject may switch from Operant #2 to Operant #3 and back again at any time.

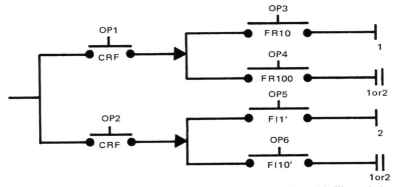

Figure 39. A Grove: The subject has a choice as to Operant #1 or #2. The emission of either will result in the reversible option of either of two other responses. The completion of one of those two options will result in recycling to only one of the original choice operants; and completion of the other option will result in a choice between Operants #1 and #2 again.

FR
Abbreviation for a "fixed-ratio schedule of reinforcement."
See **Schedule, Fixed-Ratio**.

Free Operant Rate of Response
The rate with which a free operant is emitted. See **Operant, Free**; and **Rate (of Responding)**.

Function
Y is a function of *X* if for every value of *X*, *Y* is uniquely determined. Unless the value of the dependent variable *Y* can be determined for a given value of the independent variable *X*, then a functional relationship cannot be said to exist. Example: To determine whether or not rate of responding to produce a certain reinforcer (say food) is a function of the amount of reinforcement (spoonfuls of soup, for example) we would vary the amount of soup from day to day and note any changes in rate of responding. If we found that as we increased the amount of reinforcement the rates of responding would predictably go up, then we may state that rates are a function of reinforcement magnitude. Two things should be noted. First, while rates of responding may be a function of reinforcement magnitude, this does *not* say that rates may not *also* be a function of other variables (frequency of reinforcement, amount of sleep the night before, deprivation level with respect to that reinforcer, etc.). Second, when testing the functional relationship between any two variables, great care must be exerted to keep all other variables constant. If we did not make sure that our subject always had approximately the same amount of sleep before each session, for example, then we could not be sure whether the changes in rate were really a function of reinforcement magnitude, or changes in the number of hours sleep.

Generality
Any case in which a characteristic or property of an object or event is extended beyond the specific context in which it was observed and taken to be applicable or meaningful in the

context of those other (usually unobserved) objects or events.

E.g., to say, after observing the children in one or several classrooms emitting higher rates of math fact solving behavior under a contingency of teacher "praise," that "children" will respond favorably under contingencies of teacher "praise," is an instance of generality.

NOTE: Generalities are *always* tenuous; and can never be completely validated unless the entire class of objects or events are observed (which is rarely possible). The "validity" or "meaningfulness" of a generality should be judged in terms of the number of observations actually made, their continuity, the extent of the generality, and the usefulness or necessity (from a practical standpoint) of the generality.

Generality, Intersituation
Any case of generality between two or more different situations. E.g., from a third grade classroom to a sixth grade classroom. An attempt should be made to identify the commonalities and differences between the two or more situations. See **Generality**.

Generality, Interspecies
Any generality made from one species to another species. E.g., if a pigeon reacts in this manner under these conditions, then so might man. See **Generality**.

Generality, Intersubject
Any generalization made between one subject and another, generally taken to be of the same species, and in the same situational context, but not necessarily so. E.g., if Johnny in this class reacts this way, then so might Billy. See **Generality**.

Generality, Intrasituation
Any generality made from one set of circumstances to another *within* the same general situation. E.g., from one third grade classroom to another third grade classroom. An attempt should be made to identify the commonalities and differences in the situations. See **Generality**.

Generality, Intraspecies
Any generality made from one to another member of the same species. E.g., if one pigeon reacts in this manner, then so might all pigeons. See **Generality**.

Generality, Intrasubject
Any case of generality made from one situation to another within the same subject. E.g., if Johnny performs better on his math facts when these conditions are set up, then he might

also perform better on his spelling under the same conditions. See **Generality**.

Generalization Gradient

That curve which describes the relative rates of responding under each of a set of related stimuli; only one of which has gained control over behavior through conditioning, the others through the process of generalization. Usually any one curve describes the relative rates as a function of only one stimulus parameter, but occasionally more than one parameter value is changed from one instance of the stimulus to the next. See Figure 40. See also **Generalization, Stimulus**.

Generalization, Stimulus

A process through which a stimulus acquires or loses the capacity to elicit a response (in respondent conditioning), control a discriminative response, set up an emotional state (in operant conditioning), etc., because of its similarity to a stimulus which has acquired or lost such a capacity through other means. The degree of generalization is measured by the rate or probability of responding under the former in relation to the rate of responding under the latter. *Some* generalization is likely to occur whenever an organism is conditioned to respond in the presence of a discriminative stimulus. If generalization is *not* desirable (e.g., a boy who calls *every* man "Daddy"), other stimuli (S△s) should be presented during the

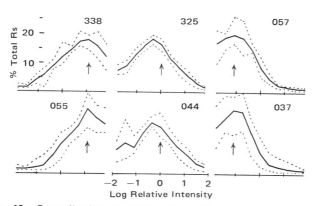

Figure 40. Generalization Gradients: These figures represent the generalization curves for six pigeons. Light intensity is the variable, and the value at which conditioning took place is indicated in each case by an arrow. Note that the highest rates of responding occur at (or near) the value originally conditioned, and that response rates decrease with intensities further from that value.[6]

---

[6] Figure reprinted from "Generalization and preference on a stimulus-intensity continuum," by D. S. Blough, *Journal of the Experimental Analysis of Behavior*, 1959, *2*, 307—317. Copyright © 1959 by the Society for the Experimental Analysis of Behavior, Inc. Used by permission of the author and publisher.

conditioning period and reinforcement *not* presented for responding in the presence thereof. This will produce the process of discrimination. If generalization *is* desirable (e.g., saying "thank you" in response to *any* gift or service received), then all stimulus conditions should be varied except those which define the concept to be formed, and responding in those various conditions reinforced (e.g., "setting up" situations with many different people in many different places where the phrase "thank you" will be appropriate and reinforced). See also **Discrimination** and **Concept Formation**.

Goal
Synonym for "aim." See **Behavior, Target**.

Group Data
Any data which is the result of more than one person working on the same type of behavior. Example: The data which results from an entire class counting the correct and incorrect responses emitted on daily math-fact quizzes. The individual data would be the number of incorrect and correct math-facts for *each* child; the group data would be the total or range, middle and quartiles of all the data for all the children put together. While it is sometimes useful to look at the whole class in group data, it is usually still important that each child's data is charted individually also so that he may be considered apart from the group.

Grove
A behavioral chain in which one or more of the components is an option which in turn leads to at least one more option. Figure 39 shows a grove diagramed according to the Findley notational system. See **Findley Diagrams.**

Hold
The period of time for which reinforcement set up by the termination of an interval is held available (delivery contingent upon the next response), and after which the organism must wait for the duration of the next interval before reinforcement is again available.

May also be used as a synonym for "maintenance" in Precision Teaching. See **Maintenance** under **Plan Function.**

Hold, Limited
Where the hold period following the expiration of an interval schedule is limited in duration. If the organism fails to respond during this period then it must wait until another reinforcement is set up. E.g., on an FI 15' w/10" hold the organism is reinforced for the first response to occur after five minutes

have elapsed since the last reinforcement. If the organism fails to respond within 10" after reinforcement is available, however, then the interval begins timing again.

Hypothetico-Deductive Method (or) Model
A general method for the organization or expansion of knowledge or data that is based upon a small number of empirically founded principles or definitions (hence, hypothetical) and is expanded by *deduction* into a larger body of testable theorems or corollaries. The accepted method for behavioral studies.

■

"If and Only If" Relationship
A relationship between two events in which one event will occur if, and only if, the other event occurs. Formally stated as: "If event A occurs then event B will occur; and if event A does not occur, then event B cannot occur."

This type of relationship reflects a "true" contingency (i.e., where one event is totally dependent upon another event).

Many arrangements or contingencies reflect "if-then" relationships, but would be generally more effective if they reflected "if and only if" relationships (i.e., if the arranged events, reinforcers, or consequences were *only* available following the emission of the specified response). See also **"If-Then" Relationship**.

"If-Then" Relationship
A relationship between two events in which one event is dependent upon the other event. Formally stated as: "If event A occurs, then event B will occur."

Implied in an "if-then" relationship is the condition that if event B has not occurred, then event A could not have occurred. The inverse, however, is not implied; that is, if event B has occurred, then it may *not* be said with certainty that event A has occurred. It may be the case, for example, that event B can also be determined by some other (third) event.

Example: The relationship between the event of "rain" and the event of "wet ground" may be considered an "if-then" relationship. That is, "if it rains, then the ground will be wet." Implied in this statement is that if the ground is not wet (not B), then it did not rain (not A). *Not* implied in this statement is the fact that if the ground is wet (B), then it rained (A), because the ground could have gotten wet by some other means (e.g., a sprinkler).

Many arrangements or contingencies reflect an "if-then" relationship (if the response occurs, then the arranged event, reinforcer, or consequence will occur). Generally speaking, however, the probabilities of successfully affecting the rate of responding would be greater if, in addition to reliably presenting (or withdrawing) the arranged event every time the behavior occurred, the manager also *prevented* the occurrence of the arranged event unless the behavior occurred. See **"If and Only If" Relationship**.

Independence

Data or phenomena are said to be independent of one another if and only if the value or condition of one in no way affects the value or condition of the other. Data collected on separate individuals, for example, are usually independent (i.e., one child's score on an examination will not usually affect another child's score on the same examination). Most behavioral data, however, collected on one individual over a period of time reflects sequential *dependency* (i.e., the value of any one given data point may influence the probable value of future data points). See **Dependency, Sequential**.

Induction, Response

A process through which a response is modified in duration, intensity, or topography to meet the particular requirements on one stimulus situation because of similarity to another stimulus situation in which a similar response was effective in procuring reinforcement. E.g., in turning a corner in one's car which one has never before encountered, one is able to induct one's responses to meet the particular stimulus requirements due to a similarity between this and other stimuli (corners) which *have* been experienced. Response induction is sometimes confused with stimulus generalization. Stimulus generalization is the tendency to respond (in a particular, and relatively invariant manner) under new stimulus conditions due to stimulus similarity; and response induction is the tendency to respond in a *different* manner under similar but different stimulus conditions.

Inductive Interaction

An *increase* in rates under one set of conditions due to an *increase* in rates under another set of conditions. See also **Interaction, Discriminated Operant**.

Information Hypothesis

An hypothesis in which it is asserted that there are two types of (informative) stimuli:

"Cues" which control differentiated performances, and "Clues" which reliably predict reinforcers.

Cues are based on S-R contingencies, and clues on stimulus pairings.

INTER

Abbreviation for "interpolated schedule." See **Schedule, Interpolated**.

Interaction

The alteration of any event or series of events (e.g., a response or series of responses and their rate of emission) as a function of some change in another event or series of events. See also **Interaction, Discriminated Operant**; and **Interaction, Undiscriminated Operant**.

Interaction, Discriminated Operant

A change in the rate of a discriminative operant brought about by a change in the schedule of reinforcement or other environmental conditions of a *different* discriminated operant.

For example: If in a MULT (FR, FI) the FI component was changed to EXT, it has been noted that concomitant with the expected *de*crease in responding under the second component (which *was* FI, and is *now* EXT), there is an *in*crease in the rate of responding under the FR (with no change in that component's condition). This would be called a condition-change interaction (see also **Behavioral Contrast**).

Condition-change interactions may be clarified in terms of the *absolute* direction of the rate change in the *un*altered component (*positive* if the rate goes up, *negative* if the rate goes down); and the direction of the rate change relative to the unaltered component (*contrast*, if the rate change is opposite to the change in the altered component; *induction*, if the rate change is in the same direction as that of the altered component). NOTE: This use of "positive" and "negative" is somewhat in conflict with the preferred usage of those terms (i.e., presentation and removal); and the terms "accelerating" and "decelerating" would be more in keeping with the rest of behavioral terminology. The use of "positive" and "negative" is, however, common in this context.

A *positive-contrast interaction*, then, would be a case in which the unaltered component *increased* (positive) in rate, and the direction of this change was *opposite* (contrast) that of the change in the altered component (i.e., in this case the rates of responding in the altered component *decreased*). See also **Interaction**; **Interaction, Undiscriminated Operant**; **Positive**; and **Negative**.

Interaction, Undiscriminated Operant

Changes in the rates of responding under one schedule of reinforcement as a function of *another* schedule of reinforcement not presently in effect where the change from one schedule to the other is not discriminated (e.g., as would be the case in a tandem or mixed schedule of reinforcement).

Interactional Diagram

Any diagram representing an interaction between an organism and any part of that organism's environment. Usually, however, in reference to a diagram used in interactional analysis.

Standard format for interactional diagrams usually includes a horizontal line (representing the passage of time), and labels on either side of that line (and to the left) indicating the parties between which interactions are to be described. The first behavior (or event, if one of the parties is the "environment") is noted on the appropriate side of the line, and the next event noted to its right (and, of course, also on the appropriate side of the line). Events and behaviors are thus noted, in order of occurrence, until the end of the period for which description is desired. Arrows are employed to indicate any event which is (necessarily) followed by any other event. Events which do not have any arrow pointing *to* them are taken to be events which require no particular antecedent; and events which have no arrow pointing *from* them (to another event) are taken to be events which are not necessarily consequated in some fashion. Figure 41 illustrates the use of an interactional diagram in the description of an interaction between teacher and pupil during spelling period.

The basic advantage in the use of interactional diagrams lies in the fact that no event must be classified as "stimulus," "response," or "reinforcer"; but rather, any event may be seen to occupy any of these positions in the natural sequence of their occurrence.

A modification of the interactional diagram may be made to include a space between the two interacting persons which represents the "environment." Events listed in that space refer, then, to events which have their origin outside the behavior of either of the two primary parties. The example of the teacher and child is re-done in this format in Figure 42.

The interactional diagram could, of course, be expanded to provide several sources of interaction (i.e., just draw a greater number of parallel lines). The number of interacting parties does, however, have practical limits governed by the sheer complexity of event descriptions and interconnecting arrows resulting from increased numbers of interacting parties.

Interactional diagrams are used most often when the specific nature of the events comprising the interactions is unknown (i.e., whether they are stimuli, reinforcers, or simply "neutral"); or where the events comprising that interaction are extremely heterogeneous, and other forms of diagramming would prove too clumsy. See also **Mechner Diagrams** and **Findley Diagrams**.

Interorganismic Generality

Synonym for "intersubject generality." See **Generality, Intersubject**.

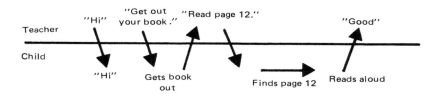

Figure 41. Two-Party Interactional Diagram: This diagram represents an interaction between a child and his teacher. The length and complexity of the interaction may, of course, be extended to meet any requirement.

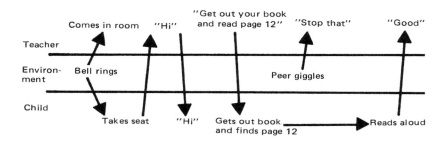

Figure 42. Interactional Diagram With "Environment": This figure represents an interactional analysis of a teacher, a child, and the "environment" (all stimuli arising from anyone or anything other than the teacher or child). The number of parties that may be added by adding more rows to the analysis is limited only by the complexity of the arrows with increased numbers of parties represented.

Inter-Reinforcement Time (IS^{R}T)

The time elapsing from the completion (end) of one reinforcement period to the start (beginning) of the next reinforcement period. Useful in the analysis of reinforcement density, program efficiency, and performance efficiency.

Theory holds that an organism should, given time to stabilize, emit that pattern of responding which will minimize IS^{R}T and maximize performance efficiency. See **Reinforcement, Operant; Conditioning, Respondent; Inter-Response Time; Reinforcement Density; Efficiency, Program;** and **Efficiency, Performance.**

Inter-Response Time (IRT)

"Inter" literally means "between," so inter-response time is in reference to that time between any two successive responses. Also called the response-response interval, but somewhat misleadingly. IRT's are only that time from the *completion* of one response to the *beginning* of the next response—excluding the time of the responses themselves. See Figure 79 under **Temporal Relationships Between Behavior and Environment; Intra-Response Time;** and **Rate, Operant-to-Operant.**

Intrapsychic

In reference to any term or theory which makes recourse to an internal and unobservable process of the "mind." Generally undesirable in behaviorism, which attempts to deal only with observable phenomena. Literally, "intrapsychic" means "within the psyche." "Psyche," originally meaning "soul," is generally interpreted today as "mind." Freudian concepts of id, ego, superego, etc., are examples of "intrapsychic" concepts.

Intra-Response Time (IRAT)

"Intra" literally means "within," so intra-response time is that time which elapses between the commencement of a response and its termination or completion. E.g., the time required to press a lever a single time. There is an inverse relationship between rate and IRATs, but this relationship is generally somewhat less than perfect; and less than the relationship between rate and IRTs. IRATs are used as a measure of responding when the overall rate is by necessity governed by an external source (e.g., correct response rate to questions orally presented by the teacher in class is limited by the number and frequency of questions; but the IRATs will decrease in magnitude with increased facility in responding). See Figure 80 under **Temporal Relationships Between Behavior and Environment.** See also **Inter-Response Time; Operant-to-Operant Rate;** and **Latency.**

IRAT
Abbreviation for "intra-response time." See **Intra-Response Time**.

IRT
An abbreviation for "inter-response time." See **Inter-Response Time**.

"Is" Analysis
The operation of writing, then observing, counting, and charting the components of the "Is" Equation. See **"Is" Equation**.

"Is-Does" Language
The "refined common-usage" language of Precision Teaching. Developed to describe with one set of terms what "is" going on in the environment without making any statements as to how events do or do not affect rates of responding; and with another set of terms to describe what "does," indeed, affect rates of responding. A language which is divided into simple descriptive ("is") and functional ("does") statements. See **"Is" Equation** and **"Does" Equation**.

"Is" Equation
In Precision Teaching, a list of environmental events and behaver behaviors which describe what "is" happening in the program setting. The first stage in the development of any plan is to fill out the "is" equation. The operation of filling out an "is" equation is called the "is" analysis. After completing an "is" analysis one is not sure that the listed events *actually* affect the behavior defined, or even that the behavior *can* be affected by environmental events. All the "is" equation does is list these events which *may* affect the movement-cycle. Events are then altered to *determine* their affect. See also **"Does" Equation**. The components of the "is" equation are shown in Figure 43.

Isomorphic
Identical or similar in form. Two "isomorphic responses," for example, would share certain critical properties with respect to topography, locus, force, critical effect, or temporal dimensions. The basis of the statement of isomorphosis should, of course, be stated (e.g., "topographically isomorphic responses").

IS^{R}T
An abbreviation for "inter-reinforcement time." See **Inter-Reinforcement Time**.

Figure 43. "Is" Equation:

Program (P): The overall, general environmental setting. Usually equated with the time of day, duration of instruction, location of the class, and any other variable which remains *constant* for the period over which the occurrence of the movement-cycle is counted and recorded. See also **Disposition** under "**Does**" **Equation**; and **Situation.**

Program Event (PE): Any event which occurs independently of the movement-cycle (can occur whether the movement-cycle occurs or not). Usually occurs antecedent (comes before) the movement-cycle, but *may* come at *any* time (before, during, or after the movement-cycle). At this stage of the analysis it is not certain that these events do indeed effect the rate of the movement-cycle. See also **Stimulus** under "**Does**" **Equation**; and **Event.**

> NOTE: The choice as to what to call a program and what to call a program event is relatively arbitrary. The two terms really only denote relative levels of discreteness. If a particular movement-cycle may be emitted at any time during the school day, for example, we are likely to call the "school day" the program and the individual subject periods (e.g., arithmetic period) program events. If, on the other hand, the movement-cycle is of concern only during arithmetic period, then it is likely that one would call "arithmetic period" the program, and the individual assignments, fact-sheets, or problems the program events. In any event, the program should denote the general context in which the movement-cycle occurs, and program events describe some activity *within* that context.

Movement-Cycle (MC): The behavior of the behaver which is to be changed. *It is not known* at this stage of the analysis if this behavior is affected by stimuli or consequences. The movement-cycle must be directly observable and countable. It must be a behavior which has a definite cycle (i.e., a beginning and an end); and cannot be a behavior which a "dead man" could emit (e.g., sitting, looking, resting, being quiet). It must also be a behavior which can be repeated (e.g., the behavior of committing suicide for example, can only be emitted *once* by any one person; and would not, therefore, meet the requirements of a movement-cycle. In this case the behaviors which should be identified are the movement-cycles that can be repeated and *lead up* to suicide).

Examples: correct single-digit, two-term addition problems; talking out of turn; getting out of seat; striking other children. See also **Pinpoint, Dead Man's Test,** and **Response** under "**Does**" **Equation.**

Arrangement (A): The relationship between the number of times the movement-cycle occurs and the number of times the arranged event occurs. At this stage of the analysis it is not certain if this relationship reflects an effective contingency or merely a coincidence of events. (NOTE: Even if this relationship is set up by the manager, thereby ruling out coincidence, it is *still* not certain that the arrangement is *effective* in changing rates of responding). In other words, the arrangement reflects a possible "if-then" relationship between the movement-cycle and the arranged event (if MC, then AE; or MC→AE).

Convention: Indicate the number of movement-cycles required to obtain an arranged event, then place a colon (:) after that number; then indicate the number of arranged events that would occur following that number of movement-cycles. Examples: 1:1 would mean that for every movement-cycle emitted, one arranged event would occur; 10:1 would mean that for every 10 movement-cycles, one arranged event would occur; 13:4 would mean that for every 13 movement-cycles, 4 arranged events would occur; 3':8 would mean that for every 3 minutes that the movement-cycle occurred, 8 arranged events would occur. See **Contingency** under "**Does**" **Equation.**

Arranged Event (AE): Those environmental events which occur just following emission of the movement-cycle and are *caused* by the movement-cycle. It is not *known* at this point in the analysis if these events actually affect the rate of responding, but they are events which may, and should be tested for that function. Called "arranged events" because they are arranged by (dependent upon) the emission of the movement-cycle. Arranged events have a higher probability of affecting rates of responding if they *are* dependent on the emission of the movement-cycle. It is best, therefore, to try to create or "build-in" a dependency between the movement-cycle and some arranged event when writing a plan to change rates of responding. A second point to remember when writing a plan is that arranged events have a higher probability of affecting rates of responding if they occur *immediately* after the movement-cycle has been emitted. See also **Consequence** under "**Does**" **Equation**; "**If-Then**" **Relationship**; "**If and Only If**" **Relationship**; and **Event**.

JND
An abbreviation for "just noticeable difference." See **Threshold, Differential**.

Job Analysis
Breaking a job down into its gross behavioral requirements. E.g., a shoe-tying task requires finding the shoes for right and left feet; putting right shoe on right foot and left shoe on left foot; lacing both shoes up; making the "base" for both bows; and tying both bows. A job analysis is supposed to provide the basis for a more organized and detailed task analysis. While the task analysis will provide the detail necessary for effective task reformulation and programming, the job analysis serves to relate all these steps into an integrated whole. See **Task Analysis** and **Task Reformulation**.

K
An abbreviation for "contingency." An element of the "does" equation in Precision Teaching. Abbreviated "K" to avoid confusion with the abbreviation for consequence which is "C." See "**Does**" **Equation**.

Label

In reference to the traditional or conventional "category" into which a behaver (person under investigation) might fall or be classified (e.g., "normal 6th grader," "trainable mentally retarded"). The use of such labels is discouraged since they are generally of too gross a nature to adequately or meaningfully describe the individual.

Latency

The interval of time between the occurrence of a stimulus and the organism's behavior which is controlled by it. See also **Inter-Response Time; Intra-Response Time;** and **Rate, Operant-to-Operant.** See Figure 44.

Learning

1. As an operation: coming into repeated contact with a defined set of contingencies and stimulus conditions which demonstrate an effect on the form or probability of behavior.
2. As a process: the alteration of behavior in a predictable manner as a result of repeated contact with a specified set of contingencies and stimulus conditions.

Learning, Errorless

1. As an operation (briefly): exposing an organism to a set of discriminative stimuli (with correlated reinforcement contingencies) which vary greatly along many parameters, and then the systematic and slow lessening of the discrepancies between those stimuli until criterion values are obtained.

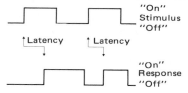

Figure 44. Latency: This figure represents two linear recordings of a response and an associated stimulus. When the linear recording is up, the response or stimulus is occurring. When the line is down, the response or stimulus is not occurring. The arrows between the two records point to the start of the stimulus and the initiation of the response. The difference between those two points represents the latency between those two events.

2. As a process: the formation of a concept or discrimination with the emission of no errors in responding (i.e., no responding under the S^Δ condition) during acquisition. Notable in this process is the absence of behavioral contrast.

Learning Sets (L-Sets)
1. As an operation: the presentation of a series of related discriminations.
2. As a process: the resultant increase in the facility with which new but related discrimination problems may be solved (i.e., new but related discrimination paradigms come to control behavior more rapidly than preceding related or new unrelated discriminations). It is said that the organism "learns to learn." More accurately, however, it may be said that the organism has formed a concept with respect to the relevant dimensions or cues necessary to solve the discrimination problems.

Least-Squares Solution
Any solution to a problem of data summary or analysis in which the sum of the deviations-squared is minimized. The mean, for example, will be that point from which the sum of the squares of the deviations of all data will be the least. The regression line will serve the same function in the dynamic case. Concurrent with the least-squares solution is the fact that the sum of the signed deviations (i.e., *un*squared) will be zero. Not all solutions (to dynamic problems) which yield a sum of signed deviations equal to zero are *least-squares* solutions, however, so the two definitions are not entirely interchangeable. Given three data points collected on three separate and successive occasions, for example, there will be three possible solutions to the problem of finding a line which will make the sum of the signed deviations equal to zero; but only one of these solutions will also minimize the sum of the squared deviations. See Figure 45.

Advantages in using the least-squares solution in analysis include the facts that the specific values of all data will be represented in the analysis (as opposed to the median solution that tends to "ignore" the specific values of extreme data); that the values of the data above the point defined by the solution will exactly "counterbalance" and "cancel" the values of the data below that point; and that the least-squares solution is quite amenable to statistical manipulation and formulation. Potential disadvantages, on the other hand, include the facts that the mean is sensitive to changes in skewness (whereas the median remains constant as long as the "middle" of the distribution remains unaltered); and that if a

Figure 45. Three "Mean" Solutions: In this figure three possible solutions to the problem of minimizing the sum of the signed deviations are given. Only one, however, will also yield the least possible sum of the *squared* deviations—solution B.

small percentage of the data are unreliable (i.e., do not accurately reflect the general nature of the phenomena being studied), the least-squares solution may be adversely affected (the median solution, on the other hand, will remain unaltered if at least 50% of the data reflect the actual phenomena). It should also be pointed out that in a perfectly symmetric distribution, the mean (least-squares) and median solutions will be identical. See also **Mean**; **Median**; and **Median Solution**.

Lindslian System
A simplified system for the analysis of behavior (and the standardization of data presentation) which utilizes (for the most part) "refined common usage" terminology. Once called COLAB (*CO*mmon *L*anguage *A*nalysis of *B*ehavior). Also called "is-does"; "Precision Teaching" and "precise behavior management."

Line, Adjusted Predicted Acceleration
There are basically three variables (other than "error" terms) which may change in performance: absolute magnitude or level of responding; the trend in the responding over time; and the variance of responding. When examining differences in performance between two experimental or observation conditions occurring sequentially in time, the predicted acceleration line *per se* is an estimate of "where responding would be" if the conditions had not changed. Unfortunately, however, changes in magnitude, variance, and trend may cancel (or magnify) any testable difference. Variance differences must be equalized by correction of the data in the second condition, but differences in magnitude may be factored out by moving

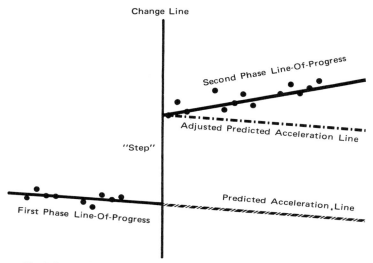

Figure 46. **Adjusted Predicted Acceleration Line**: The predicted acceleration line (an extension of the line-of-progress of the first phase) is moved up or down until it intersects the change line (denoting when the difference between the two phases was instituted) at the same point as the line-of-progress for the second phase. The difference between the original predicted acceleration line and the adjusted predicted acceleration line represents the "step" or immediate effect of the change. The difference in the slopes of the adjusted predicted acceleration line and the line-of-progress represents the "continuing effect" or change in "learning progress" created by the alteration between phases.

the predicted acceleration line up or down the difference in magnitude between the two conditions. To do this (visually), the predicted acceleration line is moved up or down until it intersects the change-line at the same point as does the line-of-progress of the second condition. The same thing may be accomplished mathematically by adding the constant of that adjustment to all points of prediction on the predicted acceleration line. The resultant line is called the adjusted predicted acceleration line. Once this adjustment has been made, comparisons between the trend in each condition may be made without the confounding effect of step (i.e., changes in magnitude between conditions). See Figure 46. See also **Line, Predicted Acceleration; Line-of-Progress;** and **Line, Phase Change.**

Line, Best-Fit
A synonym for "line-of-progress." Derives its name from the fact that a line-of-progress should represent that single line which is the "best" in "fitting" the data. Whether "best-fit" refers to a least-squares or median solution is dependent upon the specific method employed.

Line, 'Celeration
Another term used as a synonym for "line-of-progress." The term " 'celeration" is derived from the terms "acceleration" and "deceleration"—denoting lines-of-progress which are increasing and decreasing respectively. See **Line-of-Progress**.

Line-of-Progress
That line (usually drawn) through a set of data which describes the manner in which the data is changing over time (where "change" = that mathematically constant difference between successive data points when "error" or "random variation" has been removed). The line, does, then describe the general "progress" of the data.

The term "progress" implies a sequential dependency in the data; and it should be noted that while there are several techniques available for analyzing data with sequential dependency, the majority of these techniques *remove* that dependency rather than describe it (e.g., the exponentially-weighted-moving-average). The purpose of the line-of-progress, on the other hand, is basically descriptive (albeit, once the description has been made it will bear implications for predictive analyses and significance-testing). There are virtually no mathematical operations which have been designed and *validated* specifically for the purpose of progress description and analysis with behavioral data; but in general, the regression model may be employed to derive a least-squares solution to a line-of-progress; and the median slope method to derive the median-solution. Studies have not yet been completed, however, which define the applicability of these techniques in prediction and/or significance testing. See Figure 47. See also **Regression Line**, and **Median Slope**.

Line, Phase-Change
A line drawn on a graph or chart to separate the data collected in one phase from the data collected in other phases. Although the phase-change-line may be positioned anywhere between the last data point in one phase and the first data point in the next phase, it is most advisable to place the line on or just before that place on the chart which corresponds to the time when the change in conditions was actually instituted.

Line, Predicted Acceleration
That line, drawn as an extension of a line-of-progress or best-fit line, that serves as the best estimate of how performances will change in the future. If performances have been steadily increasing, for example, and are best described by a linear function, then the best estimate of where they would be in the future (given that all conditions remain reasonably the

Figure 47. Lines-of-Progress: This figure demonstrates three possible solutions to the description of trend in a data set. Notice that the regression line (least-squares solution) is most effected by the first "deviant" data point, and gives, therefore, the steepest estimate of trend. The median slope solution is the next steepest, due primarily to the fact that there is a trend in variance in the data (the data are becoming progressively more stable). To account for that trend, the median slope will shift to one side of the distribution or the other, and in this case, the lower side. The most conservative of estimates with this data is the corrected median slope. Based on essentially the same logic as the median slope, the corrected median slope is computed *after* the trend in deviations has been artificially removed, and is not, therefore, subject to its influences.

same) is an extension of the line describing that function. The validity of a predicted acceleration line rests on two basic assumptions. First, that the function of which it is an extension is, in itself, valid (i.e., *does* describe the general nature of change in the *known* performance data); and that the performances will continue to change in the same manner for the period over which prediction is desired (i.e., that the performances will not reach a "ceiling" or "floor," above or below which they may not go; and that the conditions in the environment controlling the performances remain constant). Actually, such assumptions are never completely without risk; but for all practical purposes, they may be made in a great many cases. See also **Line-of-Progress**; and **Line, Adjusted Predicted Acceleration**.

Line, Rate
Any line drawn between two data points. The slope of a rate line reflects the acceleration that has occurred between those two points. In Precision Teaching, rate lines are *not* drawn across no-chance days or phase-change lines; but *are* drawn between two rated days separated only by ignored days. See Figure 48. See also **Day, No-Chance**; **Day, Ignored**; and **Line, Phase Change**.

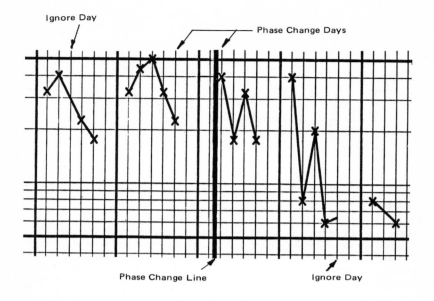

Figure 48. Rate Lines: The lines connecting successive data points are called "rate lines." Notice that rate lines do not cross no-chance days (i.e., days on which the behavior could not occur and which are left blank on the chart) or phase change lines (i.e., the line indicating when a change in the project was made). Rate lines *do*, however, cross ignore days (i.e., days on which the behavior occurred, but for some reason was not counted or rated). Should a no-chance day and an ignore day fall next to each other, the rate line crosses the ignore day and "points" at the next rated day, but does not cross the no-chance day. An example is provided in the figure.

Line, Sunday

The dark(er) vertical lines which are printed on the Standard Behavior Chart found in Precision Teaching which indicate the Sunday of each week. Other days are labeled (M, W, F) at the top of the first week on the chart paper. In Precision Teaching one never charts out of sequence (e.g., charts Monday's data point on a Sunday Line). See Figure 49.

Linear Record

A record of the occurrence of one or more events (some or all of which may be behavioral events) in which a line is extended across a paper (usually resembling a cash register or adding machine tape) at a constant rate (therefore recording the passage of time) and the pen drawing that line is deflected to one or the other side whenever the event being recorded occurs. The pen's deflection may be momentary (indicating

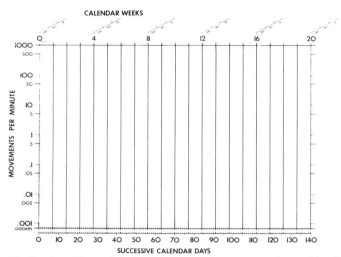

Figure 49. Sunday Lines: All day lines have been removed on this chart to emphasize the Sunday lines. Normally the Sunday lines appear as thicker and darker lines than those denoting the other days of the week to facilitate their discrimination.

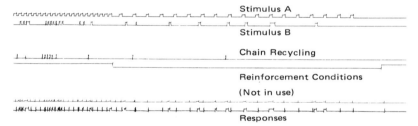

Figure 50. Linear Records: This figure represents a portion of a linear record obtained from a subject responding under a chained schedule of reinforcement. Deflection of the pen to the "up" position indicates that the event or condition being monitored by that pen is occurring; and resetting to the "down" position indicates that the event or condition has terminated. The paper moves under the pens at a constant rate to mark the passage of time. The two records at the top record certain stimulus conditions. The third line down marks the points at which stimulus conditions were recycled to the beginning of a chain. The fourth record indicates which reinforcement contingency is in effect; and the lowest line records individual responses. Note that the duration of those responses is not constant—some are momentary (the pen is only deflected for an instant), and some have considerable duration (the length of the line drawn by the pen while in the "up" position records the length of that duration). The line directly above the response pen was not in use; and deflections of that line are only produced by deflection of the response pen.

only one point of the event—e.g., the beginning) or extended (perhaps for the duration of the event). Information obtained from linear recorders, while more time-consuming to read and interpret, is usually more amenable to detailed analysis (e.g., of IRT's) than cumulative records. See Figure 50. See also **Cumulative Curve.**

89

Linear Recorder
A device designed to create a linear record concurrent with the occurrence of the event being investigated. See **Linear Record**.

M
Abbreviation for "movement" or "maintenance." See **"Is" Equation**.

Magazine
A mechanical device which delivers reinforcers to an organism during periods of reinforcement.

Magazine Training
Subjecting the experimental organism to the apparatus which delivers the reinforcer until such time when it approaches the delivery mechanism and takes the reinforcer each time it is operated without a display of disruptive emotional behavior.

Manager
A member of the Project Team. See **Project Team**.

Manipulanda
Any movable object the displacement of which may serve as a response.

Matching-to-Sample
A procedure in which a response to a stimulus or stimulus object that matches a specified sample is followed by a reinforcer.

Mean ($\overline{X}$)
A measure of central tendency which is the arithmetic average of the values of all data. The mean is equal to the sum of the individual data values divided by the number of data. The mean is more formally defined as that point from which the sum of the signed deviations or sum of the deviations-squared is least. See also **Median**.

Mechner Diagrams
A system for the diagrammatic representation of certain relationships which may exist between an organism and its

environment. Most commonly used for the representation of schedules of reinforcement. There are only two basic components in the Mechner diagram (other than the specification of response and stimulus components)—the arrow and bracket.

The arrow denotes causation. "A→B," for example, states that event B is caused by the occurrence of event A, and can be read as "if event A, then event B." The inverse is not true, however, and one may not infer the occurrence of event A given only the knowledge that event B has occurred. See **If-Then Relationship** and **If-and-Only-If Relationship** for clarification. The simplest usage of this notation is its application to the diagramming of positive reinforcement, i.e., the emission of response "R" causes the reinforcing event "S^{R+}" to occur. See Figure 51.

A bracket denotes simultaneity of occurrence. If event A and C occur in brackets, it is read as "if A and C occur at the same time"; or, "if A occurs in the presence of C." See Figure 52.

Figure 51. Positive Reinforcement   **Figure 52. Brackets**

Putting the bracket and the arrow together, one may construct a simple diagram for discriminated positive reinforcement. The diagram below is read as "if response R occurs in the presence of stimulus S^D, then R will be followed by the reinforcing event S^{R+}. See Figure 53.

The arrow may be manipulated to show special types of dependencies. In the case below, for example, an arrow is drawn from S^R to the bracket containing S^D and R—denoting the fact that once reinforcement has been delivered the original stimulus conditions are reinstated and the operations may be repeated. See Figure 54.

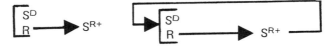

Figure 53. Discriminated   Figure 54. Recycling Discriminated
Positive Reinforcement   Positive Reinforcement

If a horizontal arrow is intersected by a vertical arrow, then the former is "interrupted" or "terminated." In the paradigm below, for example, the horizontal arrow denotes the fact that when ten seconds have passed a punishing stimulus (S^{R-}) will occur. If, however, response R is emitted "in the presence of"

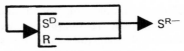

Figure 55. Avoidance Paradigm

(i.e., during) that ten seconds, then it will cause that operation to be interrupted, and recycle the "clock" to the beginning of the ten-second interval. This set of procedures represents an avoidance paradigm. See Figure 55.

Through multiples of these basic symbols (the arrow, the bracket, and the intersection of two arrows) most reinforcement paradigms may be drawn with relative ease. Of course more than one R or S may occur in any one set of brackets; and any single event (R or S) may generate more than one arrow (thus producing more than one event). In lengthy and complex chains or concurrent schedules, however, Findley diagrams may prove more "readable"; and in relatively heterogeneous sequences of interactions (i.e., interactions involving several behavior and stimulus types) involving only a few persons, "interactional diagrams" may prove simpler and less restrictive. See **Findley Diagrams** and **Interactional Diagrams**.

Median (Md)

A measure of central tendency which is the midpoint of a distribution of data. Half the data lie at or above the median; and half the data lie at or below the median. Also called the midpoint or middle. The median is more formally defined as that point from which the deviations of the other points is such that the sum of those deviations is lower than the sum of the deviations from any other point, or that the sum of the unsigned deviations is least.

Properties of the median which may make it a desirable choice in analysis include the facts that it will, in all cases, come closest to describing the majority of the data in any distribution; that it is less sensitive to (affected by) skewness; and that it minimizes the effect of data falling at the extremes of a distribution. It is somewhat less amenable to statistical formulation and manipulation, however, and may "ignore" important features of a distribution (if those features are contained in the extremes of the distribution). It should also be noted that in a perfectly symmetric distribution, the mean and the median will be the same. See also **Mean**.

Median Slope

1. The median of several slopes—usually slopes of lines-of-progress or regression lines. The median slope in this context is used to describe the median progress or change which occurred

in a set of behaviors or subjects (e.g., as a summary of how, in general, an entire class progressed through its mathematics lessons). To determine the median slope for use as a group summary, all slopes are rank-ordered from that with the greatest deceleration to that with the greatest acceleration, and then the median of those slopes is determined in the usual manner (see **Median**).

2. That line which, when passed through a set of data, minimizes the sum of the unsigned deviations of the data about it. Used to describe the progress or trend in the data when one wishes to minimize the effects of deviant data (i.e., minimize the effect of unusually high or low data points in estimating trend, and emphasize the "usual" or "general" performances described in the data). An alternative to the use of the regression line in trend or progress description.

In order to determine the median slope for any given set of data: (A) Generate all lines which pass through at least two data points and divide (all) the data so that 50% of those data fall on or above those lines, and 50% of the data fall on or below those lines. (B) Calculate the sum of the unsigned deviations about each of the lines generated. (C) Select the line which minimizes the sum of the unsigned deviations.

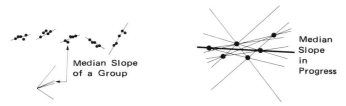

Median Slope of a Group

Median Slope in Progress

Figure 56. Median Slope: The left half of this figure represents the data from five different students with lines-of-progress for each one. Those lines are then drawn with a common origin (i.e., starting at the same place); and the median slope is determined by counting up or down the slopes until a point is found at which fifty percent of the slopes are greater, and fifty percent of the slopes are smaller.

The right half of this figure represents the method for finding the median slope for a set of data. First, all lines are drawn that pass through at least two data points and divide the data so that fifty percent of the points fall on or above the line and fifty percent of the points fall on or below the line. Since there are six data points, fifty percent is three; but the reader will note that the requirements of data on, above, and below the line will be met if either the 3rd *or* the 4th data point falls on the line (counting up and down the *deviations* from the line in question). In this case, ten lines meet the criteria (drawn in light lines on the figure). The sums of the unsigned deviations for each of those lines is then calculated, and the one that produces the least of those sums is selected as the median slope (drawn heavily in the figure). At first glance it would appear that the median slope is not steep enough to describe the trend in the data, but closer examination will reveal that most of the apparent trend in the data is caused by only one data point (the last). Since the median slope will minimize the effects of "unusual" data, it tends to "ignore" that data point and describe the "general" or "usual" trend embodied in the remainder of the data.

NOTE: The final line may be left in its original position (i.e., passing through the two data points by which it was determined) or, in some cases, may be moved up or down (keeping the slope constant) to some other point the analyst deems more descriptive. If movement is made, however, care must be taken that the data are still distributed so that 50% of the data fall on or above the line, and 50% of the data fall on or below the line. See Figure 56. See also **Line-of-Progress**, and **Slope**.

Median Solution

A solution to any problem of data summary or analysis in which the sum of the unsigned deviations in the data are minimized as opposed to the sum of the signed or squared deviations. The former is sometimes referenced as finding that point which will come closest to "hitting the most data"; and the latter as finding that point which will "balance the data so those above will exactly counterbalance those below." The median solution will minimize the effects of data falling at the extremes of the distribution; and the "mean," or "least-squares" solution will maximize the effect of the data falling at those extremes. Choice of which solution is most desirable should be based, at least in part, on how much emphasis or importance one wishes to place on the most deviant (unusual, least like the majority) data. If the data are perfectly symmetrical, the mean and median solutions will be identical. Skewness in data will affect the mean more than the median. See **Median**; **Mean**; and **Least-Squares Solution**.

Methods of Confirmation

Experimental or observational methods by which the results of a study or observation may be confirmed as representative and valid instances of the class of all such experimental manipulations or observations, the means by which we determine if what was observed is what *usually* happens, or is a more *un*usual or accidental occurrence. The most common methods of confirmation are:

I. *Replication*: Achieving the same experimental results in two or more identical manipulations of the same variables. The greater the number of replications, the greater the confirmation. Replications may be made:

A. *Between Subjects*: in which case the same manipulations are made on the same environmental variables to affect a change in the same behavior in a number of subjects; or

B. *Within a Single Subject* by:

    1. *ABA Design* where the experimental manipulations are applied (A) and removed (B) in alternation to achieve behavioral alteration, to return to the original

level of performance, to reattain the alteration, and so on in the same subject;
or
2. *Multiple Baseline* where the same experimental conditions are applied to a second type of behavior to achieve similar forms of alteration in the same subject. Used most often when experimental effects on one behavior cannot or should not be reversed (i.e., returned to their original form).
3. *Reversal* where the same experimental procedures are alternately applied to two distinctly different and competing behaviors (e.g., differentially reinforcing *high* rates; then *low* rates). See **Reversal Phase**.
II. *Stability or Predictive Value*: Where the results of the experimental manipulation are so stable as to allow a high degree of prediction across environmental conditions or time.

Middle
A term used in Precision Teaching as a synonym for "median"—that point at or above which 50% of the data in any given data set will fall. See **Median**.

Mid-Median
The arithmetic average of two medians, usually the median values for the data of two successive experimental conditions.

MIX
Abbreviation for "mixed schedule." See **Schedule, Mixed**.

Mode
The most frequent value in a set of data. There may be more than one mode in any given set of data (i.e., where several values have the same number of data points associated with them and where that number is equal to or larger than the number of data points associated with any other value).

Distributions with only one mode are called "unimodal." Distributions with greater than one mode are called "multimodal" or are identified as "bimodal," "trimodal," "quadramodal," etc.

There is no necessary relationship between the mode and other measures of central tendency (e.g., the mean and the median) in most distributions; but in the special case of a perfectly symmetrical distribution with a kurtosis equal to or greater than zero, the mode will be identical to the mean and median.

In cases where approximations are of no value, the mode is the most advisable statistic. In a horse race, for example, with six horses numbered one through six, it would not make sense to tally the number of the horse first across the finish line in each of 10 races, sum the numbers, and place a bet on the "average horse" (i.e., the mean "horse number" across the finish). Rather, the "mode horse" (i.e., the one across the finish line first, most often) would be the one most likely to yield a return on an investment. See Figure 57.

Model
That subject or device which demonstrates a performance or task to an organism in the operation of modeling. See **Modeling**.

Modeling
The training technique or operation of demonstrating a response or chain of responses to a subject, and then directing the subject to immediately imitate the performance. The trainer is said to be the model, and the trainee is said to be modeling or imitating.

Molding
The training technique or operation of physically guiding the trainee's hand, arms, limbs, etc., through the operations of a response or chain of responses with one's own hands. The operation is usually faded out by applying less and less pressure on the operating limbs or digits, and then moving one's hands further and further away from the operating limbs or digits (e.g., moving one's hands from the hands of the subject to the wrist, then the forearm, then the upper arm, etc., until all physical control is removed). NOTE: "Molding" is an excellent example of an "event during." See **Event During**.

Movement-Cycle
An element of the "Is" Equation in Precision Teaching. See **"Is" Equation**; and **Pinpoint**.

Unimodal
Distribution

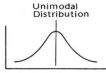

Bimodal
Distribution

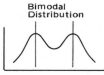

Figure 57. The Mode: In the distribution on the left there is only one mode (i.e., most frequent value or score); whereas in the right-hand distribution there are two values with the same frequency which are greater than all others. It should be noted, however, that frequently people refer to bi- or multimodal distributions in which the "modes" are not all exactly the same frequency. In this case "modes" would refer to "peaks" in the distribution. It is assumed that if this is the case, the "peaks" are all "essentially" the same, and that the differences between them are not analytically important.

Note also that in the left distribution the curve is perfectly symmetric and, since it is unimodal, the mean, median, and mode will all have the same values.

Movements Per Minute
A synonym for "responses per minute" in the "is" analysis found in Precision Teaching. Also (in Precision Teaching) in reference to the labeling up the left (the vertical axis, ordinate, or y-axis) scale on the chart. In reference to the number of movement-cycles which occur on the average in one minute. May be less than one. The charted scale ranges from .001 (corresponding to a frequency of one movement-cycle every 1000 minutes) to 1000 (corresponding to a rate of 1000 movement-cycles every minute). See also **Chart**; **Up the Left**; **Cycle**; and **Rate**.

MULT
Abbreviation for "multiple schedule." See **Schedule, Multiple**.

"Mu" (μ)
A Greek letter used to denote a population mean (i.e., the actual mean of all values comprising a defined set or population). Usually μ is not attainable (i.e., it usually is not possible to measure all values in a population), but may be estimated from a sample of values drawn from that population. See $\overline{X}$ and **Mean**.

Negative
In the behavioral sense, "remove," "terminate," or "take away." "Negative reinforcement," for example, is an operation which reinforces a response by "taking away" an aversive stimulus. "Negative" in behavioral usage, should not be confused with "bad" or "punishment."

Negative Interaction
A *decrease* in responding under one set of conditions as a result of a change in *another* set of conditions. See **Interaction**, **Discriminated Operant**.

No-Count Day
Synonym for "Ignore Day"; see **Day, Ignore**.

Number of Items
In Precision Teaching, the number of sub-units of which a program event may be comprised. Example: One arithmetic

fact sheet (the program event) may be comprised of 20 arithmetic facts (items). Frequently the number of items corresponds to the maximum number of movements which may be emitted under that program event, but not necessarily so. In the above example the movements might be considered the writing of each number in the answer of each problem. If *two* numbers were required for each problem, then the maximum number of movement-cycles would be 40; and if the number of sheets that the behavior may work on is unlimited, then there would be *no* limit to the number of movement-cycles he could emit. This case of no limits is by far most desirable.

Observer Inference
The amount of subjective interpretation that an observer is required to make in the process of recording an event during observation. Usually taken to be measured by the discrepancy between the reports of two or more observers who gathered their data under identical conditions. See also **Observer Reliability**.

Observer Influence
Alterations of the events being observed solely as a result of the process of observation.

Observer Reliability
The degree to which two or more observers agree exactly in the reports of their observations; or, alternatively, the degree to which the reports of a single observer agree when those reports are all based on repeated exposure to the same phenomena (e.g., repeated viewings of a video-tape). The degree of reliability is usually reported as the correlation between the reports in question.

Ontogenetic History
The individual organism's experiences in its interaction with the environment. Often equated to history of reinforcement. Since it is virtually impossible for two organisms to have experienced exactly the same environment in exactly the same temporal order, it is also impossible for two organisms to have the same ontogenetic history. Individual ontogenetic histories are often used to explain individual differences.

Operant
Any behavior or class of behaviors whose rate or probability of occurrence is governed (at least in part) by its history of consequences (i.e., by the events which did in the past occur *following* their emission). Operant classes are frequently

defined in terms of the consequences they produce; and, in fact, all members of that class *must* produce the same or similar consequences.

Operants are usually distinguished from "respondents" in that the latter are controlled by antecedents (i.e., eliciting stimuli) and are present in the organism's behavioral repertoire at birth or develop as a function of physical maturation. Operants, on the other hand, are considered "learned behavior." Operants and respondents may, however, have identical physical characteristics and be distinguishable solely on the basis of the environmental events controlling them at the time of identification.

Although the term "response" is generally considered to be an acceptable synonym for "operant" (or, in a different context, "respondent"), a distinction may be made between them in level of complexity. "Responses" are considered by some to be a small unit of behavior consisting of essentially one muscle movement (i.e., the type of behavior easily controlled respondently) while "operants" are considered conditioned amalgamations of responses, complex enough for relatively sophisticated (but functionally unitary) interactions with the environment. A single "knee jerk," for example, would be called a "response," while a *series* of "knee and hip movements" would be called an "operant" (i.e., "walking"). See also **Respondent; Conditioning, Operant; Conditioning, Respondent;** and **Response**.

Operant, Discriminated

Any operant, the rate of which is determined or altered by the presence or absence of some stimulus. See s^D; s^Δ; and **Operant**.

Operant, Free

Any operant which may be emitted at any rate free from external physical constraint. Any operant, the rate of which is not physically and absolutely determined externally.

Operants whose rates are determined by stimulus conditions and/or reinforcement schedules may still be designated *"free"* as long as it is *physically* possible for differing rates of responding to obtain.

Manipulanda and procedural idiosyncracies in all environments usually place constraints on the possible rates of responding which may obtain. If these constraints allow "reasonable" variability in rates of operant emission, however, the operant may still be considered "free." Since "reasonable" is a relative and subjective term, it is advisable that these limits of possible rates be clearly specified. See **Operant, Paced; Stimulus Control; Record Floor;** and **Record Ceiling**.

Operant Level
The rate or probability of responding prior to any known conditioning; or, prior to a specific experimental manipulation.

Operant, Negative
An operant, the emission of which will *prevent* or *postpone* the occurrence of a negative or positive reinforcer. The *failure* to emit a negative operant for a specified period of time will result in the occurrence of a negative or positive reinforcer. See also **Operant**; and **Operant, Positive**.

Operant, Paced
Any operant whose rate of emission is absolutely determined by external physical constraint. Should not be confused with an operant under stimulus or contingency control, but where it is still *physically* possible for rates to vary. See also **Operant, Free**; **Stimulus Control**; **Contingency Control**; and **Rate (of Responding)**.

Operant, Positive
An operant, the emission of which (or repeated emission of which—dependent upon the schedule of reinforcement) will lead to a consequence (either a positive *or* negative reinforcer). See also **Operant**; and **Operant, Negative**.

Operant Structure
The entire operant paradigm as a unit, including antecedent stimuli, schedules of reinforcement, subsequent stimulus events, etc. Sometimes called the "operant reflex."

Operant-to-Operant Interval (OOI)
The elapsed time between the start of one instance of behavior and the start of the next instance of the same behavior. May be used to estimate operant-to-operant rate or averaged rate of responding—both estimates of the number of responses which may be emitted in a given unit of time. Sometimes the operant-to-operant interval is confused with IRTs or IRATs—quite incorrectly (see the definitions for each). See also **Temporal Relationships Between Behavior and Environment**.

Operants, Concurrent
Two or more responses, of different topography at least with respect to locus, capable of being executed with little mutual interference at the same time or in rapid alternation, under the control of separate programs. E.g., a child in school may have a "choice" of working on his arithmetic or talking to his neighbor. Each operant is controlled by different reinforcers and contingencies (i.e., teacher or peer approval); and each

may be emitted in rapid alternation with the other. In observing concurrent operants, one should collect data or rate of responding in each, the rate of alternation between the two, and the stimulus or environmental conditions which are most highly correlated with the process of changing from each to the other.

Option

A point in a sequence of contingencies and behaviors at which the organism may engage in any one of two or more behaviors. An *irreversible option* is one in which the organism, having started to engage in one of the choice behaviors *cannot* "return" and engage in one of the other options. A *reversible option* is one in which the organism, after having engaged in one of the choice behaviors *may* return to engage in another choice. Options may also be a combination of reversible and irreversible choices; that is, if the organism makes one choice it may later take another, but once that second behavior is begun, the other options are lost, etc. See Figures 33, 34, and 35 under **Findley Diagrams**.

Ordinate

The vertical, or Y, coordinate of a graph. In psychology the response measure is usually plotted on the ordinate. See example in Figure 1.

Paradigm

A systematic representation or model. In behaviorism, usually in reference to a representation or description of some interaction between an organism and its environment.

There are several standard paradigms in behaviorism (e.g., reinforcement, avoidance, shaping, chaining), and, in turn, several methods for the schematic representation of these paradigms. In Figure 58 Mechner and Findley diagrams are used to describe an interaction in which the emission of a single behavior results in both the avoidance of a punishing stimulus and the attainment of a positively reinforcing stimulus—thus demonstrating how "standard" paradigms may be combined to create new paradigms.

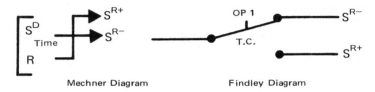

Mechner Diagram   Findley Diagram

Figure 58. Paradigms

Parameter

An independent variable that is held constant at some level while another independent variable is varied. Subsequently, the parameter may be held constant at another level while the experiment is repeated. When a parameter is held constant at different levels, a parametric study is performed. A parameter is often defined as any variable which is independent of at least one other variable which is dependent upon it; and which is (for that reason) deserving of study or investigation in and of itself as an independent variable.

Peak Shift

A phenomenon of responding observed in tests for stimulus generalization in which the maximum rate of responding is observed to fall at a point on the tested continuum which lies to the left or right (i.e., at a higher or lower value of the stimulus parameter) of the originally conditioned stimulus value. Usually due to aversive contingencies applied to responding to values or selected values on the side opposite that of the peak shift, or positive contingencies applied to values or selected values on the same side as the peak shift.

(%)

Abbreviation for "percentage schedule." See **Schedule, Percentage**.

Penultimate Component

The second-to-last component of a series—usually where "last" is defined as that which results in reinforcement. Frequently the penultimate component bears properties or characteristics of responding unusual to the other components. For example: Responding is frequently highest in the penultimate component of a sequential schedule under the control of an interval outside schedule.

Performance

The sum total of all specific characteristics defining the nature of the behavior of an organism at any given time or in any given situation, and the relationships which exist between successive instances of that behavior. The *behavior* in question, for example, might be "looking at a watch"; and the *performance* of a particular subject described as "the emission of that behavior with increasing rates as the time of an appointment approaches." The description of a performance always includes or references the description of behavior; but the inverse is never true. One may speak of *behavior* as being defined by the characteristics of any single instance of an interaction between an organism and its environment; and *performance* as being defined by the characteristic relationships between repeated instances of those interactions; or at least, the relationships between the behavioral event in question and some one or more other events in the environment.

The distinction between "performance" and "behavior" is not strictly followed in the literature, however; and the specific meaning of either term must generally be determined by the context in which it is employed. See also **Behavior**.

Performance, Competitive

A performance which, while not physically incompatible with another performance, will detract from (e.g., reduce the rate or probability of) another performance; and which has an above chance probability of being emitted in the same or similar stimulus conditions as the other performance. See also **Performance, Incompatible**.

Performance, Incompatible

Two or more performances are incompatible when it is physically impossible to engage in them at the same point in time. E.g., the behavior of reaching for a book on the table is incompatible with clasping one's hands behind the head. Caution is advised in labeling two behaviors as incompatible merely because it is highly *unlikely* that they would occur at the same time. For example, it is highly unlikely that a child would be doing his arithmetic if he were talking. It *is* possible, however, that a child talk and at the same time be writing the answers to his arithmetic problems. These behaviors would *not*, therefore, be incompatible; rather, one would say that they are *competitive* (one tends to distract from the other, but not necessarily *prohibit* the other). Reducing or increasing the rate of one would not *necessarily* have any effect on the other. See also **Performance, Competitive**.

Performance, Steady-State

An organism is said to have reached steady-state when his performance characteristics reach a point where they no longer change from session to session (i.e., when rate remains stable and patterns of responding no longer change temporal distribution or physical properties). Also called "stable-state performance." See also **Performance**.

Performance, Target
That set of response characteristics, including the relationships which should obtain between successive instances of those responses (e.g., the rate of their emission) which the behavior modifier or manager wishes to establish. Also called the performance "aim" or "goal." See also **Performance**; **Performance, Terminal**; and **Behavior**.

Performance, Terminal
That set of response characteristics which obtains at the end of any given interval of time (e.g., the end of a session, observation, or school year). One should not confuse "terminal" performance with "target" performance; the latter being what one *wishes* to establish, but which may or may not actually be achieved by the end of the time available. See also **Performance**; **Performance, Target**; and **Behavior**.

Permanent
Synonym for "therapeutic." See **Therapeutic**.

Phase
A period during which a particular and specified plan or set of experimental or environmental conditions is in effect. In Precision Teaching, differentiated on the chart from other phases by two vertical lines one at the beginning, and one at the end. See Figure 59. See **Line, Phase Change**; **Phase, Before**; **Phase, During**; **Phase, Between**; **Phase, After**; **Phase, Reference**; **Phase, Experimental**; **Baseline**; and **Reversal Phase**.

Phase, After
In Precision Teaching, a period of continued rate recording after the procedures of the during phase have been discontinued. The purpose of the after phase is to check on the permanence (therapeutic value) of the effects produced in the during phase(s). E.g., after having produced acceleration of reading rates in the during phase by consequating each page read with a penny, the pennies are discontinued in the after phase to determine if the higher rates will maintain without them. A synonym for "last reference phase." See also **Phase, Before**; **Phase, During**; **Phase, Between**; and **Phase, Reference**.

Phase, Before
A phrase, originating in Precision Teaching, in reference to a period during which the manager of a project records the rate

of responding and finds the line-of-progress of a behavior before altering any events to *change* the rates of responding or progress. NOTE: "Before" is in reference to "before-*alteration*"; and should not imply that it is a phase "before *anything*"—the manager may, in fact, be doing several things which affect rates of responding, but simply had not previously undertaken a specific project to define and alter those interactions. During the before phase the manager (and everyone else, for that matter) continue to do whatever *was* being done; the purpose of the phase is to establish what the specific effects of those interactions are before *changes* are made.

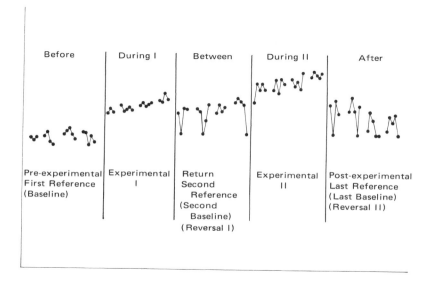

Before	During I	Between	During II	After
Pre-experimental First Reference (Baseline)	Experimental I	Return Second Reference (Second Baseline) (Reversal I)	Experimental II	Post-experimental Last Reference (Last Baseline) (Reversal II)

Figure 59. Phases of a Project: The phase labels used in Precision Teaching are given at the top of the chart. Labels used by various other disciplines are given below. "Baseline" and "reversal," however, are placed in parentheses to indicate that they bear certain functional connotations which should be investigated before those labels are used. Briefly, the order of events in this project are: (1) A preliminary phase in which the value of the dependent variable is determined prior to the first experimental alteration; (2) The first experimental phase in which the value of the dependent variable is determined as a function of the experimental alteration; (3) A "check" phase in which conditions are returned to those which obtained in the first phase or "reversed" expressly for the purpose of producing the opposite of the reaction that was produced in the first experimental phase; (4) A second experimental phase in which the same or different changes are imposed to determine their affects on the dependent variable; and (5) A last "check" phase in which conditions are again returned to original or reversed. The purpose of the check phases is to lend credence to the fact that the change produced in the experimental phases was due to the planned experimental alterations and not to chance or uncontrolled variables.

The implementation of a before phase serves the purposes of defining the affect of procedures already in practice; determining if, in fact, a project is actually needed (or if the rates are already progressing in the desired direction); establishing a "base" against which the effectiveness of future changes may be assessed; and aiding the manager in determining when a project should be instituted (e.g., if there are certain days on which the child is always better, it is common practice to start a project on one of those days—when there is already a tendency for rates to move in the desired direction).

The before phase is *not* equivalent to the traditional "baseline phase." A baseline implies that the rates of responding are stable and/or predictable, and that the environment remains constant throughout the duration of the phase. Neither of these conditions need obtain in a before phase, however; and may, in fact, not be possible due to practical limitations. A before phase *is* essentially equivalent to a "first reference phase." See also **Phase, During; Phase, Between; Phase, After;** and **Phase, Reference.**

Phase, Between

In Precision Teaching, following an unsuccessful during phase, the between phase is that phase in which conditions are returned (as nearly as possible) to the original conditions in the before phase to obtain another estimate of the rate with which the movement-cycle is being emitted. This allows the manager to have a new reference against which he may determine the effectiveness of new alterations tried in the second during phase. Between phases are the same as before phases, except they occur between two during phases instead of at the very beginning of a project. NOTE: In a curriculum project there may be a series of during phases *without* intervening between phases.

Phase Detail

An instance wherein one line-of-progress does not satisfactorily describe the apparent acceleration that occurs within any one phase, and where more than one line-of-progress is drawn. The degree of "detail" is dependent upon the number of lines-of-progress drawn. No more lines should be drawn, however, than are "absolutely" necessary to adequately describe what is occurring in the phase. See Figure 60. See also **Line-of-Progress.**

Phase, During

In Precision Teaching, the period in which an attempt is made to affect the desired change in the rate with which the movement-cycle or response is being emitted. The commencement of the during phase is noted on the chart by drawing a vertical line in the space just preceding the first day in the during phase. The termination of the during phase is noted on the chart by drawing a vertical line on the chart in the space just preceding the first day of the next phase. More than one during phase may be needed, each representing a different attempt at the alteration of the behavior. Each new change in any part of the "is-does" equation requires a new during phase. Whenever more than one during phase is needed, however, a between phase should occur between them. A synonym for "experimental phase." See also **Phase, Between; Phase, Before; Phase, After;** and **Phase, Experimental.**

Phase, Experimental

That portion of an experiment in which the experimental condition is imposed (i.e., the independent variables are altered) and data collected to determine its effect on the dependent variable. Also called the "during phase." See also **Phase, Reference.**

Phase, Reference

Any period of investigation in which "natural" or "pre-experimental" conditions are allowed to obtain in order to get data against which the experimental phase data may be compared. The reference phase data is, therefore, that to which reference is made when the effects of various changes in conditions are evaluated. A reference phase may *precede* the initial experimental change (the phase would then be called a "first-reference phase"); *between* successive changes (then labeled "second, third, etc., reference phase"); and *after* the last experimental phase (then labeled "last reference phase"). Reference phases are sometimes called "baselines" or "before, between, and after" phases, but as each of these terms has other denotations, they should be used with discretion.

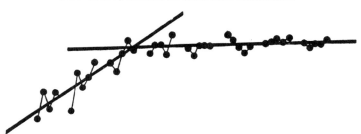

Figure 60. Phase Detail: In this project high initial acceleration eventually drops off to a much lower rate of acceleration. Although several lines-of-progress *could* be drawn, only two appear to be needed in order to describe the data with reasonable clarity. Should the data continue to be as flat as the last two weeks here, however, a third line-of-progress might be advisable later.

Phylogenetic History

The evolutionary history of the species in which the survival of individuals with particular genetic features produces a selection of genetic patterns. Often referred to as the "inheritance" of the organism or the basis for "natural selection."

Pinpoint

In Precision Teaching, in reference to the operation of or result of the operation of identifying and describing a movement-cycle. The description of a movement-cycle must be discrete enough to allow the inclusion of only one unique form of behavior under that description. If *more* than one type of behavior may be included under the description of the movement-cycle, then the behavior has not been adequately "pinpointed." Example: "Arithmetic behavior" would *not* be a pinpointed movement-cycle since there are a tremendous variety of arithmetic behaviors which are obviously different from one another (adding is not the same as subtracting; adding two numbers is not the same as adding 73 numbers; etc.). "Correct answers written for two-term, single-digit addition problems" *is* a relatively well pinpointed movement-cycle. See also **Movement-Cycle** under "**Is**" **Equation**.

Plan

In Precision Teaching an "Is" or "Does" equation which has been written or devised for the express purpose of changing or maintaining rates of responding. A statement of how events will be rearranged or changed to affect rates of responding. An *ineffective* plan (one which failed to change rates of responding), or a plan which has not yet been tried is written in the "Is" equation form; and an *effective* plan (one which has been tried and which *did* affect rates of responding) is written in the "Does" equation form. See "**Is**" **Equation** and "**Does**" **Equation**.

Plan Functions or Aims

The effect on the rate of responding by a particular plan. Example: If a plan is instituted and the rate of responding increases, then the plan function is acceleration (Ac).

The plan function is not necessarily the *desired* result (aim), e.g., one may have *intended* the rates of responding to decrease, but the plan may have served the *function* of increasing the rates. So it should be made clear as to whether one is noting a result (function) or an aim.

> **Acquisition (AQ):** To institute a behavior where it does not already exist. The response rate must be at zero at

the start of a program with this function. For example: If teaching a child to write the letters of the alphabet and he was unable to do so before, the plan is one of acquisition.

Acceleration (AC): To increase the rate of responding of a response. In this case the rate would have been greater than zero prior to the alteration of the plan, but not as high as would be desirable. The child may be able to solve arithmetic problems, for example, but not fast enough.

Deceleration (DE): To decrease the rate of responding. This may apply to "deviant" (social) behavior, or "error" (academic) behavior. The child may have a relatively high arithmetic problem solving rate, for example, but commit too many errors; or he may talk out of turn too frequently. It is usually a good idea to identify those behaviors which *are* emitted instead of the behaviors which should be accelerated and write a plan to decelerate them at the same time (and vice versa). See also **Double Equation**.

Fluctuation (FL): To make less stable, or to increase the limits of variation in the rate of responding. For example: To change responding that varies between 50 and 60 responses per minute to rates that vary between 10 and 100 responses per minute. The average rate remains approximately the same, but the performance is less stable. NOTE: This rarely is *desired* as a function (i.e., an aim), but if it occurs, it should be noted as a result.

Maintenance (MT); Also called **Hold (H)**: To keep the rate of responding at the same level. A plan designed to "fade out" the conditions of a previous during phase, for example, or to try out a new plan without disrupting the rate of responding, would be designated a maintenance or hold plan.

Stabilization (ST): To make more stable, or to decrease the limits of variation in the rate of responding. For example: To change responding that varies between 10 and 100 responses per minute to rates that vary between 50 and 60 responses per minute. The average rate remains the same, but the performance is more stable.

In Precision Teaching, the conventions are as follows: The aim, or *desired* function of a project is noted by placing an arrowhead on the chart on the date the aim was decided upon pointing up or down (the direction in which it is desired rates go); and draw a horizontal line through the arrowhead at the desired rate (see **Behavior, Target**.) The *result* of a plan (regardless of the aim) is noted when the effective "Is" equation elements are translated into the "Does" equation. For example: A program which was found to accelerate the rate of responding would be designated AcD (the program becomes a *D*isposition).

Positive (+)
In behavioral usage "to add," "additive," or "by addition." A "positive reinforcer," for example, is a stimulus which reinforces by its "addition" to the environment (i.e., by happening or being presented as opposed to being ended or removed). "Positive" in the behavioral sense should not be confused with "good" or "preferred." See also **Negative**.

Positive Interaction
An *increase* in the rate of responding under one set of conditions as a function of a change in *another* set of conditions. See **Interaction, Discriminated Operant**.

Precision Teaching
A set of standard procedures for the analysis of behavior introduced by O. R. Lindsley in 1964. Differing from the traditional or Skinnerian model primarily in the area of terminology. See **"Is" Equation**.

Precision Teaching, Basic Steps in
Those steps or operations which are implicit in any Precision Teaching project. In brief, the steps are:
1. *Pinpoint*: the precise identification of the movement-cycle. See **Movement-Cycle** and **Pinpoint**.
2. *Record and Chart*: the collection of rate data, and the recording of those data on the standard chart. See **Rate** and **Chart**.
3. *Change*: the alteration of any specified component of the "Is" equation in an attempt to affect rates of responding. See **"Is" Equation**.
4. *Try, Try, Try Again*: the continued specification and alteration of "Is" Equation components until the desired effect is attained.

Preference
The probability that an organism will emit one behavior to obtain one reinforcing event as opposed to another behavior to

obtain another reinforcing event (where the organism is physically capable of emitting either behavior; and where both reinforcers are available at the same time). Where probability appears to be 1.00 in favor of one reinforcer to the exclusion of all others, additional information may be gained by applying a "response-cost" to the reinforcer with the highest probability (i.e., the subject must emit two responses to obtain the most favored reinforcer and one response to obtain the least favored, then 3:1, 4:1, etc.) until the point is found where the probability that the subject will emit "X" responses to obtain the previously favored responses is the same that he will emit one response to obtain the least favored (i.e., half the time he chooses to "earn" one reinforcer, and half the time he chooses the other). By this technique we may find, for example, that a child will study arithmetic for 63 minutes if his only other choice is to study spelling for 10 minutes. Arithmetic, in the case, would be "preferred" 6.3 times more than spelling. It must be noted, however, that both behaviors may have low preference when held in comparison to another behavior (such as model building). It should also be noted that in the above example the actual reinforcers were not specified (i.e., it is not known why arithmetic is, in itself, or produces a reinforcer more powerful than that of or produced by spelling), but that is not necessary to obtain estimates of relative preference.

Preference, Position
Where the probability of an organism responding to a specific stimulus is greater merely because of that stimulus' position in the stimulus field. Any stimulus in that position would have a higher probability of controlling a response.

Premack Principle
A procedure whereby the emission of one operant is reinforced by the *opportunity* to engage in some previously established high rate behavior. The assumption is that the "reinforcing operant" (the previously established high-rate operant used to reinforce the other operant) must either be "self-reinforcing" or reinforced by some means not (usually) controlled by the experimenter or therapist. This assumption can be made by virtue of the fact that it *is* being emitted at a high rate. By making the opportunity to emit this response contingent upon another response, a type of artificial "chain" of responses is formed which will terminate in *some* sort of reinforcer already demonstrated to be effective (i.e., that reinforcer . . . whatever it is . . . *already* maintains the high rate "reinforcing operant"); and, the completion of that chain will,

in turn, reinforce the operant initiating that chain.

$$R_1 \longrightarrow \begin{bmatrix} S_2{}^D \\ R_2 \longrightarrow S_3{}^{R+} \end{bmatrix}$$

Where R_1 is the response to be generated and maintained.

$S_2{}^D$ is the stimulus condition (opportunity) in which R_2 may be emitted.

R_2 is the response (reinforcing operant) which is *already* in the repertoire of the subject; and which is emitted at a high rate whenever the opportunity to do so ($S_2{}^D$) is afforded.

$S_3{}^{R+}$ is the reinforcer (usually unknown) which maintains R_2. $S_3{}^{R+}$ is already *known* to be effective because of the manner in which R_2 is maintained.

EXAMPLE: It is known that a child will read a particular magazine for hours at a time whenever permitted to do so. The reason that this behavior is maintained (i.e., the reinforcer obtained) is not known. Making the opportunity to read the magazine contingent upon doing homework will increase the rate with which homework is completed.

The advantages of using the Premack principle to reinforce behavior are that: (1) whether or not the specific reinforcer that maintains the "reinforcing operant" can be specified, it is *known* to be effective and can be employed via the chain described above; and (2) the reinforcer in that chain is more likely to be "natural" and easily obtained for the maintenance of the behavior after specific training is terminated. The potential *dis*advantages to the use of the Premack principle are the facts that (1) it is usually more time consuming to allow a high rate behavior to occur than to dispense a more conventional "concrete" reinforcer; and (2) while the reinforcer obtained for the high rate behavior may be great enough in magnitude and/or frequency to maintain the "reinforcing operant," it may *not* be great enough to maintain a longer *chain* of operants (i.e., the behaviors which must be emitted to gain the opportunity to emit the "reinforcing operant"). See also **Chain**.

Pretest-Posttest Design
An experimental design in which a test is given to the experimental subjects before and after the "treatment" or manipulation of the experimental variable. This design permits

the investigation of overall effect only, and cannot be employed to investigate "process" (i.e., the moment-to-moment or session-to-session changes in performance which define the manner in which the overall effect was achieved). A "control" group (not exposed to the experimental variable) is also necessary to rule out the possibility that the change reflected by the difference between the pretest and the posttest did not occur independently of (despite) the manipulation of the experimental variable. See also **Experimental Design, Time-Series**.

Probability

Probability may be calculated in two basic forms: *Theoretical* probability, or *Empirical* probability. Theoretical probability is calculated on the assumption that each event of concern has an equal probability of occurring on any single trial; or that the probability of that event may be otherwise determined without recourse to the observation of its actual frequency; and the probability of any single event, therefore, is solely a function of the number of other possible events on any single trial (occasion) and the number of trials. Empirical probability, also called a "frequency ratio" or "observed probability" is calculated purely on the basis of data collected on the *actual occurrence* of the event in concern relative to the number of alternative events. Since it is a basic premise of the behavioral sciences that behavior is *not* random in nature, (and, therefore, each behavioral event does not have an equal probability of occurring on any single trial) it is usually empirical probability that is of the most concern. Empirical probability is calculated by dividing the number of events for which the probability is desired by the number of times that event *might* have occurred or had the opportunity to occur:

$P(A) = a/n$ "the probability of event A equals the number of times event A was observed to occur (a) divided by the number of times event A had the opportunity to occur (n)."

Probability may only range from (0.0) to (1.0). If a man were observed to stop his car every time he encountered a red light, then the number of times the "stopping a car at a red light" behavior occurred is equal to the number of opportunities, and the probability would be (1.0). If another man were observed never to stop at a red light, then the numerator (a) in the fraction would be zero, and the resultant probability would be (0.0). If another man stopped 75 times out of an observed 100 possibilities, then the probability of his stopping behavior would be 75/100 or (.75).

In the calculation of empirical probability it must be remembered that:

1.   All possible events must be considered. The categorization of these outcomes may be simplex (e.g., stopping or not stopping at a red light) or complex (e.g., stopping at a red light from a speed between 0 and 25 miles per hour; from a speed of 26 to 35 miles per hour; from a speed of 36 to 45 miles per hour; etc.). The number and choice of categories is purely arbitrary, but the total number of events in all of the categories put together must equal the number of possible events (n).

2.   The observational situation must be defined and remain constant, e.g., the observational situation above is a red light and the presence of the man observed in his car. Other stops and other red lights are not counted.

3.   The degree to which the empirical probability approaches the actual probability of an event is a function of the number of events observed. With a single flip of a coin, for example, observed probability of a head may turn out to be (0.0) or (1.00); whereas the actual probability of a head on any single trial is (.50). As the number of observations increases the error decreases. By 100 flips of the coin the number of heads might be 43, and the resultant empirical probability (.43)—much closer to (.50) than (0.0) or (1.00). To clarify the significance of the probability estimate, therefore, the number of observations upon which the estimate was calculated should be noted. E.g., the observed probability of a head on any single flip of a coin was (.43) based on 100 trials; or the probability of a man stopping at a red light was .75 based on 100 trials. Figure 61 demonstrates how the empirical probability of "heads" in a coin-flipping experiment approaches the known (theoretical) probability of .5 with more trials.

Probability, Relative

A special case of empirical probability in which the probability of a certain event is calculated as the ratio of the rate of that event to the rate of that event plus the rate of another event. The resultant probability is read: "given that one of two events occurs (X or Y), the probability of event (X) is . . ."

$$\text{The relative probability of event } X = \frac{\text{the rate of event } X}{\text{the rate of event } X + \text{the rate of event } Y}$$

EXAMPLE: If a pigeon "pecks" at a rate of 3.8 responses per minute, and "coos" at a rate of 16.2 responses per minute; then the probability of "pecking" is (3.8/3.8 + 16.2 =) .19 relative to "cooing." The number of behaviors to which the probability is made referent may be increased to any number. For example: One may know the rates of talking, arithmetic, and out-of-seat behavior, and then calculate the relative probability of arithmetic behavior as:

$$\frac{\text{rate of arithmetic problem solving}}{\text{rate of talking} + \text{the rate of arithmetic problem solving} + \text{the rate of out-of-seat}}$$

See also **Probability**.

Process
Any change in the form, probability, or rate of responding. Many operations (e.g., reinforcement) are defined in terms of the process they produce in the organism. Process denotes the change in performance, and not necessarily the maintenance or long term effect of that change.

Proficiency
Those characteristics of responding which are necessary to guarantee that the organism is capable of achieving some predetermined type of interaction with the environment. Note that the interaction in question need not be reinforcing *per se*, only that the interaction be of a specified type. For example: If it is desirable that all second grade children be able to read the price of an item in a store, select the right coins for the purchase (or, if no coins are available, then select the correct

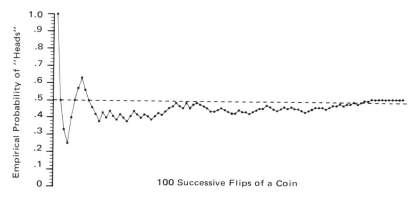

Figure 61. The Empirical Probability of Heads: This chart represents a simple experiment in which a coin was tossed 100 times and the empirical probability of "heads" calculated after each toss. The dotted line at .50 represents the "theoretical" probability of heads (if, of course, the coin is "fair"). Notice that at the beginning of the experiment there was a considerable discrepancy between the empirical and theoretical probabilities; and that with more and more trials it became more difficult to alter the overall empirical probability with any single flip of the coin. This obtains because each successive flip represents a smaller percentage of the total number of flips than any previous flip.

bill), and be able to determine if the right change has been administered with 100% accuracy, then proficiency can be determined as those behavioral characteristics a child must display in the "test" situation that guarantees the desired interaction. It may be found, for example, that of all the children who practice "paying and change-receiving" behavior in the classroom, those that never make errors in a store are those that are able to emit those behaviors at or above a rate of 2 per minute in the classroom. "Proficiency," then, would be defined as a rate of 2 per minute with no errors in the classroom. "Proficiency" should not be confused with "aim," where the latter term describes what is desired (i.e., to make payment and receive change correctly); and the former is a description of the response characteristics necessary to achieve the aim. Aims are arbitrarily determined (i.e., what do you want), but proficiencies are determined by their ability to achieve the aim (i.e., what is necessary to get there). There are several methods of defining proficiencies—among them are error rates, correct rates, a combination of error and correct rates, probability of responding, progress through a program, and the behaviors necessary for only a single interaction with the environment. Once the aim has been clearly specified, however, the criteria of proficiency should be reasonably easy to determine. See also **Behavior, Target; Proficiency, Dynamic**; and **Proficiency, Static**.

Proficiency, Dynamic
A proficiency statement in terms of the progress an individual is making toward the accomplishment of some aim. The aim must, therefore, include not only a statement of the desired results, but also *when* the results are desired. Then it may be determined if the student is progressing at a rapid enough pace to achieve the aim by the specified time. To say that an organism has achieved dynamic proficiency does *not* mean that he has already achieved the final objective, but only that he is progressing at a rate which has a high probability of reaching the desired level by the desired date. See also **Proficiency; Behavior, Target**; and **Line-of-Progress**.

Proficiency, Static
A proficiency level stated only in terms of "magnitude" or "type" of responding necessary to achieve a certain aim, and in which there is no statement of *when* the aim should be achieved. See also **Proficiency**; and **Proficiency, Dynamic**.

Program
An element of the "is" equation in Precision Teaching. See "**Is**" **Equation**.

Program Event (PE)
An element of the "is" equation in Precision Teaching. See "Is" Equation.

Programming
Arranging a set of reinforcing contingencies, including schedules, stimuli, etc., usually with the intent of maximizing or minimizing the probability of a particular performance.

Programming, Independent
A program developed for use by a single individual, and designed to be carried out in the absence of other persons (e.g., a math program in which the child works alone—without interaction with the other students). The term independent does not, however, exclude the possibility that another person is not part of the program *per se* (e.g., a teacher could orally test the student as part of the program); but independent *does* mean that the child or person responding under the program does so alone (i.e., no other person is also responding as part of that individual's program).

Programming, Individual
A case in which a program has been developed and implemented specifically for one individual. This does *not* mean that the individual must work *alone* (part of the program plan might specify working *with* someone)—just that the program was designed for that individual's particular response superiorities and/or deficiencies (as opposed to being a general plan applied to all students or persons without alteration). See also **Programming, Independent**.

Progressive Relaxation Training
A relatively involved method of Relaxation Training. See **Relaxation Training**.

Project (in Precision Teaching)
Any effort by any person or group of persons to alter the rates of any movement-cycle or response emitted by that person or group of persons, or any other person. NOTE: In labeling such an effort a "project" it is inferred that the operations and procedures employed in the attempted alteration are those prescribed by Precision Teaching. See **Precision Teaching, Basic Steps in**.

Project Team (in Precision Teaching)
The project team is composed of all persons related, directly or indirectly, with the planning or implementation of a project. The title of each project team member serves only to describe the basic function that person performs, and the level of

involvement with the behaver or data that function entails. In no way does one title or another imply the relative "importance" of any single member of the project team. Any one person may perform any number of functions, and, therefore, have any number of titles. The members of a project team are:

Behaver: The individual whose behavior is being charted.

Manager: That individual who is directly responsible for the implementation of the plan to affect a change in the rate of the movement-cycle. Usually a teacher or other practitioner who works directly with the behaver, but not necessarily so. If there *is*, however, *anyone* who works directly with the behaver as part of the plan, then that person is called the manager.

Supervisor: That individual who is in a supportive position to the manager and advises the manager on the significance or interpretation of the behaver's data.

Trainer: Any individual who is responsible for the training of managers or supervisors. A person who teaches the principles and procedures of Precision Teaching to someone else.

Depositor: The individual who prepares and submits project reports for storage and/or analysis in some central facility (e.g., Precision Teaching's "data bank" located in Kansas City, Kansas and operated by Behavior Research Co.).

Charter: The individual who charts the rates of responding on the standard behavior chart. Usually the charter is the behaver or manager—preferably the former.

Counter: The individual who counts the movement-cycle during the course of its emission; or who is responsible for determining that information after its emission through the examination of permanent records (e.g., fact sheets with written answers).

Prosthesis

Literally prosthesis is the process of instituting something where it did not previously exist. In behavioral usage, however, we speak of prosthesis as the alteration of an environment to shape, condition, or maintain a specific performance which the organism would not otherwise emit or be able to emit. It is definitive of a prosthetic change that once the environment is restored to its former state the behavior will extinguish or otherwise fail to maintain or be emitted. Often it cannot be determined whether a change is prosthetic or therapeutic until such time as the alteration is removed or reversed and the behavioral result observed. One may speak of prosthetic environments, prosthetic devices, prosthetic contingencies, etc. See also **Therapeutic**.

Prosthetic
Of or pertaining to prosthesis. See **Prosthesis**.

Prosthetic Device
A device especially designed and constructed to permit or maintain behaviors in an organism which it would not otherwise emit or be able to emit. Removal of the device will result in the discontinuance of the behaviors it supported or permitted. An artificial leg would be, for example, a prosthetic device to allow a person to walk who would not otherwise be able to do so. See **Prosthesis**.

Punishment
1. As an operation: the presentation of an aversive stimulus immediately following the emission of a response. Contingency is implied but not necessary (i.e., punishment may be accidental or coincidental).

2. As a process: the resultant reduction in probability or rate of responding for the punished operant. NOTE: Reduction in probability or rate may or may not be permanent or maintain over a long period of time. Do *not* confuse punishment with negative reinforcement, which has the opposite behavioral result.

Quartile Deviation
Synonym for "interquartile range." See **Range, Interquartile**.

Range
A measure of central tendency, that is, a measure of how a set of numbers are grouped together. Specifically, the range refers to the difference (sometimes called the distance) between the

highest and lowest rate values or data points in any given data set. The range is used to describe how variable or stable the data are in that period.

To find the range simply subtract the lowest data value from the highest data value in that set. If the highest datum were 10, and the lowest datum were 7, then the range would be:

$$10 - 7 = 3$$

This range would be considered indicative of a relatively stable data set (i.e., each data point is about the same as each other data point).

If the highest datum were 189, and the lowest datum were 12, then the range would be:

$$189 - 12 = 177$$

This range would generally be considered indicative of a relatively *unstable* or variable set of data points. (I.e., each data point may be considerably different than other data points).

If the data are charted (and therefore interpreted from their appearance) on a logarithmic chart (e.g., the standard 6-cycle chart of Precision Teaching), then it is more in keeping with the visual analysis to express ranges in terms of the number by which the lowest data point must be multiplied to obtain the value of the highest point. For example, in the case where the lowest data point were 7 and the greatest 10 (as before), one would divide 10 by 7:

$$10/7 = 1.42857 \text{ (or) } 1.43$$

Then the range would be expressed as "times 1.43" (i.e., the lowest number, 7, must be multiplied by 1.43 to obtain the highest number, 10). The advantage of expressing ranges in this manner lies in the fact that equal ratios on log charts appear to be the same (e.g., a times-two ratio between any two numbers will always occupy the same amount of vertical space on the chart regardless of the absolute magnitude of difference between the two numbers). See Figure 62 for examples.

Range, Interquartile
That range of values which includes 50% of all data in any given data set, and extends from that point at or below which 25% of the data fall to that point at or above which 25% of the data fall. See **Range**.

Rate
The average frequency of a specified event during a standard unit of time (usually one minute). The rate of responding, for example, would be the average number of responses emitted by the behaver during one minute. To calculate rate divide the

number of events (e.g., responses) by the number of units of time (e.g., minutes). Example: If 45 responses were observed to occur over an interval of 10 minutes, then the rate of responding would be:

$$\frac{45 \text{ responses}}{10 \text{ minutes}} = 4.5 \text{ responses per minute}$$

NOTE: Rates can also be calculated for other events for purposes of analysis (e.g., if the rate of some event increases, what happens to the rate of responding?).

Rate Finder

A device, developed in Precision Teaching, used for the calculation of rates of responding directly on a chart. Must be used on a "ratio" (semilog or log/log) scale such as the standard Precision Teaching behavior chart.

The use of the rate finder is identical to that of a slide rule. Place the number on the rate finder that corresponds to the number of minutes observed next to the number on the chart that corresponds to the number of responses counted. The rate of responding will be equal to that point on the chart which is then next to the "one" on the rate finder scale. Figure 63 demonstrates these operations. NOTE: A portion of the "acceleration finder" (of Precision Teaching) may be used as a rate finder on the standard Precision Teaching behavior chart. See also **Acceleration Finder**.

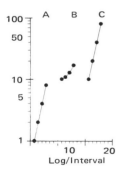
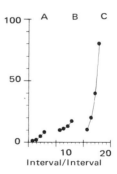

Figure 62. Range: Three data sets (A, B, and C) are shown on two charts—a log/interval chart, and an interval/interval chart. The range of data set A could be described as a "times 7" or a "plus 7"—each describing the relationship between the lowest and highest data point. The range of data set B, on the other hand, is simply a "plus 7"; and data set C is a "times 7." On the log/interval chart A and C appear to be the same and both are "times 7." Expressing ranges in ratios, therefore, will afford the greatest consistency between verbal and visual description of those data. On the interval/interval chart, however, data set B looks most like A, and both may be expressed as "plus 7." On this type of chart, therefore, expressing ranges in terms of the arithmetic difference between the high and low data points would be most advisable.

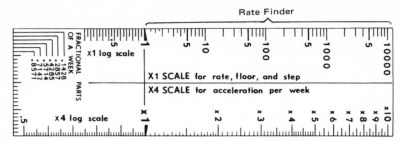

Figure 63. Rate Finder: The "times one" scale of the acceleration finder may also be used as a rate finder. Operating on the principle of a slide rule, the number of behaviors counted is found on the chart, and the number of minutes observed is noted on the acceleration finder. Placing those two points together (the count on the chart and the minutes on the finder) then indicates the rate (count divided by time) where the "one" on the rate finder scale falls. Using scales in this manner is only valid on logarithmic paper, and the scale on the rate finder must be exactly the same as the scale on the chart with which it is to be used.

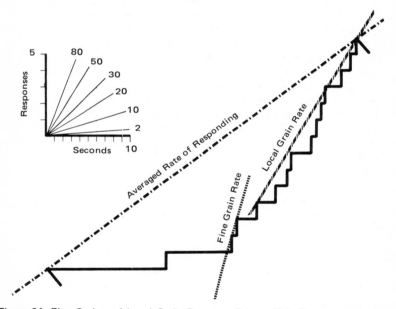

Figure 64. Fine Grain and Local Grain Response Rates: This figure, representing a blow-up of a cumulative record, demonstrates the difference between average, fine grain, and local grain rates of responding. The average rate of responding may be found as the slope of the line connecting the beginning of the record with the end of the record. Connecting any two successive responses results in a slope representing a fine grain response, and taking any section of the curve with reasonable consistency in responding results in a local grain estimate. The small figure in the upper left hand corner notes the scale for vertical and horizontal movements of the pen, and provides a few reference slopes for comparison.

From this figure it may be seen how average response rates can sometimes "neglect" a great deal of information in the response pattern.

122

Rate, Fine Grain
The rate of responding over a small unit of time, usually between any two responses. Also called "operant-to-operant rate." See Figure 64.

Rate, Local Grain
The rate of responding measured over a short period of time, and in which more than two responses have occurred. See Figure 64.

Rate, Mean
Rate of response over an interval of time in which changes of local rate have occurred. Nearly all rate statements are mean rates. See **Rate of Responding**.

Rate, No Count
A term, originating in Precision Teaching, in reference to any rate of "zero" which has been computed on a count of zero, but where there may be some doubt as to whether the rate is *actually* zero, or just falls below the record floor. In Precision Teaching, no count rates are charted just below the record floor, *not* on the zero line. See Figure 65. See also **Record Floor**.

Rate (of Responding)
The number of responses emitted by the organism during a unit of time, where the unit of time is usually a minute. Arithmetically, the number of responses divided by the number of minutes. E.g., if an organism emits 100 responses in five minutes, the rate of responding is equal to $100/5 = 20/\text{min}$.

Rate (of Responding), Averaged
An estimate of the number of responses that will (on the average) occur within a given unit of time (usually one minute). Calculated as the number of responses divided by the time the behavior was observed.

E.g., averaged rate per minute = the # of responses observed/the number of minutes observation.

As the frequency of the behavior approaches 1, however, the accuracy of the estimation decreases. More accurate estimates may be achieved by beginning the observation time with the emission of one response and ending with the emission of another; and then dividing the number of responses observed -1 by the observation time:

corrected average rate = (# of responses -1)/time from the beginning of the first response to the end of the last.

OR, a more accurate estimate may also be obtained by utilizing the operant-to-operant interval. See **Operant-to-Operant Interval** and **Rate, Operant-to-Operant**.

Rate of Responding, Relative
That proportion of responses in a specified interval or situation which are of a specified type. The relative rate of responding of operant "X" to the total number of responses emitted in a situation where "X_2" and "X_3" may also be emitted would be:

$$\text{relative rate } X_1 = \frac{\text{rate or number of } X_1}{\begin{array}{l}(\text{rate or number of } X_1) + \\ (\text{rate or number of } X_2) + \\ (\text{rate or number of } X_3)\end{array}}$$

Rate, Operant-to-Operant (OOR)
An estimate of the number of responses emitted in any given minute, obtained by dividing 1 by that time which elapses from the beginning of one response to the beginning of the next response. Operant-to-operant rate = 1/beginning-to-beginning time. The usual "averaged" rate of responding will approach the actual operant-to-operant rate as N (the number of responses) increases:

averaged rate = the # of responses/the time observed

In averaged rates, however, there are two intervals undefined by responses (i.e., the beginning of the interval ending with the *first* response observed; and the end of the last interval beginning with the *last* response observed). The discrepancy between averaged rate and the mean of a set of operant-to-operant rates may increase, therefore, as N approaches 1 (and the ratio of these two intervals to all other intervals increases). This discrepancy can be eliminated, however, if observation time always begins with the beginning of one response and ends with the termination of another response (where $N \geq 2$).

The operant-to-operant rates are generally more informative than averaged rates (e.g., the distribution of operant-to-operant rates can be plotted as a very discrete measure of changes in responding), but considerably more difficult to obtain (each interval must be timed and recorded—especially difficult with high response rates). Don't confuse OOR (operant-to-operant rates) with IRTs (inter-response times) or IRATs (intra-response times). Also called a special case of "fine grain rate." See **Rate**; **Inter-Response Time**; and **Intra-Response Time**.

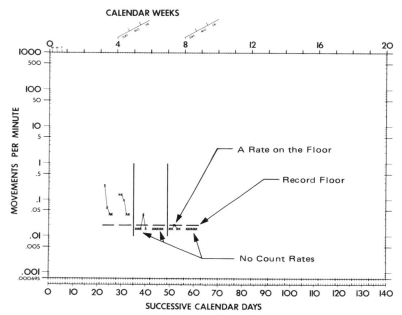

Figure 65. No Count Rates: The record floor, calculated as 1 divided by the number of minutes observed, indicates the lowest rate (other than zero) that may be determined within the time observed. If the rates fall below that level, they are all recorded as "zero." To remind the analyst that rates may simply be below the "floor" and not really "zero," rates calculated on a count of zero (i.e., no behavior occurred during the time the subject was observed) are charted just below the floor — not at zero. A rate falling *on* the record floor indicates a count of one (i.e., one behavior was observed). More recently some people have been charting no count rates as little question marks to further explicate the fact that the rate may be greater than zero, but is simply unknown.

Rate, Overall
Rate of responding for a relatively large interval of time, the size of the interval usually taken to be the time between reinforcements, time in session, the entire day, or some other discrete unit.

Rate Pause
A period of no responding, usually in contrast to periods of high (or higher) rates. E.g., following reinforcement on a fixed-ratio schedule there is usually a rate pause, that is, a short interval of time when the organism does not respond. See Figure 66.

Rate, Running
A rate of responding which is sustained and relatively stable over a specified interval of time. Often the only important single rate except zero (as in the typical ratio performance). See Figure 66.

125

Figure 66. Rate Pause and Running Rate Under an FR Schedule: Rate pauses are noted as flat, horizontal lines, and responding as vertical movement. The steeper the slope of vertical movement, the higher the rate of responding. Note that in these fixed ratio performance records there are basically only two rates—zero and about 300 per minute. The former is called a "pause" and the latter "running rate." Notice also that the running rates in both schedules are the same, and that only the length of the pauses differ. Schedule A is an FR200 and schedule B is an FR120. The organism in both cases is a pigeon.[7]

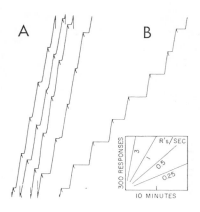

Rate, Single-Movement
A term, originating in Precision Teaching, in reference to a special case of rate in which the count is always one, and the observation time is always taken as the time it takes to emit a single instance of the behavior in question.

Single-movement rate = 1/(time from beginning to end of one movement)

The single-movement rate was originally designed to accommodate, in rated format, data that would usually be expressed in duration. "Late to work in the morning," for example, is a behavior which may occur only once on any given day; and the most critical dimension of the behavior is *how late*. Although it would be possible to chart the number of minutes late *per se*, the calculation of a single-movement rate keeps that data comparable with *standard* Precision Teaching data— rate of responding. Actually, the data expressed in a single-movement rate are identical to a record floor where the observation time is always the time it takes to emit a single movement-cycle. See also **Movement-Cycle, Record Floor,** and **Rate of Responding.**

Rate, Terminal
The rate of responding at, or just prior to, the moment of reinforcement. See Figure 67.

Ratio, Suppression
The ratio between a measure of responding during one stimulus condition and the same measure of responding

[7] Figure from Ferster, C.B. and Skinner, B.F. *Schedules of reinforcement.* New York: Appleton-Century-Crofts, page 52. Copyright © 1957. Used by permission of Appleton-Century-Crofts, Educational Division, Meredith Corporation.

Figure 67. Terminal Rate: This figure represents a portion of the cumulative records of a pigeon's performance under an FI 16, TO 5 schedule of reinforcement. Note that the final rate is relatively stable and unchanging. It is this rate, ending with reinforcement and back as long as it is stable, that is called the "terminal rate."[8]

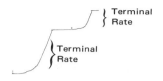

Terminal Rate

Terminal Rate

applied during the time just preceding the stimulus condition in question.

E.g., if one is interested in the effects of 5″ of shock on responding, a "suppression ratio" could be calculated by dividing the number of responses during the 5″ of shock by the number of responses during the 5″ just *preceding* the shock.

Suppression ratio = (# responses during 5″ shock)/(# responses in 5″ just *before* shock)

Some experimenters have chosen arbitrary time intervals for comparison (e.g., *10″* before shock and *5″* shock) which are not necessarily the same; in addition, certain experimenters choose to include the shock time in *both* estimates (e.g., 5″ shock time divided by 10″ before shock + 5″ shock time = 5″/15″) either of these latter arrangements induce idiosyncratic limits on the outcome, however, whereas the method discussed first (above) always has the limits of (0 → 1)—assuming that suppression does, in fact, occur. If there is a possibility that the time preceding the stimulus event in question will *not* contain more responses, then the limits differ accordingly. (NOTE: It is probably this last condition which prompts some experimenters to always include the count from *both* time intervals in the denominator of this ratio. If this practice is assumed, however, the possible limits of the ratio must be fully explained.)

Reactive Measures
Measures which in and of themselves cause a change in what they are measuring. E.g., scales designed to measure attitudes often change the attitudes they are supposed to measure.

Reciprocal Inhibition
A process produced by the simultaneous occurrence of two stimuli, each normally controlling or eliciting a response incompatible with the response controlled or elicited by the other. If both stimuli are of equal "strength," then neither

---

[8] Figure from Ferster, C. B. and Skinner, B. F., *Schedules of reinforcement*. New York: Appleton-Century-Crofts, p. 237. Copyright © 1957. Used by permission of Appleton-Century-Crofts, Educational Division, Meredith Corporation.

response will occur. If one stimulus is "stronger" than the other, then the response controlled by it will occur, but with reduced magnitude.

Reciprocal inhibition is often induced in behavioral therapy for the treatment of phobias or maladaptive anxieties. See, for example, **Systematic Desensitization**.

Reconditioning

When a behavior has been conditioned and subsequently extinguished, it may be reconditioned by repeating the operations of deprivation and reinforcement. Original conditioning is usually accomplished on a schedule of continuous reinforcement; reconditioning is often accomplished with other schedules, and usually obtains in less time than the original or preceding conditioning trials.

Record Ceiling

A term, originating in Precision Teaching, in reference to the highest possible rate of responding which may occur under certain specified conditions. E.g., if the response is "problem solved" on a particular fact sheet that had 100 problems on it; and if 10 minutes were allowed to work on the fact sheet (no more, no less), then the highest possible calculated rate of responding would be:

$$\frac{100 \text{ problems}}{10 \text{ minutes}} = \text{a record ceiling of 10 responses per minute}$$

If the response being counted were "correct answers to questions asked by the teacher during arithmetic period," then the record ceiling would be the rate of "question asking," since the behaver's rate cannot be higher than the rate with which those questions are asked.

There is probably a record ceiling for every response. Sometimes, however, it is impossible to determine what that ceiling may be. If the only apparent limitation to the rate of responding is the capacity of the behaver to respond faster, then usually no record ceiling is noted. If, however, some *external* factor (presentation of material, limited amounts of material to work on, etc.) appears to limit the maximum rate of responding, then that limit should be calculated and recorded as the record ceiling.

Record ceilings are generally considered undesirable, since they place an artificial limit on responding, and thereby limit the amount of information we can gain about a behaver. Additional disadvantages, indicated by some data sets, include a "pacing" phenomenon and "slowing" phenomenon. The "pacing phenomenon" is described as a process in which the child learns just how fast he must go to complete the problems under the limit; and even when the ceiling is removed, that child will tend to respond at the same rate (even though now it would be possible for him to accelerate). The "slowing phenomenon" is observed as a deceleration in progress as the ceiling is approached (but not yet reached). Even though a child with no ceiling might accelerate consistently for several weeks, many children will slow down as they *approach* the ceiling (even though they have not yet reached it) and actually *de*celerate. Projects with no ceiling, on the other hand tend to have longer periods of high acceleration, fewer instances of "pacing," and fewer cases of "regression" (deceleration following periods of acceleration). Whenever possible, therefore, it is advisable to eliminate any known record ceiling.

When record ceilings are completely unavoidable (e.g., there are only a set number of fact sheets at any one level available), then the manager should do one of two things. First, the behavers may be allowed to start over again after finishing the available materials. There will be some "practice effect" or "memory" of the answers already given; but in general these effects will be small if the repetition is only once every 100 problems or so. Second, the behavers may be timed to completion (i.e., instead of having a constant record floor, keeping track of whatever time it takes the behaver to finish). This latter suggestion is less desirable since it will introduce a variable record floor (see **Record Floor**).

To determine roughly how many problems should be given a behaver to minimize the practice effect of repetition and/or the problem of the record ceiling the manager should avoid any á priori estimates of what a behaver is "capable" of doing. Rather, select a behaver that already possesses the skill in question (e.g., in math facts, it could be the math teacher) and determine how fast that behaver is able to emit the response. Then, to allow for the possibility that the rate achieved does not necessarily represent the "best," multiply that rate by 1.5 or 2. If, for example, a teacher were able to perform the math facts at a rate of 40 per minute, then the materials and timing should allow the behaver to proceed at a rate of 60 or 80 per minute before repeating problems. There has been more than one case where a student has outperformed the teacher. Don't underestimate the behaver!

Whenever a record ceiling can be noted, it is quite often the case that it is not the distance between the rate of responding and the record floor that is important, but the difference between the rate of responding and the record ceiling— whenever a child is responding as rapidly as is physically possible, it really doesn't matter how fast that is.

In Precision Teaching the record ceiling is noted by placing a dashed line across the Sunday lines on the chart at the level of the record ceiling. If the record ceiling varies considerably within the week (e.g., as would be the case if the ceiling were determined by the number of questions asked), then the record ceiling is recorded on a separate chart (e.g., the rate of "question asking"), and comparisons are made between the charts by overlaying them. See Figure 68. See also **Record Floor.**

Record, Constant
A term, originating in Precision Teaching, in reference to the record floor of a predetermined recording time. Any record floor which is calculated on a record length which remains constant from observation to observation. E.g., if it were

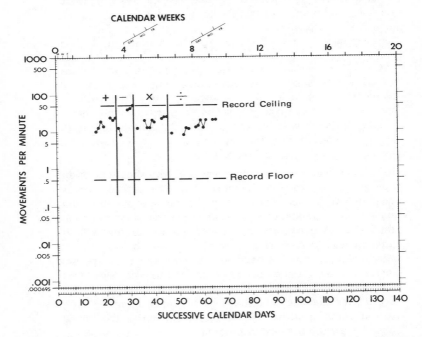

Figure 68. Record Ceiling: This chart demonstrates the use of record ceiling, and some of the potential drawbacks. The behaviors charted are two-term math facts of the type noted at the top of each phase. With a record floor of .5 we know that the time sample was a constant 2 minutes; and with a record ceiling of 50 facts per minute it is apparent that there were only 100 problems on which the child could work. In all but one of the phases the child's rates fell well below the ceiling, but in the subtraction phase the maximum rate was obtained. In addition to the fact that the child's maximum rate will never be known for that phase, there are some data which indicate that ceilings tend to reduce overall responding as those rates *approach* the ceiling. Although they are generally undesirable, of course, record ceilings should be noted if they exist.

determined in advance that the teacher would count an academic behavior for exactly 10 minutes each day, the constant record would be (1/10 = .1); or, if it were determined in advance that a management behavior problem would be counted for exactly 20 minutes each day, then the constant record would be (1/20 = .05). The convention and calculation for the constant record is identical to that of the record floor. See **Record Floor.**

NOTE: Constant records are ideal because they simplify interpretation of data. A changing record floor may affect rates of responding. If the floor is constant, on the other hand, then this variable (at least) can be eliminated as a possible contributor to any changes in rate.

Record Floor
A term, originating in Precision Teaching, in reference to the lowest measurable or recordable rate other than zero. Since the lowest count other than zero is 1, then the lowest measurable rate for any given observation would be 1 divided by the number of minutes in the record length. E.g., if the record length is 10 minutes, then the record floor would be:

$$\frac{1}{10 \text{ minutes}} = .1 \text{ (record floor)}$$

Rates of responding cannot fall below the record floor without being calculated as zero. In fact, however, the rates may *not* be zero, but just less than the value of the record floor. The record floor acts, therefore, as a measure of the "sensitivity" of the record length, i.e., one is not sensitive to (cannot measure) rates between zero and the record floor.

If rates consistently "bounce back and forth" from above to below, then back above the record floor, it is advisable to attempt to increase the record length (thereby lowering the record floor) to determine if rates are actually going to zero, or just can't be measured. In Precision Teaching rates which fall below the record floor are charted *just below* the record floor, *not* on the "zero" line.

Following is a list of the advantages for charting the record floor:
1. The record length (observation time) may be determined for any single data point at a later time: Record length = one divided by the record floor.
2. The count from which any single data point was calculated may be found at a later date: Count = rate divided by the record floor.
3. The record floor can serve as a "qualification" for changes that may occur in rates. E.g., if error rates increased from .1 to .2, but both fall on the record floor, then the data still reflects

just one error; and the increase in rate might have just been an artifact of raising the record floor.

4. The record floor can be used to assess the relative reliabilities of data points. The longer the record length (i.e., the lower the record floor), the more reliable the data point.

5. The record floor can indicate when it is necessary to increase the record length (observation time). When rates "bounce back and forth" between points above the record floor and zero (below the record floor), then it is wise to try to increase the record length. The rationale for this is simply that the rates may *not* actually be going to zero, but rather are just less than the record floor and cannot, therefore, be measured. By increasing the record length (i.e., decreasing the record floor), it may be possible to determine the actual value of what would have been previously considered no count rates.

NOTE: Highly variable record floors increase the difficulty of data analysis. It is wise, therefore, to attempt to keep the record floor constant. See Figure 69. See also **Record, Constant**; **Record Ceiling**; and **Rate, No Count**.

In Precision Teaching the record floor is noted on the standard behavior chart by a short dashed line across the day to which that floor applies. In the preferable event of a constant record floor, the floor is indicated by a line extending from each Monday-line to each Friday-line of each week in which there are data. In both cases, of course, the line is placed at the level of the rate defining the floor.

Although the use of the record floor is found most often in Precision Teaching, and is applied exclusively to rate data, there does, in fact, exist a record floor for virtually *all* forms of data.

In percentage, for example, the lowest percentage (other than zero) which may obtain is equal to one divided by the number of events forming the percentage base. If one observes 50 children and then wishes to give the percentage of those children with certain characteristics, then the lowest percentage (other than zero) which may be obtained is 1/50, or, 2%. Virtually any statistic which may be expressed in the form of a ratio (i.e., one number divided by another) may be qualified by the expression of a record floor.

In cases where comparisons are desired between subjects or various observations, the record floor is particularly important. In recent literature, for example, there has been a trend toward the calculation and reporting of "exact probabilities" of certain events. To say that .001 is more significant than .01 does not make sense, however, if both lie on the record floor (i.e., if both were calculated on an observed frequency of one). See also **Record Ceiling**.

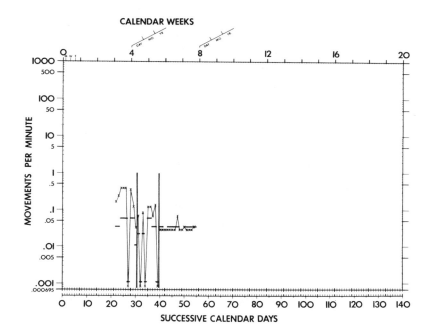

Figure 69. Record Floor: The first two phases in this deceleration project have variable record floors—the time observed each day changed from day-to-day. The last phase, however, has a constant record floor. Although there are certainly advantages in looking at a behavior for as long as possible, it may also be seen from this chart that interpretation of the data is far more clear with the constant record floor (the third phase).

Record Length

The number of minutes during which the data are collected. Only those minutes of actual observation during which the behavior may occur should be counted in the record length. Example: If during a school day of 6 hours a child is being observed and the behavior counted during *all* times, then the record length is:

(6 hours) times (60 minutes in an hour) = 360 minutes

If, however, the child is *not* observed during lunch (60 minutes) and recess (two periods of 15 minutes each), then the record length is:

The school day (360 minutes) minus lunch (60 minutes)
minus two recess periods (2 × 15 = 30 minutes)
= a total 270 minutes record length.

133

Reflex

A relationship between an eliciting stimulus and an elicited response such as the contraction of the pupil of the eye as a result of shining light on it, the jerk of the knee as a result of tapping the patellar tendon, etc. The reflex describes both the behavior of the organism (response) and its environment (stimulus). See **Respondent**.

Reflex Strength

That hypothetical entity which determines the relationship (at any given moment) between the intensity of the stimulus and the latency, magnitude, fatigability, and threshold of the response.

It is better to state the former in terms of some combination of the latter rather than making a vague reference to "reflex strength" alone.

Regression Line

Any function (or line representing that function) which describes the set of all mean predictions of one variable given knowledge about another variable. Standard linear regression is expressed in the equation:

$$\widehat{Y} = a + bX$$

where: $\widehat{Y}$ is the estimate of the value of the variable Y to be formed from knowledge of the value of X

X is the value of the variable which is known

a equals the intercept of the regression line at X = 0 (the Y axis)

b equals the slope of the regression line

The specific values of a and b may be determined from the following formulas:

$$b = \frac{N\Sigma XY - (\Sigma X)(\Sigma Y)}{N X^2 - (\Sigma X)^2}$$

$$a = \overline{Y} - b\overline{X}$$

In addition to linear regression (yielding a straight line), curvilinear regression formulas may also be constructed (yielding curves). All regression lines represent a least-squares solution to the problem of minimizing the deviations squared of actual data (in the Y dimension) about it. See **Least-Squares Solution**.

Reinforcement, Accidental

A coincidence of a response and a reinforcing event. Although there is no causal relationship as in programmed or contingent reinforcement, such a coincidence will have the same effect on rate of responding; and, if the coincidence is repetitive, (i.e., happens again) or dramatic (i.e., involves a very powerful reinforcer), it will lead to superstitious behavior. Also called "incidental" or "spurious reinforcement." See **Behavior, Superstitious**.

Reinforcement, Collateral

The operation of generating and maintaining behavior through reinforcement programmed for another behavior which occurs in close temporal proximity. A form of accidental reinforcement where the reinforcement was, in fact, programmed, but for another behavior. See **Reinforcement, Accidental**.

Reinforcement, Delayed

Reinforcement is generally defined as a temporal phenomenon (i.e., the occurrence of a reinforcing event immediately following the emission of a response). Violation of this temporal relationship should, therefore, obviate the use of that term with respect to the behavior in question. There are cases, however, where the delivery of a specific reinforcer (i.e., the occurrence of a specific reinforcing event) may be delayed substantially without decelerating effects on the behavior—usually after a period of prolonged or "strong" reinforcement in the usual sense. In these cases it is hypothesized that other environmental events (perhaps the behavior itself) which invariably occur concurrent with or immediately following the behavior have become conditioned reinforcers (via the process of respondent conditioning) capable of maintaining response rates in the absence of immediate, more substantial reinforcement; or that "mediating behaviors" are learned by the organism which "bridge the gap" between the (ultimately) reinforced behavior and the reinforcing event. In these cases the mediating behavior may be considered a superstitiously conditioned chain with the behavior upon which reinforcement is actually contingent as its first component.

The actual affect of any given delay between a response and the reinforcing event is dependent upon the length of the delay, type and duration of previous conditioning, availability of conditioned reinforcers, and the method by which the delay is imposed. For example, if a delay is imposed gradually (i.e., starting with a small delay and increasing it very slowly), the probability of achieving (ultimately) a long delay with little or no decrease in performance is greater than if the long delay is immediately imposed.

One should note that delayed reinforcement is *not* equivalent to a ratio or interval schedule of reinforcement (although either of those or another schedule may, in fact, also be in effect). A schedule of reinforcement defines the nature of contingency between responding and reinforcement, and the specification of "delay" only defines when the reinforcement will occur *after* the conditions of responding expressed in the schedule have been met.

While the purpose of an artificially imposed delay in reinforcement is usually to increase the probability that the organism will emit certain responses in the absence of immediate consequation (i.e., as one is normally expected to do in the "real world"), reinforcement delays may also be employed as a means of decreasing the rate or probability of responding. As noted above, if a relatively large delay is immediately instituted, there is a good probability that performances will be affected in much the same way as they would be under the conditions of extinction. In a situation where it is not feasible to literally *prevent* consequation for a response (a response, that is, for which deceleration is desired), it may be possible to delay it and achieve the same results. If a child begins to "cry and whine" for dinner, for example, one may not wish to actually eliminate dinner altogether, but may be able to avoid effective consequation of that behavior by simply *delaying* the meal.

Reinforcement Density
The number of reinforcements obtained by an organism per unit of time, or, per unit of behavior. If 10 reinforcements were obtained in a 20-minute interval the density would be 1:2 min. (I.e., one reinforcement for every 2 minutes of responding.) If 10 reinforcements were obtained after 1000 responses, the density would be 1:100R (i.e., one reinforcement for every 100 responses). The abbreviation for reinforcement density is $S^R D$. If the density is expressed in reference to time, then the abbreviation may be expanded to $S^R D_T$. If density is expressed in reference to responses, then the abbreviation becomes $S^R D_R$. These abbreviations are not widely used, however; and the user would be wise to explain their usage with their first appearance in any written material.

Often the choice of whether to express density in terms of time or number of responses is arbitrary. If, however, it is known that reinforcement is contingent upon the number of responses, then density should be expressed in those terms, etc. The advantage of referring to reinforcement density rather than a specific schedule of reinforcement (e.g., referring to the above samples as VI 2 and VR 100) lies in the fact that reinforcement density does not explicitly define the schedule of reinforcement; and thereby allows for the possibility of accidental reinforcement, or reinforcement on a time basis where it might appear to be a function of the number of responses, etc. In all situations where the actual schedules or contingencies are in doubt, one should note the frequency of reinforcement in terms of density. NOTE: If one wishes to compare the relative effects of two different types of schedules (e.g., FR vs. FI), one should attempt to equalize reinforcement densities so that *only* the contingencies differ.

Reinforcement, Differential
Reinforcement which is contingent upon (1) responding in the presence of a given property of a stimulus, in which case the resulting process is discrimination; or (2) the presence of a given intensive, durational, or topographical property of a response, in which case the resulting process is differentiation, or (3) a given rate of responding. All other, related or unrelated, responses are not reinforced.

Reinforcement, Episodic
A schedule of reinforcement in which the reinforcer is absent until a behavioral criteria has been met (see **Reinforcement, Intermittent**)—as opposed to conjugate reinforcement in which the reinforcer is *present* until *failure* to meet the behavioral criteria. In the former, one may speak of the reinforcement as being *presented*; and in the latter as being *removed* or terminated. See also **Schedule, Conjugate**.

Reinforcement, Intermittent
Noncontinuous reinforcement. A schedule of reinforcement according to which not every response is reinforced. See **Reinforcement, Schedules of**.

Reinforcement, Negative
1. As an operation: The removal or termination of an aversive stimulus following the emission of an operant response. Such removal or termination may be contingent or accidental (see **Behavior, Superstitious**).
2. As a process: The resultant increase in the probability or rate of responding of the operant in question. Aversive stimuli are often defined in terms of their ability to produce the process of negative reinforcement. Do *not* confuse negative reinforcement with punishment, which has the opposite behavioral effect. NOTE: It might be helpful to remember that "negative" and "positive" in operant terminology do not mean

"bad" or "good" as they often do in the colloquial language; but, rather, "remove" or "add," as they do in arithmetic. In this case, then "negative reinforcement" means to "make stronger by subtracting something," or, "taking away an aversive stimulus to strengthen responding." See also **Reinforcement, Positive**; and **Punishment**.

Reinforcement, Operant

1. As an operation: The removal or presentation of a reinforcing stimulus immediately following the emission of a response. Removal or presentation need not be contingent, but may occur coincidentally or accidentally (see **Behavior, Superstitious**).

2. As a process: The resulting increase or decrease in probability or rate of responding, or the maintenance of probability or rate of responding at a level above or below operant level. See also **Conditioning, Respondent; Reinforcement, Positive**; and **Reinforcement, Negative**.

Reinforcement, Positive

1. As an operation: The occurrence of a positively reinforcing event following the emission of an operant response. The two events may occur as a function of a program, or be coincidental. See **Behavior, Superstitious**.

2. As a process: The resultant increase in rate or probability of responding, or maintenance of rate or probability of responding above that of operant level. See also **Stimulus, Positive; Conditioning, Operant**; and **Reinforcement, Negative**.

Reinforcement, Schedules of

The manner in which reinforcement is delivered or made contingent upon responding. See the following:

1. Differential Reinforcement of High Rates (DRH)
2. Differential Reinforcement of Low Rates (DRL)
3. Differential Reinforcement of Other Behaviors (DRO)
4. Differential Reinforcement of Paced Responding (DRP)
5. Extinction, Respondent
6. Extinction, Operant
7. Reinforcement, Accidental
8. Schedule, Adjusting (ADJ)
9. Schedule, Alternative (ALT)
10. Schedule, Chained (CHAIN)
11. Schedule, Conjugate
12. Schedule, Conjunctive (CONJ)
13. Schedule, Continuous Reinforcement (CRF)
14. Schedule, Fixed Interval (FI)
15. Schedule, Fixed Ratio (FR)
16. Schedule, Interlocking (INTERLOCK)
17. Schedule, Interpolated (INTER)
18. Schedule, Mixed (MIX)
19. Schedule, Multiple (MULT)
20. Schedule, Percentage (%)
21. Schedule, Tandem (TAND)
22. Schedule, Variable Interval (VI)
23. Schedule, Variable Ratio (VR)
24. Schedules, Concurrent (CONC)

Reinforcement, Set-Up
To make reinforcement available, the delivery of which is contingent on the next response.

Reinforcer
Any stimulus or stimulus event which, when used in a reinforcement paradigm, is found to produce the phenomena of conditioning. Any stimulus or stimulus event which, when presented or withdrawn, is found to increase or decrease probability or rate of responding, or maintain the probability or rate of responding above or below that of operant level. See also "**Does**" **Equation** for **Arranged Event** and **Consequence**.

Reinforcer Building
The operation of making a neutral stimulus (S^N) into a (conditioned) reinforcing stimulus (S^r) by pairing it (as in respondent conditioning) with a stimulus already possessing that property (an S^R or previously conditioned S^r); or making an (S^N) into an (S^r) by prolonged and unusual deprivation. In the latter of these cases the S^N must have, in fact, had reinforcing properties, but was simply ineffective at the organism's normal level of deprivation with respect to it. See also **Reinforcer, Conditioned**; **Stimulus, Neutral**; and **Deprivation**.

Reinforcer, Conditioned (S^r)
A stimulus which has gained reinforcing properties solely through a history of being consistently paired (as in respondent conditioning) with another stimulus already possessing those properties. Also called a secondary, second-order, or higher-order reinforcer. See also **Reinforcer**; **Conditioning, Respondent**; and **Stimulus, Conditioned**.

Reinforcer Durability
The degree to which a reinforcer remains constant in reinforcing properties over time. See **Reinforcing Ability**.

Reinforcer, Generalized
A type of conditioned reinforcer which does not owe its reinforcing properties to being paired with only one previously effective reinforcing stimulus, but rather has been paired with many other reinforcing stimuli. Due to its multiple history the generalized reinforcer does not depend upon any one state of deprivation to be effective. Money is a generalized reinforcer (i.e., with it many other reinforcers may be purchased: food, clothing, etc.). Generalized reinforcers are usually quite durable. See also **Reinforcer**; **Reinforcer Durability**; and **Reinforcer, Conditioned**.

Reinforcer, Negative (S^R−)

Any stimulus which will produce the process of negative reinforcement. An aversive stimulus which immediately follows the emission of a response. If antecedent to the emission of a response, it is called an aversive stimulus. Also called a "punishing stimulus." See **Stimulus, Aversive; "Does" Equation**; and **Reinforcement, Negative**.

Reinforcer, Positive (S^R+)

Any stimulus which will produce the process of positive reinforcements. A positive stimulus which occurs following the emission of a response (as in positive reinforcement). Also called "accelerating consequence." See also **Reinforcement, Positive** and **Stimulus, Positive**.

Reinforcer, Primary (S^R)

A stimulus which has reinforcing properties (i.e., will produce the process of reinforcement), and which is not dependent upon a history of conditioning for those properties. Primary reinforcers are often termed "innate," "unconditioned," "unlearned," or "biological" reinforcers. Primary reinforcers usually hold the same basic properties in all members of a given species. S^R is the abbreviation for a primary reinforcer. S^R+ is the abbreviation for a positively reinforcing primary stimulus, and S^R− is the abbreviation for a negatively reinforcing primary stimulus. See also **Reinforcer, Conditioned**; and **Reinforcement, Operant**.

Reinforcing Ability

The degree to which a stimulus or stimulus event may reinforce a response. Empirically determined by the amount or type of responding in which an organism will engage to obtain that reinforcer. Reinforcing ability may vary as a function of deprivation/satiation, further conditioning, the presence or absence of other reinforcers or punishers in the environment, and other variables. See also **Reinforcer Durability**.

Relaxation Training

A set of procedures designed to train a client to produce a state of muscle relaxation. Usually accomplished by having the client alternatingly tense and relax gross muscle groups; and then, as greater control is gained, to tense and relax smaller and smaller muscle groups until all muscles may be controlled in multiples or singularly.

Competing stimuli and responses are limited, and "suggestions of relaxation, and calmness" are often made by the therapist. Practice between sessions is usually encouraged.

Relaxation training is most frequently used in systematic desensitization and other related therapies.

Repertoire

The total number of performances or responses which the organism may emit under the various conditions present in its environment and as a result of its history of interactions with that environment.

Repertoire, Fine-Grain

An operant performance which changes under the control of small variations in the stimulus conditions present. The phrase "point to point correspondence between changes in a stimulus and the corresponding changes in a performance" is in reference to a fine-grain repertoire. E.g., drawing from a copy, or steering a car. Also see **Induction, Response**.

Research, Applied

The collection of data (and subsequent analysis) for the express purpose of resolving some immediate practical problem. Data collection procedures tend to be less rigorous than in "basic" research, but not necessarily so. Similarly, the usefulness of the data, while more immediate, tends to be less generalizable than that which obtains from "basic" research; and, therefore, tends to be "ephemeral, not eternal." Neither of these latter conditions are definitive, however, and only the criterion of immediate applicability may be used for the absolute classification of "applied research" as such.

Research, Basic

Any operation of data collection and subsequent analysis which is conducted for the ultimate purpose of quantitative formulation of verifiable and generalizable "laws." In turn, the purpose of those "laws" is to establish the relationships which exist between a wide variety of phenomena in a manner which will allow the properties of specific phenomena to be deduced from a limited set of general principles. Unlike "applied research," basic research is not necessarily concerned with the immediate (or, for that matter, the ultimate) *applicability* of its findings, only the "truth" of those findings. Although precision in control and significance testing has been associated with basic research, it need not be *limited* to this form of research; and so may not actually be considered a differentiating characteristic.

Respondent

A response which is elicited (i.e., "caused" or evoked) by antecedent stimuli. A respondent is *not* learned and is intact at birth (or developed as a function of biological maturation) as an integral function of the nervous system. The organism has no control (strictly speaking) over the emission of the respondent, and must emit the response every time the eliciting stimuli occurs (if physiologically capable of doing so). E.g., every time a bright light is directed into the eye the respondent of "pupil constriction" must occur if physiologically possible. NOTE: It *is* possible to "mask" a respondent by operant control of the organs involved (e.g., by tensing the leg muscles before a tap on the knee), but strictly speaking the respondent behavior (while not easily observable) still occurs. Also called "Type S," "Pavlovian," "reflex-action," "classical," or "reflex response."

Respondent Conditioning, Temporal Relations Between the CS and UCS During Conditioning. (Presented in order of their ability to produce the process of respondent conditioning.)

1. *Simultaneous*: Where the CS and UCS are presented at the same time, or overlap in their presentation. See Figures 70 and 71.

2. *Delay*: Where the UCS is presented immediately following the termination of the CS. See Figure 72.

3. *Trace*: Where the UCS is not presented until some time has elapsed since the termination of the CS. See Figure 73.

4. *Backward*: Where the CS is presented after the termination of the UCS. See Figure 74.

NOTE: Little or no respondent conditioning will occur with this temporal relationship between the CS and UCS— depending upon the "gap" between them, and whether or not the reflex has terminated or is continuing when the CS is presented.

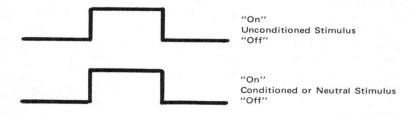

"On"
Unconditioned Stimulus
"Off"

"On"
Conditioned or Neutral Stimulus
"Off"

Figure 70. Simultaneous Conditioning, Complete: In these figures and those to follow, the unconditioned stimulus is presented in the top recording (line up, stimulus occurring; line down, stimulus not occurring); and the conditioned stimulus is represented in the lower recording. Complete simultaneity obtains if the occurrence of both stimuli exactly overlap (i.e., start and stop at the same times).

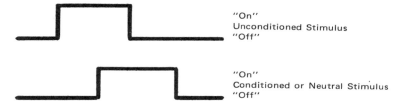

"On"
Unconditioned Stimulus
"Off"

"On"
Conditioned or Neutral Stimulus
"Off"

Figure 71. Simultaneous Conditioning, Partial: The unconditioned and conditioned stimuli overlap, but the unconditioned stimulus begins *before* the conditioned stimulus.

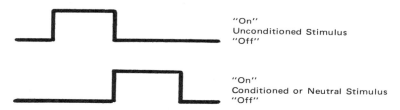

"On"
Unconditioned Stimulus
"Off"

"On"
Conditioned or Neutral Stimulus
"Off"

Figure 72. Delay Conditioning: The occurrence of the neutral or conditioned stimulus follows the termination of the unconditioned stimulus exactly.

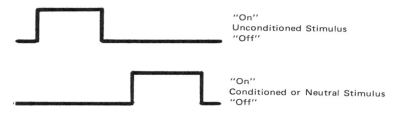

"On"
Unconditioned Stimulus
"Off"

"On"
Conditioned or Neutral Stimulus
"Off"

Figure 73. Trace Conditioning: The conditioned or neutral stimulus occurs after some time has past since the termination of the unconditioned stimulus.

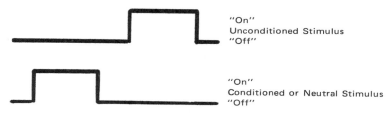

"On"
Unconditioned Stimulus
"Off"

"On"
Conditioned or Neutral Stimulus
"Off"

Figure 74. Backward Conditioning: The neutral or conditioned stimulus occurs *before* the unconditioned stimulus.

Respondent Laws, Primary

1. *Law of Threshold*: There is a range of stimulus intensities below which no response (reflex) will occur and above which a response will always occur. Within this range itself responses will occur with some uncertainty. An arbitrary point within this uncertainty region (say, that intensity which elicits the response 50% of the time) is called the threshold, and intensities above that point are called eliciting stimuli.

2. *Law of Intensity-Magnitude*: As the eliciting stimulus is increased in intensity, the magnitude of the elicited respondent also increases. They are said to be directly related.

3. *Law of Intensity-Latency*: As the eliciting stimulus is increased in intensity, the time (latency) between the onset of the eliciting stimulus and the onset of the respondent decreases. They are said to be inversely related.

Respondent Laws, Secondary

1. *Law of Reflex Fatigue*: When a reflex is repeatedly elicited within a short interval of time by a constant stimulus intensity, the respondent magnitude gradually declines, and eventually the response may cease altogether.

2. *The Law of Temporal Summation*: Stimuli with intensities below the normal threshold of a response may elicit that response if a number of them occur in rapid succession. They are said to temporally summate.

Responding, Intermediate

Responding which is periodic or interrupted with or without the control of the responding organism. See also **Response Seizure.**

Response (R)

An instance of an identifiable and measurable part of behavior, or a class of such instances. See also **Operant; Respondent; Movement-Cycle** in the **"Is" Equation;** and **Response** in the **"Does" Equation.**

Response, Alternative

A response which will produce the same type or magnitude of reinforcement as another (different) response. One method to aid in the reduction of the rate or probability of a (presumably deviant) response is to shape or otherwise institute a more desirable alternative response.

Response Building

1. As an operation: The imposition of reinforcers and explicit reinforcement contingencies upon the emission of a specified behavior or class of behaviors which, although presently being emitted at high or predictable rates, are not

under an identifiable schedule of reinforcement or maintained by any identifiable reinforcer.

2. As a process: The establishment of that behavior as an operant (subject, therefore, to the operations of positive and negative control and extinction). For example: Some studies have indicated that facial "ticks" may be brought under operant control by first reinforcing them; and then, once control is established, they may be extinguished. One may hypothesize that the initial reinforcement operations teach the organism to control the response; and then, since it is an "undesirable" response to begin (and not, therefore, generally reinforced by the organism), the organism will be able to control the response to the extent necessary to produce the process of extinction. These suppositions are not, however, necessary to the successful employment of response building, and serve only to add theory to demonstrable behavioral process.

Response, Chained
A sequence of responses in which one response produces conditions essential to the next, as in making the next response possible or more likely to be reinforced. Successive responses may or may not have the same topography. See also **Schedule, Chained**.

Response, Conditioned (CR)
In respondent conditioning, the response that is elicited by the conditioned stimulus. Physically it may be identical to the corresponding unconditioned response, but usually varies in intensity, latency, or duration.

Response Controlled Discriminative Stimulation
A prosthetic technique for persons appearing to have intermittent attention of behavioral seizures where discriminative stimuli (e.g., speech, movies, etc.) are presented and continued only as long as a specified response rate in the organism is above a certain threshold. Similar to conjugate reinforcement, except that the stimuli being maintained by responding need not be reinforcing in and of themselves. For example, a movie designed to teach a child about a certain subject could be made to incorporate a discriminative stimulus to which the student must respond to guarantee the continuation of the film. Questions with multiple choice answers every few minutes of the film (easy enough for the student to answer if he was "attending") could require a choice response on one of several keys. The correct response makes the film advance, and an incorrect answer "signals" that the student was not attending and "backs the film up" to the point of the last

question. Responding, then, controls the stimulus film presentation. Calling this procedure "response controlled discriminative stimulation" as opposed to simply a "teaching machine," however, connotes that the subject is prone to intermittent responding beyond his control (e.g., epileptic seizures); and that the purpose of the questions is not to "test" his ability to interpret the material, but only his physiological ability to receive the stimulus input. Such a distinction is, to say the least, quite "hazy" in the majority of instances.

Response Controlled Narration
A narration which only progresses for the period of time that the listener is actively responding to it, stops when responding stops, and continues when responding continues at the point where narration was last terminated. A special case of "response controlled discriminative stimulation."

Response Drift
The process of a performance changing (gradually) in form, rate, or other characteristics over a period of time, usually as a result of noncontingent reinforcement or contingencies which allow a large range of response characteristics to be reinforced and do not explicitly or implicitly favor one particular form. This does not include responses which change in form as a result of contingencies or contingency changes which explicitly or implicitly favor such a change (i.e., contingencies which will reinforce more often or in greater amount those responses which approximate one form over another). Superstitiously reinforced or conditioned behavior will usually "drift"; and is often taken as an indicator of that type of behavior. Drift is not *necessarily* a property of superstitiously reinforced behavior, however. See **Differentiation**; **Response**; and **Shaping**.

Response Externalization
The operation of interposing a response manipulanda between the organism and the environment for the purpose of defining or quantifying an otherwise unobservable behavior. (E.g., externalizing the movie-looking behavior of an infant by requiring the child to maintain a steady response rate on a kick-board to keep the image lit on the screen.) Such externalizations are rarely "perfect" (e.g., it would be possible for the child to maintain the kick-board rate without looking at the movie), but they are better than the subjective, interpretive accounts usually describing such behavior.

Response Regression
The emission of a variety of response classes in succession where:

1. All the responses have a history of reinforcement with respect to a common reinforcer type;

2. The organism is in a state of extreme deprivation with respect to that reinforcer; and

3. Each successive class of responses emitted by the organism represents a more primitive response (with respect to the recency and degree of conditioning) than the responses previously emitted and extinguished.

For example: A man may, in a situation, try using logic to dissuade someone from committing an offense against his family (assuming that logic was the most recent behavior appropriate to that situation conditioned into his repertoire); and failing, try verbal threats and name-calling (an earlier, more child-like conditioned response); and finally crying (one of the most primitive "defense" behaviors). All behaviors emitted are associated with the same reinforcer (avoidance of physical harm); and are emitted in the sequence of most recent to least recent in acquisition (and, presumably, most to least effective in procuring the reinforcer in the immediate history of the organism).

Response regression is often cited as an example of how a previously "intrapsychic" concept (in this case, Freudian) can be translated into observable and testable form, and demonstrated to exist in a manner conducive to the identification of environmental events which are effective in the alteration of the process.

Response-Response Interval (RRI)

The time elapsing between the initiation of any two successive responses. Do not confuse RRI with IRT or IRAT which refer to the time between and within responses respectively. RRI is also called "operant-to-operant interval." See also **Inter-Response Time; Intra-Response Time;** and **Rate, Operant-to-Operant.**

Response Run

A series of consecutive responses with the same (or nearly the same) topography and locus and the same or similar IRT's (inter-response times; i.e., the time between responses are approximately the same). For example: After a brief pause following reinforcement there is usually a stable and sustained "run" in an FR schedule of reinforcement.

Response Seizure

A period in which the organism is incapable of responding due to organismic variables beyond its control. A time when the organism is periodically but uncontrollably unresponsive to a situation, e.g., as an epileptic might be.

Response Shift
Responding by an organism which is *not* differentiated or discriminated in an environment in which the organism had demonstrated discrimination or differentiation in the past.

Response-Shock Interval (RS)
In avoidance conditioning, the time elapsing between the last response and the time of the next programmed occurrence of shock or aversive stimulus. See also **Behavior, Avoidance.**

Response Strength
The probability or rate of responding, degree of stability in performance, or the time necessary to reduce the rate of probability of responding to operant level through the operation of extinction (usually in comparison to rates, probability, etc., of competing responses). None of these definitions are entirely satisfactory, and the reader is cautioned to be precise and explicit in defining exactly what is meant when he uses the term response strength.

Response Suppression
A process in which rate or probability of responding is decreased for a short period of time—usually for the duration of a particular contingency, during the presentation or removal of a reinforcer, the duration of a particular (aversive) stimulus event, or for a short period of time following one of the above events. E.g., punishment will usually suppress responding when first introduced, but rarely eliminates the response from the repertoire of the organism for any significant period of time. See Figure 75. See also **Adaptation.**

Response Tendency
It is always desirable to maintain data collection or observation of a performance until it reaches stability (i.e., until the form and performance characteristics have remained approximately the same over a number of observations). It may be necessary, however, to terminate observations before this happens. In such an instance it is proper to indicate the direction in which the response characteristics were changing (e.g., the rate was steadily increasing, the force becoming more attenuated, etc.). Such an observation is called "reporting the response tendency." See also **Response Drift.**

Response Topographies, Widened
Where the topography of a requisite response is altered to allow the same critical effect to be obtained with a response of a more gross character (e.g., a typewriter is constructed so that the keys may be banged with the fist).

Figure 75. Response Suppression: After approximately 2 months of conditioning under an FI 5' schedule of reinforcement, the pigeon whose performance is represented in this figure was punished (as well as reinforced) for responding by electrical shock at the intensities noted. Note that after an immediate suppression of responding after the institution of shock or greater intensity of shock, responding increases as the pigeon adapts to the punishment. Only after *severe* punishment (90 volts) does the response suppression maintain at a low level. Notice also that after shock is removed altogether that the rate of responding increases to a point *above* that which obtained before punishment was started.[9]

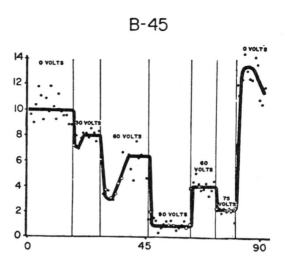

B-45

Response, Unconditioned (UR) or (UCR)

In respondent conditioning, that response which is elicited by the unconditioned stimulus.

Restraint

The control of an organism's behaviors through physical means (e.g., tying, holding, chaining, locking in a small room), or otherwise limiting the number of behaviors an organism is able to emit by such means. Also called "confinement." Restraint is only capable of suppressing the behaviors in question. Unless the means of restraint are aversive enough to generate avoidance behaviors (incompatible with the behaviors controlled) those suppressed behaviors will be reinstated with the termination of restraint.

Reversal Phase

That period in the experiment in which the previously established response or response form is placed on extinction, and reinforcement is made contingent upon a form of response which is opposite or nearly opposite (at least in one dimension: e.g., rate, form, intensity, etc.) to that response

---

[9] Figure reprinted from "Punishment during fixed-interval reinforcement," by N. H. Azrin and W. C. Holz, *Journal of the Experimental Analysis of Behavior*, 1961, **4**, 343–347. Copyright © 1961 by the Society for the Experimental Analysis of Behavior, Inc. Used by permission of the authors and publisher.

which previously produced reinforcement. The object of the reversal phase is to demonstrate that responses shaped and maintained earlier in the experiment were a function of the experimental manipulations, and not due simply to chance or some unknown variable. The simple removal of an experimental condition (e.g., the reinforcer or contingency) is often called a reversal, but is more properly called a "post-experimental phase" or "second (third, etc.) reference phase"; for while simple extinction may reverse the rate of performance it does not (strictly speaking) reverse the contingencies. Subsequent changes in the form or rate of the performance would not, therefore, necessarily reflect the function of the contingency, but may only reflect the function of reinforcement density. See also **Baseline; Phase, Experimental; Phase, Reference; Reinforcement Density;** and **Methods of Confirmation.**

RS

An abbreviation for "response-shock interval." See **Response—Shock Interval.**

S

Abbreviation for "stimulus" or "stabilization." See **Stimulus; "Is" Equation;** and **Plan Functions or Aims (Stabilization).**

Salience

The degree to which a stimulus or part of a stimulus event controls behavior independently of the remainder of the stimulus environment. Equated to "distinctness" as opposed to "intensity or magnitude."

Satiation

1. As an operation: Making food or other reinforcers available (contingently or noncontingently) in relatively large quantities over a long period of time.

2. As a process: A reduction in the effectiveness of the reinforcer; and a corresponding reduction in the rate or probability of responding which produces that reinforcer. See also **Deprivation;** and **Satiation Method.**

Satiation Method

A method for determining preferences or subhungers in which the organism is successively satiated upon two or more potential reinforcers and later, following deprivation, satiated on the same reinforcers in reverse order (e.g., reinforce pecking responses with corn until satiation, and then present wheat as a reinforcer; subsequently, satiate on wheat first and then corn). Alternatively, two groups of subjects may be used, each receiving the potential reinforcers in a different order. Preference is determined by comparing the "strength of response" during the second satiation trials. See also **Response Strength** and **Satiation**.

S^D ("S-dee")

1. In operant terminology: A stimulus in the presence of which the emission of a specified operant, class of operants, or chain of operants will (eventually) be followed by either a positive reinforcer or a punisher (or the removal of either); and in the absence of which the contingency and occurrence of these subsequent events is indeterminable (except as noted below). Rates and/or probabilities of responding will be highly predictable in the presence of an S^D, and less predictable or indeterminable in its absence (except as noted below). Whether rates and probabilities of responding increase, decrease, or maintain at a higher or lower than operant level in the presence of the S^D is dependent upon the contingencies—reinforcing or punishing—with which the S^D is correlated; and the degree of increase or decrease will depend upon the degree of correlation between the S^D and the contingencies (i.e., is *every* response consequated; a certain *ratio* of responses; a certain percentage; etc.). In the special case where the S^D is present during all instances of consequation, one may speak of its absence as an S$^\Delta$, and complete stimulus control will obtain. This special case is *not*, however, inherent in the definition of an S^D. Since the term "stimulus" is used, it is assumed that anything labeled an S^D has known functions, and *does* control responding. If the function is unknown, on the other hand, "E-Dee" (E^D, discriminative event) would be the appropriate label (i.e., for an event which is correlated with some consequence, but the effect on behavior of which is not known). See also **Stimulus**; **Event, Discriminative**; and **E^D**.

2. In respondent discrimination: A stimulus in the presence of which the occurrence of a conditioned stimulus will always be followed by the occurrence of the unconditioned stimulus; and in the absence of which the occurrence of the unconditioned stimulus following the occurrence of the correlated conditioned stimulus is indeterminable. An S^D in respondent

conditioning will increase the probability that the conditioned stimulus will elicit the conditioned response in its presence; and decrease or not affect the probability that the conditioned stimulus will elicit the conditioned response in its absence. In the special case where an S^D is present during *all* pairings of the conditioned and unconditioned stimulus, we speak of the absence of the S^D as an S^Δ, and complete stimulus control will obtain. This special case is *not*, however, inherent in the definition of an S^D. The use of the term "stimulus" implies that an S^D *does* control the behavior of the organism. If the actual function is unknown, then the use of the term "event" (E^D, discriminative event) is more appropriate (i.e., it *is* an event that *is* correlated with the pairings; but whether or not it actually controls responding is unknown). See also **Stimulus; Event, Discriminative**; and **E^D**.

S^Δ ("S-Delta")

1. In operant discrimination: A stimulus in the presence of which the emission of an operant, class of operants, or chain of operants will never be reinforced or punished (i.e., never consequated in any way); and in the absence of which the availability of consequences is indeterminable (except as noted below). An S^Δ will produce highly predictable rates or probabilities of responding in its presence and less predictable rates of responding in its absence. Whether rates of responding increase, decrease, or maintain at a point higher or lower than that of operant level is dependent upon the contingencies whose absence the S^Δ signals (i.e., reinforcing or punishing). In the special case where the S^Δ is present during every case in which consequation is not available, we may speak of its absence as an S^D, and complete stimulus control will obtain. This special case is *not*, however, inherent in the basic definition of an S^Δ. The use of the term "stimulus" denotes function (i.e., that the S^Δ *does*, in fact, control rates of responding). If function is unknown, then the use of the term "event" is more appropriate (E^Δ, "E-Delta")—denoting an event which *is* correlated with the absence of consequation, but which is not *known* to determine rates of responding. See also **S^D**; **Stimulus; Event**; and **E^Δ**.

2. In respondent discrimination: A stimulus in the presence of which the occurrence of a conditioned stimulus will never be followed by the occurrence of the correlated unconditioned stimulus; and in the absence of which the probability of the occurrence of the unconditioned stimulus is indeterminable. An S^Δ will decrease the probability that the conditioned stimulus will elicit the conditioned response in its presence; and increase or not affect the probability that the conditioned

stimulus will elicit the conditioned response in its absence. In the special case where the S^Δ is present in *all* instances when the unconditioned stimulus will not occur, we speak of the absence of the S^Δ as an S^D; and complete stimulus control will obtain. This special case is *not*, however, inherent in the definition of an S^Δ. The use of the term "stimulus" denotes the fact that the S^Δ *will* control responding. If the function is unknown, then the use of the term "event" is more appropriate (E^Δ, "E-Delta")—denoting an event which *is* correlated with the absence of the unconditioned stimulus, but which is not *known* to control the probability of responding. See also S^D; **Stimulus; Event;** and E^Δ.

S^D Class

Any class of stimuli, each of which controls the same response or response class in the manner of a discriminative stimulus. Unless otherwise noted, all stimuli in the class must have some physical property in common—making generalization across that class likely. See also **Stimulus, Discriminative;** S^D **Class, Arbitrary;** and **Generalization, Stimulus.**

S^Δ Class

Any class of stimuli, each of which controls the same response or response class in the manner of an S^Δ. Unless otherwise noted, all stimuli in the class must have some physical property in common which would make generalization across the class likely. See also S^Δ **Class, Arbitrary;** S^Δ; and **Generalization, Stimulus.**

S^D Class, Arbitrary

A class of S^Ds which control the same response, but need have no other intrinsic relationship. Inclusion in the class is purely arbitrary. E.g., a red light, a policeman, a crosswalk with people in it, and a stop sign may all control the stopping response of a man driving a car, but the inclusion of these stimuli into that S^D class was originally arbitrary.

S^Δ Class, Arbitrary

Any class of stimuli, each of which controls the same response or response class in the manner of an S^Δ. The inclusion of stimuli into the class is arbitrary, however, and each stimulus must gain control over responding via explicit histories with the contingencies they reflect since generalization across this class is not possible. See also S^Δ; S^Δ **Class;** S^D **Class, Arbitrary.**

Scallop

A positively accelerated curve (such as usually obtains in the steady-state performance of an organism on a fixed-interval schedule). See Figure 76.

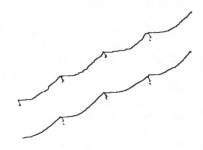

Figure 76. Scallops: "Scallops" in the cumulative record of an FI Performance.[10]

Schedule, Adjusting (ADJ)

A form of schedule in which a value, (e.g., of interval or ratio) is changed in some systematic way from reinforcement to reinforcement as a function of the performance of the organism (e.g., long inter-response times in one ratio will cause the next ratio to be larger).

Schedule, Alternative (ALT)

A schedule of reinforcement in which the organism is reinforced under whichever of two schedules in effect is satisfied first. For example, the organism is reinforced for the first response to occur after one minute has elapsed since the last reinforcement, or after 50 responses. Whichever occurs first would be an ALT (FI 1'; FR 50).

Schedule, Chained (CHAIN)

A schedule in which one response produces the stimulus conditions for the next response which in turn produces the conditions for the next response, etc., until reinforcement is procured (at the end of the chain). Resembles a multiple schedule with the exception that reinforcement follows the completion of all components instead of each individual component. A chained schedule is designated by the abbreviation CHAIN followed by the designations for the individual elements. A CHAIN (FR10, FI5, FR100) would designate a schedule under which the organism must emit 10 responses to produce a stimulus in the presence of which one response after 5 minutes have elapsed will produce a stimulus in the presence of which 100 responses will produce reinforcement.

[10] Figure from Ferster, C. B. and Skinner, B. F., *Schedules of reinforcement*. New York: Appleton-Century-Crofts, p. 146. Copyright © 1957. Used by permission of Appleton-Century-Crofts, Educational Division, Meredith Corporation.

Schedule, Complex

Any schedule of reinforcement which is comprised of a compound of two or more other schedules, or in which more than one form of behavior is required. Examples would include multiple, mixed, chained, and concurrent schedules of reinforcement. See **Reinforcement, Schedules of** for a more complete listing.

Schedule, Conjugate (CONJG)

A schedule of reinforcement in which reinforcement is continuously present (e.g., the opportunity to eat) as long as a specified response is maintained at a criterion rate. Failure to maintain responding results in the discontinuance of reinforcement (e.g., the removal of the food dish) until responding is again at criterion level.

Schedule, Conjunctive (CONJ)

A schedule in which both of two contingencies must be met to achieve reinforcement. For example, if 100 responses must be emitted, at least one of which is 10 minutes after the last reinforcement, then this schedule would be designated CONJ (FI 10; FR 100).

Schedule, Continuous Reinforcement (CRF)

A schedule in which every emission of a response in a class of responses is reinforced. Equivalent to an FR 1, or, a 100% reinforcement schedule.

Schedule, Fixed-Interval (FI)

A schedule of reinforcement in which the first response occurring after a specified interval of time has elapsed is reinforced; and where the interval begins timing from the moment when the last reinforcer was delivered. A given schedule is so designated by adding a number to the letters FI to indicate the length of the interval. FI 5' would designate a fixed-interval schedule of five minutes. It is important to remember that the reinforcer is not necessarily delivered at the end of the interval—it is only "set-up," or made available for delivery contingent upon the emission of the next response.

Schedule, Fixed-Ratio (FR)

A schedule of reinforcement in which reinforcement is made contingent upon the completion of a fixed number of responses. The schedule is designated by adding a number to the letters FR to indicate the length of the ratio. FR 100 would mean that after every 100 responses the organism would be reinforced.

Schedule, Higher-Order

A schedule of intermittent reinforcement in which a behavior or chain of behaviors specified under one schedule of reinforcement is treated as a unitary response and programmed under another schedule. Differentiated from nested contingencies in that reinforcement is only delivered upon the completion of the conditions specified by the "outside" or governing schedule. Example: An FR 100 [CHAIN (X,Y,Z)] would be a second-order schedule in which the first schedule (the CHAIN) describes the behavior to be emitted by the organism; and the second, or governing schedule (the FR) determines when that behavior will be reinforced. In this case the organism must emit 100 chains of the behaviors X, Y, and Z before it is reinforced. The complexity of higher-order schedules may be increased to any level. An FI 1000' (FR 100 [CHAIN(X,Y,Z)]) would be a third-order schedule in which the first series of 100 chains of X, Y, and Z to be completed after 1000 minutes have passed since the last reinforcement would be reinforced.

Schedule, Interlocking (INTERLOCK)

A schedule of reinforcement in which the reinforcement is determined by two schedules, where the setting of one schedule is altered by progress made in the other. E.g., in the schedule INTERLOCK (FI 5 FR 250), the organism is reinforced at a ratio which is slowly reduced from 250 to 1 during 5 minutes. If responding is rapid, reinforcement occurs only after a large ratio has been completed; if responding is slow, reinforcement occurs at a much lower ratio; if no response occurs in 5 minutes, then the first response after that is reinforced.

Schedule, Interpolated (INTER)

A single block of reinforcements in one schedule is interpolated into a sustained period of responding on a different "background" schedule. E.g., while responding on a VR1000 schedule the organism is also reinforced on an FR15 schedule. This would be designated FR15 INTER VR1000.

Schedule, Interval

Schedules of reinforcement in which reinforcement is programmed partly as a function of time (as well as, perhaps, responding or some other condition). See also **Schedule, Variable-Interval (VI)** and **Schedule, Fixed-Interval (FI)**.

Schedule, Mixed (MIX)

A schedule of reinforcement where reinforcement is programmed by two or more schedules alternating (usually at random), and where there are no correlated stimuli with the schedules to allow the organism to determine which schedule is in effect at any one time. E.g., a MIX FI 5, FR 50 represents a program in which reinforcement is sometimes available for the first response after 5 minutes and sometimes available for the completion of the first 50 responses; the possibilities of each occurring either at random or according to a predetermined pattern, but where the organism is unable to determine by any means which program is in effect.

Schedule, Multiple (MULT)
Where reinforcement is programmed by two or more schedules alternating (usually at random), and where each schedule has a correlated and unique stimulus which will allow (but not necessarily require) that the organism determine which schedule is in effect at any one time. Differs from a mixed schedule in the implementation of the correlated stimuli. E.g., a MULT FR 50, FI 5 would designate a program where reinforcement is sometimes contingent upon the emission of the first response after 5 minutes have elapsed since the last reinforcement and sometimes after the 50th response has been emitted; the possibilities of each alternating (usually at random), but where the organism is able to determine which schedule is in effect by observing the correlated stimuli.

Schedule, Nonintermittent
Any schedule of reinforcement where all responses of a class of responses are reinforced in the same manner (i.e., every time, or not at all). See **Schedule, Continuous Reinforcement**; **Extinction, Operant**; and **Extinction, Respondent**.

Schedule, Percentage (%)
1. A schedule of reinforcement under which a specified percentage of all responses are reinforced, but where the specific responses being reinforced are unknown. E.g., 20% reinforcement designates a schedule where approximately 20% of all responses will be reinforced, or, approximately 1 out of every 5, but where reinforcement may or may not occur after any one particular response.
2. A schedule of reinforcement where only a certain percentage of all normally programmed reinforcements are delivered. E.g., FR50 (20%) designates a schedule under which reinforcement is contingent upon the emission of 50 responses, but where reinforcement is actually delivered following only 20% of all successfully completed ratios; and where those reinforced ratios are randomly determined.

Most percentage schedules could be written as a VR schedule, or as a higher-order VR schedule. The denotation of (%), however, implies that the nature of variation is unknown (even to the programmer) whereas in a VR schedule the programmer is usually aware of the variables determining the reinforcement. To the organism there should not be a *functional* difference, however, between VR and (%) schedules.

Schedule, Ratio
Schedules of reinforcement where reinforcement is made contingent upon the number of responses emitted by the organism since the last reinforcement. See also **Schedule, Fixed-Ratio (FR)** and **Schedule, Variable-Ratio (VR)**.

Schedule, Sequential
A form of second-order schedule in which several schedules of reinforcement are linked in a sequential manner to comprise the elements of a new, more complex schedule. Explicit in the term "sequential" are the additional requirements that a unique S^D be associated with each of the component schedules (as opposed to no stimulus or brief stimulus at the beginning of each component); and that the sequence of components be fixed and invariant (as opposed to the random occurrence of any one component following the completion of any other or even the same component). If the "outside schedule" (i.e., that schedule which determines the number of components which must be completed to obtain the final reinforcement) is a fixed-ratio, then the sequential schedule may be properly termed a chained schedule. If, on the other hand, the ratio is variable or an interval schedule is employed, then the number of components necessary for final reinforcement is indeterminable (from the standpoint of the organism), and the sequence *cannot* be properly called a chain. See also **Schedule, Higher-Order; Schedule, Fixed-Ratio; Schedule, Fixed-Interval; Schedule, Variable-Ratio; Schedule, Variable-Interval; Schedule, Chained; Schedule, Tandem.**

Schedule, Strained
A schedule of reinforcement in which reinforcements occur so intermittently, or in which such great amounts of behavior are required that performance drops off to extremely low rates or ceases altogether.

Schedule, Tandem (TAND)
A schedule of intermittent reinforcement in which a single reinforcement is programmed by two or more schedules acting in succession *without* correlated stimuli. Similar to a "chain," with the exception of correlated stimuli.

Schedule, Variable Interval (VI)

A schedule of reinforcement where reinforcement is made contingent upon the first response to occur after a specified interval has elapsed since the last reinforcement; and where the length of the interval varies from trial to trial at random between two arbitrary extremes and with a specified mean. E.g., V 15' would designate a schedule of reinforcement under which the first response occurring after an interval which was 5 minutes long *on the average* would be reinforced, but where the size of that interval might vary from 1 minute to 10 minutes from trial to trial. NOTE: When designating a VI schedule it is advisable to explicate the high and low extremes of variation.

Schedule, Variable Ratio (VR)

A schedule of reinforcement where the reinforcer is made contingent upon the number of responses emitted since the last reinforcement; and where the size of the ratio varies from trial to trial at random between two arbitrary extremes and around a specified mean. E.g., VR10 would designate a schedule of reinforcement under which *on the average* every 10th response would be reinforced, but where the size of the ratio might vary from 1 to 20 from trial to trial. NOTE: When designating a VR schedule it is advisable to explicate the high and low extremes of variation.

Schedules, Concurrent (CONC)

Two or more schedules of reinforcement independently arranged but operating at the same time on different operants. The organism may operate under one or more of these schedules at the same time or in rapid alternation. A situation in which a child may be consequated on a VR10 for behavior X, and on a VI 4' for behavior Y (where both schedules are in effect at the same time) would be designated CONC [VR10(X); VI 4'(Y)]. See also **Operants, Concurrent**.

SE

Abbreviation for "subsequent event." See **Event, Subsequent**.

Self-Control

1. The emission of behaviors by an organism for the express purpose of producing a change in the environment which will in turn alter the frequency of certain behaviors in its own repertoire.

2. The failure of an organism to acquire, consume, or otherwise take advantage of known reinforcers presently available in the environment; and will, as a result, obtain or avoid larger or more powerful reinforcers at a later time.

Punishment, for example, may produce immediate (but temporary) suppression of deviant responses emitted by a child in a classroom. If the teacher exerts self-control and ignores the deviant responses while positively reinforcing appropriate responses she will, in effect, be refusing the immediate reinforcement of "response suppression" for the purpose of obtaining the long-term (but delayed) reinforcement of "response elimination" through the processes of extinction and reinforcement of incompatible and alternative responses.

Setting
A functional term in reference to the general and relatively constant environmental context in which a behavior occurs or is observed. Usually defined as the "where" and "when" of the occurrence or observation (e.g., a "Skinner box" from noon to one each day; or a "classroom" from 9:00 to 9:30 each day Monday through Friday, with 26 students and one teacher). Of course the detail with which the setting is described can vary from a very gross description (e.g., "Skinner box") to a very detailed definition (e.g., giving the dimension of the box, the color of its walls, sound attenuation qualities, etc.). Usually only the variables which are believed to noticeably affect the performances are noted. If the function of the setting is unknown (i.e., how it affects the behavior), then it is called a "situation." The equivalent terms in Precision Teaching are "program" (affect unknown) and "disposition" (affect known). Any single element of the setting may be called a "setting-element" or "stimulus." Since "stimulus" is sometimes used in shorthand reference to a "stimulus-event," however, the use of the former term (setting-element) is generally preferred. See also **Situation; Setting-Element;** and **Stimulus.**

Setting-Element
A functional term in reference to any single part of the environment which remains constant throughout the time during which the behavior occurs. It is assumed that the function of the setting-element is known (i.e., how it affects the rate or probability of responding). If the function is *unknown*, then the element is more properly called a *"situation*-element." See also **Setting.**

Setting Event
A stimulus-response relationship that affects the probability of the occurrence of a response. E.g., satiation and deprivation with respect to the reinforcer controlling the response, the critical periods of sleep and fatigue cycles, etc. Sometimes confused with a priming stimulus, which is a specific induce-

ment to responding. Also called, somewhat more meaningfully, "setting factor." See **Stimulus, Priming;** and **Setting.**

Shaping

1. As an operation: Reinforcing that class of responses in an organism's present repertoire which most resembles a specified target behavior *not* presently in the repertoire; and the continuance of reinforcement, with each successive reinforcement made contingent upon a behavior which *more* closely approximates the target than the previously reinforced behavior. NOTE: This operation is often referred to as "shaping by successive approximations."

As each new class of behaviors is reinforced, those classes of previously reinforced behaviors (representing earlier approximations of the desired behavior) are placed on extinction. Since the extinction usually results in increased response variability, it serves the dual purpose of reducing (presently) undesired responding *and* increasing the probability that newer and closer approximations of the desired response will be emitted.

2. As a process: The resultant change in the form and/or frequency of the ongoing operants to more closely approximate, and finally acquire the specified characteristics of the target behavior. See also **Auto-Shaping.**

Shock-Shock Interval (SS)

In avoidance conditioning, the interval between any two successive shocks when no response is made during that interval. See also **Behavior, Avoidance.**

Situation

A descriptive term in reference to all parts of an environment which remain constant (unchanging) during the course of any observation or series of observations. Examples might include the position of walls, their color, the number of desks in the room, the position of the room in the school, and the size of type in a book being read. The designation of "situation" does not mean that the condition in question *cannot* change, only that it *does not* change during the period in which the behavior is being observed. For example: The fact that a certain size print is used in a book from which a child reads *can* be changed, but *does not* change (usually) while the child is reading in any one session.

As a descriptive term, the designation of "situation" implies that the function of that set of environmental constants is unknown. When the function of the situation *is* known (i.e., it is known how those constants affect rate of responding), then it is more properly called a setting (it is now known that those constants "*set* the conditions" for a certain type and level of responding). A synonym for situation in Precision Teaching is "program." See also **Situation-Element; Setting;** and **Event.**

Situation-Element
A descriptive term in reference to any single part of an environment which remains constant during the time in which the behavior is observed. The function of the situation element (i.e., how it affects the rate or probability of responding) is assumed unknown. If the function of the element *is* known, then it is more properly called a "setting-element." See also **Situation.**

Skinner Box
A small experimental space in which an organism (usually infrahuman) may be placed for operant study. See also **Experimental Space.**

Slope
The rate of change described by a line, where, in fact, that line may in turn be a summary of the rate of change occurring between any two or more data points. The slope of a line is always equal to the vertical difference between any two points on the line divided by the horizontal difference between the same two points; or, height divided by base. Prior to the calculation of the slope, however, all transformations implied by the scales of the chart on which the data in question are displayed must be made. If, for example, the standard Precision Teaching behavior chart is being used, the rate data must be converted to logs before calculations are made. In this case the formula for the slope of a line is taken as:

$$\text{Log (slope)} = \frac{\text{Log (second rate)} - \text{Log (first rate)}}{\text{Number of weeks over which the change occurred}}$$

EXAMPLE: If a line-of-progress went from a rate of 1/min. to 100/min. in two weeks,

$$\text{Log (slope)} = \frac{\text{Log (10)} - \text{Log (1)}}{2}$$

$$= \frac{2.0 - 0.0}{2}$$

$$= \frac{2.0}{2}$$

$$= 1.0; \text{ which is the log of 10, so the slope would be "x10 per week."}$$

For any given chart an "acceleration finder" may be constructed to eliminate the need for actual calculation. See **Acceleration Finder** for an example. See Figure 77.

S⁻
Abbreviation for an "aversive stimulus." See **Stimulus, Aversive.**

Sᴺ
Abbreviation for "neutral stimulus." See **Stimulus, Neutral.**

S⁺
Abbreviation for a "positive stimulus." See **Stimulus, Positive.**

Spontaneous Recovery
A temporarily higher than operant-level rate sometimes observed at the beginning of a session, following a session where lower rates obtained (e.g., perhaps because of extinction). This term suggests that the earlier rate has "recovered" during the intervening time. A more plausible explanation is that stimuli closely associated with the beginning of a session control higher rates because of earlier conditions of reinforcement, and because there has not yet been an opportunity for this

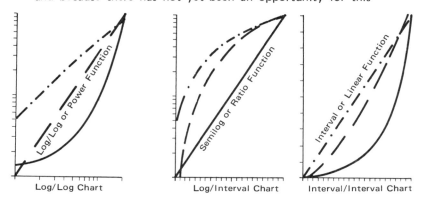

Log/Log Chart	Log/Interval Chart	Interval/Interval Chart
Log Slope Log Height/Log Base	Log Slope Log Height/Base	Slope Height/Base

Figure 77. Slope: The denotation of "slope" as a description of a line implies that line is straight. Virtually any function may be drawn as a straight line, however, if the appropriate scales are used for the chart. These three charts represent the most common. Notice that on each chart only one of the three functions turns out to be a straight line—the function that matches the scales of the chart. The slope of that straight line is determined by choosing any two points on the line and dividing the vertical differences between those two points by the horizontal difference between them (height/base). If one or both of the scales on the chart are non-linear, however, then the appropriate transformations must be performed on the data before the division. Similarly, if the data are transformed, then the slope will be expressed in units of the transformation (e.g., if a log transformation is made, then the slope will be expressed as a logarithm).

effect to be altered by the experimental changes made during the bulk of the preceding session.

S^R−
Abbreviation for "negative reinforcer." See **Reinforcer, Negative**.

S^{R+}
Abbreviation for "positive reinforcer." See **Reinforcer, Positive**.

S^r
Abbreviation for a "conditioned reinforcer." See **Reinforcer, Conditioned**.

S^R
Abbreviation for "primary reinforcer." See **Reinforcer, Primary**.

SS
Abbreviation for "shock-shock interval." See **Shock-Shock Interval**.

State of the Organism
A general term used to denote a condition in which wide varieties of behaviors are being emitted by the organism which are all under the control of a relatively few number of stimulus-reinforcer contingencies. For example: A pigeon will often flap his wings, strut around the cage, and bob his head simultaneously in the presence of a single pre-adversive stimulus. The sum of these actions (usually termed "anxiety") is called a "state of the organism."

Static Analysis
An analysis of data in which all data points are assumed (for purposes of analysis) to have occurred at the same point in time (or otherwise are classed into a single group). Analysis is then made between one group and one or more other groups on the basis of one or more "static" descriptions (e.g., the mean and variance of each group).

The analysis is "static" in that the best estimate of what the values in one group will be (if no effective change occurred in conditions) is what the values in another group *were*. Then, if the values are, in fact, *not* the same, it is assumed that the change in conditions was effective in changing the resultant data. The "null hypothesis" is, then, "no-change," or, that the data will be "static" with respect to the parameters compared (e.g., mean and variance).

When "group data" are compared (e.g., the math-fact scores for 30 elementary school students) then the static analysis is usually appropriate; but when individuals are analyzed over time (e.g., following just one student through the entire math-fact curriculum), then there is usually some means of estimating trend—and the "static" measures are no longer valid predictors. See also **Dynamic Analysis**. Examples of "static" analysis would include the F-test and analysis of variance.

Step

A term, originating in Precision Teaching in reference to a large change in rate between any two successive observation periods. Usually occurring as a result of changes in the plan (phase changes) but not necessarily so. A "drop" in rate is called a "step down" and a "jump" is called a "step up." To calculate the value of the step on a log chart (e.g., the standard Precision Teaching behavior chart) divide the greater number by the lesser number (the largest rate by the smallest rate); then label the answer "dividby" ($\div$) if a "drop" occurred, and "times" (x) if a "jump" occurred.

Example: If rate dropped from a line-of-progress with a value of 8 to a rate of 2. then.

$$\frac{8}{2} = 4 = \text{a step down} \div 2''$$

If the line-of-progress had a value of 8, and the rate was 24, then

$$\frac{24}{8} = 3 = \text{a step up} \times 3''$$

On an interval chart steps would be calculated as the simple absolute difference between points (i.e., subtract the smallest number from the largest number, and label the change as "+" or "−"). See Figure 78. See also **Acceleration Analysis**.

Step, First

A term, originating in Precision Teaching, in reference to a measure of the initial change in rate between the last week in one phase and the first week in the next phase. Calculated in the same manner as any step, but where the "data points" are the *end* of the line-of-progress in one phase, and the *beginning* of the line-of-progress in the next phase. The first step is eliminated in the acceleration analysis. The first step is usually taken to indicate changes in "motivation" (e.g., how he "gets something" for doing it) or changes in "opportunity" (e.g., the material is now easier) rather than changes in "ability"—which should be reflected in the slope of the line-of-progress for that phase.

Stimulus (S)

All objects (e.g., a book or a dog) and events (e.g., the closing of a book, or the barking of a dog) in our environment are considered to be stimuli due to the fact that we are aware of them only inasmuch as they "stimulate" our senses (i.e., we must hear, see, touch, or smell them before we know them to exist). Generally speaking we refer to an object or event as a stimulus if it occurs prior to or simultaneously with the response. If the object or event occurs after the response, and has been demonstrated to affect the rate of responding, then we refer to it as a reinforcer. NOTE: It is quite possible for any given response to serve as a stimulus for any other (similar or different) response. Whether or not a response may serve as a stimulus or reinforcer for *itself*, however, (in the absence of any other environmental or organismic reaction) is arguable. But the use of the term "stimulus" implies that it does, in fact, alter the rate or probability of certain responses. See also S^D; S^Δ; S^N; S^+; S^-; **Event**; and **Program Event** (under "Is" Equation); and **Stimulus** (under "Does" Equation).

Stimulus, Adjustable

A stimulus which the organism may alter in some respect as a function of his responding. E.g., a short line may act as an S^D for responding on one key which will lengthen the line to

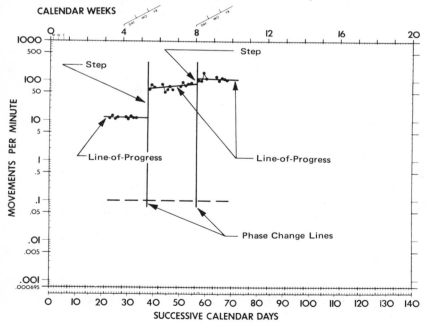

Figure 78. Step: The "step" in a project is taken as the difference between the points at which two lines-of-progress (from two different phases) meet the phase change line separating these projects. Note that the change line is drawn just before the first data point in the second phase. If the line were drawn anywhere between the last data point in one phase and the first data point in the second phase, then the value of the step might change.

match a sample whereupon reinforcement is delivered; a child may pile blocks on one another until they match the height of a chair whereupon a board may be placed between them to form a bridge; and a carpenter may file the leg of a table until the table rests evenly without rocking.

Stimulus, Aversive (S−)

A stimulus, the removal of which is reinforcing (i.e., will increase the rate or probability of that response which just preceded its removal); or, which may suppress responding which just precedes its presentation. The former is negative reinforcement, the latter punishment. Due to the fact that negative reinforcement generates stable and consistent rates of responding over a long period of time (and the effects of punishment may be transitory), an aversive stimulus is usually defined by negative reinforcement. Such a definition reflects the stability of the stimulus' reinforcing properties, rather than by rates changing as a function of adaptation. Also called "negative stimulus." See **Reinforcer, Negative**.

Stimulus Building

1. As an operation: Consistently pairing (as in respondent conditioning) the occurrence of a neutral stimulus with the occurrence of an already effective unconditioned or conditioned stimulus, discriminative stimulus, or reinforcing stimulus.

2. As a process: The resultant gain in the effectiveness or capacity of the previously neutral stimulus to serve the same function as the stimulus with which it is paired.

Stimulus, Conditioned (CS)

1. In operant conditioning: A stimulus which has gained the ability to alter some property of behavior by being paired consistently in the past with another stimulus which already possessed that ability, or, by being paired with some explicit reinforcement contingency.

2. In respondent conditioning: A stimulus which has gained the ability to elicit a conditioned response by being paired consistently in the past with another stimulus which already possessed that ability.

Also called "second-order stimulus" and "higher-order stimulus." See also **Stimulus, Unconditioned** and **Reinforcer, Conditioned**.

Stimulus Control

A stimulus is said to exert control over behavior whenever rates or probabilities of responding vary as a function of the presence or absence of that stimulus in the environment. See also S^D; S^Δ; **Stimulus, Discriminative; Stimulus Control, Partial**; and **Stimulus Control, Complete**.

Stimulus Control, Abstract
The process by which a stimulus controls behavior through an abstract property such as shape, position, or relative size. In each case the controlling property of the stimulus is found in a class of stimuli, and reinforcement is determined by a general rule rather than a specific form of the stimulus.

Stimulus Control, Complete
A stimulus is said to exert complete stimulus control over the emission of an operant when it functions as an S^D by its presence, and as an S^Δ by its absence (or vice versa). In such a case rates or probability of responding would be high in one condition and extremely low or nonexistent in the other, and highly predictable in both. See also S^D; S^Δ; **Stimulus Control; Stimulus Control, Partial**; and **Stimulus, Discriminative**.

Stimulus Control, Partial
A stimulus is said to exert partial stimulus control over the emission of an operant whenever rate or probability of responding is highly predictable or stable in the presence of that stimulus; but indeterminable or unstable in its absence. E.g., as would be the case if a stimulus functioned as an S^D or an S^Δ by its presence or absence, but not both. See also S^D; S^Δ; **Stimulus Control; Stimulus, Discriminative**; and **Stimulus Control, Complete**.

Stimulus Cue
The specific property of a stimulus that differentiates that stimulus from the class of all related stimuli as a discriminative stimulus. See also **Salience**.

Stimulus, Discriminative
1. In operant discrimination: A stimulus which is paired consistently with the presence or absence of a reinforcement contingency.
2. In respondent discrimination: A stimulus which is paired consistently with the pairing or nonpairing of the unconditioned stimulus with the conditioned stimulus.
    See also S^D and S^Δ.

Stimulus, Emotional
A stimulus which alters many ongoing performances in the organism's repertoire other than those expressly affected by reinforcement or extinction. "Flushing of the face" and "perspiring," for example, are emotional responses sometimes called "embarrassment." Since neither of these responses are

generally consequated by explicit reinforcement contingencies (at least in the immediate history of the organism—discounting any phylogenetic rationale for the behavior), any stimulus which produces these responses may be considered emotional.

Problems arise in the classification of "emotional stimuli" when one considers the possibility that certain responses may have been conditioned in the history of the organism—if not to the stimulus in question, to one sharing certain properties with present stimulus conditions. "Wing flapping," for example, is often cited as an "emotional response" emitted by pigeons under conditions of extinction or pre-aversive stimulation. While wing-flapping bears no direct relationship to the specific conditions at hand, however, "flying" behavior most certainly *could* have been conditioned in the history of the organism as a response to situations where food is no longer available or danger threatens. Is the response "emotional," then, or merely "inductive" or "regressive"?

Stimulus Event, Catalytic
A stimulus event which predictably generates a particular behavior or behavioral pattern. Not to be confused with an S^D since it may be an S^Δ as well (i.e., the catalytic event might be the removal of aversive contingencies). Example: It is said that recess time in school is a catalytic stimulus event for disruptive physical behaviors which would be punished during any other school period.

Stimulus, Expanded
Any stimulus which is of a longer duration (e.g., a light on for a longer period) or more drawn out (e.g., slower speech), but which does not differ from the usual or normal stimulus with respect to intensity, tone, pitch, or any other relevant dimension.

Stimulus Fading
Sometimes used as a synonym for "stimulus building," but incorrectly so. See **Fading**.

Stimulus Field
The set of all stimuli which may affect an organism at any one time, i.e., all stimuli that the organism may see, feel, hear, or smell at any given moment.

Stimulus, Integral
A complex stimulus in which there are many components which, although they could be separated physically, must occur in conjunction (and, perhaps in a particular sequence) in order to control responding in the designated manner (i.e., as an S^D, S^Δ, S^{r+}, or S^{r-}). Determination of the function must

be made via the technique of event sampling as well as time sampling. Prior to the determination of function (i.e., before evidence is available to make certain the function of the integral stimulus), it is called an "integral event."

Stimulus Magnitude
The size or intensity of a stimulus. In respondent behavior the stimulus magnitude and response magnitude are directly proportional (i.e., when one increases the other increases, etc.). In operant behavior this relationship is arbitrary when the stimulus is above physiological thresholds, and is solely dependent upon an explicit history of reinforcement (e.g., one could differentially reinforce high-pressure responses on a lever to a stimulus of low intensity, and low-pressure responses to a stimulus of high intensity, etc.).

Stimulus, Neutral (S^N)
1. In operant conditioning: A stimulus which has no effect on behavior. Strictly speaking this would require that the organism were totally unaware of the presence of the stimulus, or at least that it had never been paired in any way with any contingency. In a more general sense, however, we may consider a stimulus neutral with respect to one set of circumstances or behaviors and discriminative with respect to another. A green traffic light, for example, may be discriminative with respect to driving behaviors, for example, but have no effect (i.e., be neutral with respect to) reading behavior.
2. In respondent conditioning: A stimulus which has never been paired with an unconditioned stimulus, and which is ineffective in eliciting a reflex or altering respondent behavior in any way. Many of the same qualifications mentioned above in the operant usage also apply here.

Stimulus, Paced
Any situation in which the stimulus conditions necessary for responding are not present continuously, but rather, are "paced," or presented in a fashion which restricts the possible range of rates of responding to that stimulus.

Pacing may be independent of or dependent upon responding. In the first case, usually called program pacing, the stimulus is presented as a function of some variable "external to the organism" (e.g., a machine is set up to present a new math problem to a student every 10 seconds—regardless of whether or not the student has emitted any response to the preceding problem). In program pacing the upper limit of rate of responding is determined by the pace at which stimuli are presented. In the example above, if the problems are presented at a rate of one every 10 seconds, the upper limit of "problem-solution" behavior rates would be 6 per minute. Such artificially imposed "record ceilings" are usually undesirable.

The second category of pacing is usually called response-dependent pacing, or, response pacing. In this case the next stimulus is presented when the response to the last stimulus has been made (e.g., a teacher presents a new spelling-list flash card after the student has responded to the last one). The denotation of "pacing" in this situation implies that there is some time delay between stimulus presentations that still places a limit on responding, although this limit is usually much harder to determine than the limits imposed by program pacing. In the spelling-card situation, for example, the student might be able to work faster with a typed list of the words, thereby eliminating the teacher-imposed delay of presenting the next flash card. As minor as this may seem, data suggest that such program revisions *can* significantly affect response rates. See also **Operant, Paced**; and **Stimulus-Response Relationship, Functionally Dependent**.

Stimulus Perseveration
1. The tendency to repeat incorrect choices (responses to incorrect stimuli) on subsequent trials of the same problem.

2. The failure to alter the form, mode, or frequency of responding with changes in the discriminative stimuli of the environment.

Also called "response perseveration," somewhat more correctly, since it is defined by the response of the organism.

Stimulus, Positive (S⁺)
Any stimulus which will increase the rate or probability of responding, or maintain responding at a point above operant level for any response that immediately precedes its occurrence, or decrease the rate or probability of responding, or maintain responding at a point lower than operant level for any response which just precedes its termination. In the former case it is called a positive reinforcer. The antonym of a positive stimulus is negative stimulus (S⁻). See **Stimulus, Aversive**.

Stimulus, Pre-Aversive
A stimulus which is presented consistently just prior to the introduction of a primary or previously conditioned aversive stimulus. May come to function as an S^D or conditioned aversive stimulus through the process of respondent conditioning. See **Suppression, Conditioned**.

Stimulus, Priming

A stimulus generally intended to induce or cue responding, but which is not continually presented once responding has started and has come under the control of other events or reinforcement. E.g., a teacher may use the priming stimulus of a command to induce a child to begin his arithmetic, but once arithmetic behaviors have begun to be emitted, the teacher no longer commands him to begin. Also called a "setting stimulus."

Stimulus Property

A single dimension of the stimulus which may control a performance differentially from other dimensions of the stimulus. E.g., color, size, position, etc.

Stimulus-Response Relationship, Functionally Dependent

Any stimulus-response relationship in which the specific value of the stimulus determines the general nature of the response; and the specific nature of the response determines the next value of the stimulus, etc.

Example: The stimulus of a curve will determine the nature of a general turning response on the wheel of a car; which in turn determines the next stimulus (of the car's relation to the curve); which in turn determines the nature of the next wheel-turning response, etc. Also, a teacher may present a flash card to which a student is to respond; the nature of the response may determine the next card to be read, which in turn determines the next response, etc. It is this type of relationship which is enjoyed in most adjusting schedules or instances of response induction.

Stimulus Set

The class of all related stimuli which function to elicit a specific respondent behavior (reflex). To be differentiated from a cue set or stimulus *class* which elicits an operant response.

Stimulus Shaping

1. As an operation: Altering some dimension of a neutral stimulus to the point where it becomes noticeable to an organism; and differentially reinforcing the emission of an operant already in the organism's repertoire in the presence (or absence) of that stimulus to make it function as an effective S^D (or S^Δ). All other parts of the operant structure must be intact (i.e., the response, contingency, and reinforcer); and the subject must be capable of responding.

2. As a process: The resultant formation of stimulus control.

Also called "stimulus fading," somewhat incorrectly. See also **Stimulus Control; Stimulus Building;** and **Stimulus Fading.**

Stimulus Shift, Extradimensional
Where the relevant dimension of the discriminative stimulus is altered. Results in negative transfer. E.g., where the relevant dimension in one S^D is *color*, and then is changed to form. Color and form are two separable dimensions. See also **Stimulus Shift, Intradimensional;** and **Transfer, Negative.**

Stimulus Shift, Intradimensional
Where the relevant cue of a discriminative stimulus is altered, but within the same dimension (e.g., where the specific color is changed, but the relevant dimension remains color). Results in positive transfer. See also **Stimulus Shift, Extradimensional;** and **Transfer, Positive.**

Stimulus, Subliminal
Any stimulus with an intensity below that required to elicit a response. Below threshold. NOTE: A stimulus may be subliminal with respect to *one* response, but still effect another response. "Subliminal advertising," for example, presents a stimulus subliminal to the extent that the subject is incapable of emitting a response to specifically identify *when* the stimulus occurs, but that stimulus may *still* effect the "buying response" of the subject. See **Threshold** and **Respondent Laws, Primary.**

Stimulus, Unconditioned (UCS) or (US)
In respondent conditioning, the stimulus which elicits the unconditioned response without having had to be paired with another stimulus in the past. A UCS is frequently defined as one which is effective at the birth of the organism, but as physiological capabilities of responding alter with maturation, this distinction is not entirely correct.

Strain
The decreased frequency of a performance that occurs as a result of schedules with a particularly low reinforcement density or that require a great deal of effort in responding. See **Abulia.**

Subhunger
A preference for a member of a class of reinforcers: e.g., a pigeon might prefer corn to several other grains, or a person might prefer the music of Mozart to that of other composers. Preference is usually defined by the relative frequencies of the

responses that produces the different reinforcers. See **Preference**.

Subliminal
Below threshold. See **Threshold** and **Respondent Laws, Primary**.

Supervisor
A member of the project team in Precision Teaching. See **Project Team**.

Suppression
Any reduction in rate of responding which is temporary in nature. Usually associated with a temporary (and usually aversive) change in the environment.

Suppression, Conditioned
1. As an operation: Repeatedly presenting a stimulus (S_1) during or prior to the onset of an aversive stimulus.
2. As a process: The temporary suppression of responding during subsequent presentations of that stimulus (S_1). NOTE: (S_1) is then called a "pre-aversive stimulus."

Systematic Desensitization
A specific sequence of operations designed to reduce or eliminate phobias or maladaptive anxiety. Comprised of three basic steps: First, the subject is trained in "deep muscle relaxation"; second, a graded list of stimuli is compiled representing the stimuli which elicit the anxiety or phobia in order from least to most anxiety-producing; and third, the stimuli are reproduced in the mind of the client through imagery while in a state of deep muscle relaxation. Presentation of new, higher-level stimuli is made contingent upon complete relaxation in the presence of milder (lower-level) stimuli. The rapidity with which new stimuli are presented is governed entirely by the client.

Systematic desensitization is considered one of several related types of counter-conditioning techniques, differentiated primarily by the detail with which the list of eliciting stimuli is formed and the means of stimulus presentation. Other, similar therapies, include: "deconditioning," "graded tasks," "dosing anxiety," "reconditioning," "hypnotic desensitization," "paradoxical intention," and "autogenic training."

Systematization
The integration of all relevant data and information pertaining to any specified issue. The collation and ordering of information to achieve a single body of data in which all aspects of the issue are described and related to all other aspects, and with

which the entire issue may be examined and investigated as a whole or complete subject matter.

TAND
Abbreviation for "tandem schedule." See **Schedule, Tandem.**

Task Analysis
Breaking down a job or job analysis into its fine stimulus-response components. Each unique response is stated in order of its emission, with its correlated stimulus. E.g., to lace a shoe:

Stimulus	Response
1. sight of shoe	1. extend right arm to lace
2. right hand over lace	2. grasp lace between thumb and forefinger.
	. . . etc.

The purpose of a task analysis is to identify relevant stimuli which may be pre-trained or need to be augmented; and responses which may be pre-trained or altered in form or sequence to make the acquisition of the task more rapid and with fewer errors. Also see **Job Analysis; Task Reformulation;** and **Training Program.**

Task Reformulation
Altering the form or order of stimulus or response components in a task analysis to insure more rapid acquisition or more efficient performance of the entire chain. E.g., installing a counter on a machine that rings a bell when a crank has been turned the correct number of times. See also **Task Analysis; Job Analysis;** and **Training Program.**

T ("Tee")
A set and specific period during which one instance of a t^D and one instance of a t^Δ will alternate. The length of a cycle of a t^D and t^Δ. An FI 1" with a 5" hold will have a t^Δ period of one minute, a t^D period of 5", and a complete cycle (or T) of 1'5". See also t^D, and t^Δ.

t^D ("Tee-Dee")

A set and specific interval of time during which if a response is emitted it will produce or aid in the production of (depending on the schedule in effect) reinforcement. Similar to S^D, but where the only "stimulus" is the passage of time. For example, if an FI 1' (fixed interval-one minute) schedule of reinforcement with a limited hold of 5", the first response to be emitted during the five seconds following one minute since the last reinforcement will be reinforced. The 5", then, is a t^D. See also **T**, **t$^\Delta$**, and **S^D**.

t$^\Delta$ ("Tee-Delta")

A set and specific interval of time during which if a response is emitted it will never be contingently reinforced. Similar to S$^\Delta$, but where the "stimulus" is the passage of time. For example, in an FI 1" a response will never be reinforced during the first one minute following the last reinforcement. This minute, then, is a t$^\Delta$. See also **t^D**, **T**, and **S$^\Delta$**.

Temporal Relationships Between Behavior and Environment

There are several ways in which behavior may occur in temporal relationships to the environment in which it is emitted. Many times the specific temporal relationship determines the function of the interaction (e.g., event occurring *before* an instance of behavior could effect that behavior quite differently than a similar event occurring immediately *after* the same behavior). Here, however, only brief definitions of the temporal relationships *per se* will be given. To determine the potential functional implications of these relationships, the reader should consult the individual definitions of each term located elsewhere in the glossary.

NOTE: It is quite possible for one type of event to have several temporal relationships to the behavior. Categories are not, in this sense, mutually exclusive.

Relationships Within or Between Several Instances of the Same Behavior:

> *Inter-Response Time (IRT):* The time between the completion of one instance of behavior and the beginning of the next instance of the same behavior. If the behavior was "sentences written," for example, then the IRTs would be the time elapsed from the moment the last letter in a sentence was completed to the moment the first letter in the next sentence was started. See Figure 79.

> *Intra-Response Time (IRAT):* The time between the start of one instance of behavior and the end of the same

instance of behavior. If the behavior were "sentences written," for example, then the IRAT would be the elapsed time from the moment the first letter in the sentence was begun and the moment the last letter in the sentence was completed. See Figure 80.

Operant-to-Operant Interval (OOI): The elapsed time between the start of one instance of behavior to the start of the next instance of the same behavior. If the behavior was "sentences written," for example, the OOI would be the elapsed time between the moment the first letter in one sentence was started and the moment the first letter in the next sentence was started. See Figure 81.

Operant-to-Operant Rate (OOR): The inverse of the operant-to-operant interval (i.e., 1/OOI). Used to equate the OOI with the more usual measure of averaged rate of responding (see below). OOR is equivalent to an estimate of the number of operants which could occur in one standard unit of time (usually a minute) with the given OOI. Note that the OOI must be expressed in terms of the unit of time in question (i.e., the OOI cannot be

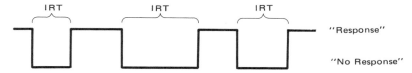

Figure 79. Inter-Response Time: In this and the figures to follow a response is indicated by a rise in the line, and the termination of a response by a fall in the line. IRTs are noted as that time which elapses between the termination of one response and the initiation of the next response.

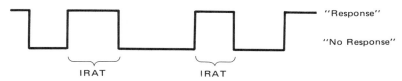

Figure 80. Intra-Response Time: The time which elapses between the initiation of a response and the termination of the same response.

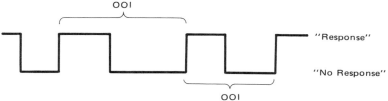

Figure 81. Operant-to-Operant Interval: The time which elapses between the initiation of one response and the initiation of the next response.

expressed in seconds and the answer expressed in minutes unless a conversion is made). Since only one value of OOI is expressed in the equation for OOR (and several different values may, in fact, have obtained in any given set of data), the OOI used is usually a summary statistic of all OOIs obtained. If the mean of all OOIs is used, then the result is an approximation of averaged rate of responding, but using the median OOI has, in some cases, been shown to give a much more stable estimate of the rate of responding (i.e., it is not as sensitive to unusually long or short OOIs as the mean; and, therefore, reflects the majority of OOIs more realistically).

Averaged Rate-of-Responding (ARR): An estimate of the number of responses which may be expected to occur in any given unit of time (usually one minute). Calculated by dividing the number of responses observed by the total time of the observation:

$$\text{\# responses/time observed}$$

As the number of responses approaches 1, however, the accuracy of this estimate diminishes; and it is preferable to calculate the OOR (mean or median) whenever possible.

Relationships Between a Behavioral Event and Another Environmental Event

Latency: The time elapsing between the onset of one event and the onset of another. Either event may be the behavioral event in question (i.e., the first or second); and both events may, in fact, be behaviors (but of different types—otherwise the relationship would be called an OOI, see above). See Figure 82.

Event Before (EB): Any relationship between a behavior and an environmental event in which the event always precedes the emission of the behavior. There may

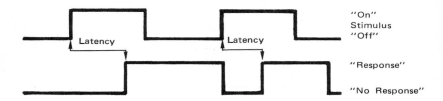

Figure 82. Latency: The time which elapses between the onset of a stimulus and the occurrence of some event (in this case, a response).

178

be some latency between the time of the event before and the occurrence of the behavior, but usually the use of the term (EB) implies that the behavior occurs soon following the occurrence of the event before.

Event Until (EU): Any relationship between a behavior and an environmental event in which the event always precedes the emission of the behavior; *and* continues to occur (either as one continuous event or a rapid repetition of shorter events) until the behavior is emitted. If, for example, a teacher said a spelling word once (and the student is then expected to write it), that would be designated an event before; but if the teacher *repeated* the spelling word until all students acknowledged completion, then that would be an event until.

Antecedent Event: Any event meeting the criteria of an event-before or an event-until. When differentiation between the categories of event-before and event-until is difficult or impossible, the term "antecedent-event" may be used to denote the possibility of either.

Event During (ED): Any relationship between a behavior and an environmental event in which the event occurs *concurrently* (i.e., at the same time as) the behavior. For example: If a teacher smiled at a student only during the time he was reading (i.e., didn't smile until the student started reading; and stopped smiling when the student stopped reading), then that would be an event during. Events during may also be qualified as "events-during-all" or "events-during-part" of the response.

Event After (EA): Any relationship between a behavior and an environmental event in which the event always occurs *after* the behavior. Note that this does not necessarily imply that the event is *caused* by the behavior—only that it occurs (if at all) after the behavior (see also **Arranged Event**). For example: If a child had the habit of always "fidgeting" (i.e., talking out of turn, getting out of his seat, and putting his books away) just before recess and lunch, then recess and lunch would be events after, even though they certainly weren't *caused* by that behavior. The designation of event after does, however, imply that the event occurs reasonably *soon* after the behavior. Also called a "subsequent event."

Event Anytime (EAn): An event which bears no particular temporal relationship to the behavior (i.e., it occurs before, during, or after the occurrence of the behavior). Events anytime can, however, still control responding by superstitious or accidental conditioning.

A teacher, for example, may smile at a child more or less randomly (i.e., at any time—regardless of the child's behavior); but smiling may (accidentally) follow "talk-out" behavior often enough for the child to believe that talking *causes* the smiling. Also called an "uncorrelated event."

Event Always (EAI): An environmental event which is continually occurring during the period in which the behavior is being emitted—so that the event always occurs before, during, *and* after each behavioral event. Examples would include the ticking of a clock and the noise of machines in the background. An event always is differentiated from an event anytime (see above) in that it has a definite "rhythm" (i.e., a consistent "on-off" pattern) which is rapid enough to insure occurrence before, during, and after (nearly) all responses; whereas an event anytime is less regular and occurs less frequently. The implication is that the event anytime has a higher probability of accidentally occurring in one position (i.e., the before, during, or after position) to the exclusion of the others, and therefore, has a higher probability of gaining superstitious control over the response. The event always is, however, still an *event* (i.e., a change in the environment—like the "tick"-"no tick"-"tick," etc., of a clock) and so cannot be classified as a situation element (see below).

Situation and Situation-Element: Any condition in the environment which remains constant (unchanging). Sometimes equated to the general "setting" in which the behavior occurs. Examples would be the walls, their color, the number of desks in a room, the position of the room in the school, and the number of people in the room. The designation of situation does not mean that the condition *cannot* change, just that it *does* not change during the period in which the behavior is being observed. For example: The fact that there are 30 students in one class may be classified as a situation-element during math period; but several of the students may go elsewhere for reading—changing the situation. As long as the 30 students are there for math, though, then with respect to math behavior, "30 students" is a situation-element. Note that "situation" is used whenever reference is made to the entire complex of non-changing environmental conditions; and "situation-element" whenever reference is made to a small part of that complex. "Situation" has also been equated to the Precision Teaching term "program."

Program Event (PE): A term, originating in Precision Teaching, in reference to any event which is not caused by the behavior. Usually the use of PE implies that there is *some* consistent relationship (before, until, during, or after) but that the relationship is not causal. It is advisable, whenever possible, to use a more specific label (e.g., see the definitions of all events given above).

NOTE: Besides each of the discrete terms listed above, it is possible for an event to have several relationships to a behavior. To describe these compounds, new complex terms may be created. For example, an event which starts before the behavior and continues *through* the emission of the behavior might be called an EBD (event before/during). Similarly, an EAU would be an event which starts *after* one instance of the behavior and continues *until* the next instance of that behavior.

Temporary
Synonym for "prosthetic." See **Prosthetic**.

Therapeutic
Of or pertaining to therapy. See **Therapy**.

Therapeutic Device
A device designed and constructed to generate behaviors which will still maintain when the device is removed from the environment. For example, exercise machines in physical therapy are designed to increase the strength of the patient so that he may engage in physical activities that will, in turn, maintain the strength of the patient without the need of special devices. A teaching machine designed to teach a child to read is another example. It should be noted, however, that a "therapeutic device" may only be labeled as such *after* its use has been terminated and it has been demonstrated that the behaviors do, in fact, maintain. Any other use of the word must be considered speculative. See **Therapeutic**.

Therapy
Literally therapy is the operation of altering something which already exists in some form. In behavioral usage, however, one speaks of therapy as the alteration of an environment to shape or condition a peformance which will maintain when the therapeutic element is removed. Often it cannot be determined whether a specific change in the environment is therapeutic until it is observed whether or not the behavior it generates maintains after the environment is restored to its original condition. One may speak of therapeutic environments, therapeutic devices, therapeutic contingencies, etc. See also **Prosthesis**.

Threshold

The minimal value of any stimulus dimension (e.g., intensity, size, duration, etc.) which will render that stimulus noticeable to the organism; or, that value which the stimulus must have in order to exert a specified control over behavior.

Threshold, Absolute

The smallest stimulus intensity that a subject can discriminate. Since the absolute threshold may change slightly with varying conditions in the environment and organism, the absolute threshold is usually taken as that point which allows discrimination 50% of the time.

Threshold Differential

Just Noticeable Difference (JND), the smallest difference between the values of two stimuli that the subject can discriminate. Since the specific value of a JND may change slightly with varying conditions of the environment and organism, the JND is usually taken as that difference which may be discriminated 50% of the time.

Threshold Penumbra

The range of stimulus intensities which may or may not be sufficient to elicit a respondent behavior (dependent upon specific conditions in the environment and organism). That range of stimulus values between the point where the organism will *always* respond and that point where the organism will *never* respond. See **Threshold** and **Respondent Laws, Primary**.

Time-Rule Check List

A method of observation in which the occurrence or non-occurrence of a specified event during a specified time period is checked off (or coded) on a list of possible events (or events of concern). Repeated observations will result in a probability estimate of at least one occurrence of a specified event in a defined period of time. The resultant data are *not* rate, but approximate rate as the size of the time base decreases. Time-rule check lists are usually ipsative measures. See **Data, Ipsative**.

Time Sampling

A method of descriptive analysis in which the temporal order of events and responses and their frequency of occurrence within a specified interval are recorded. By comparing the results of two or more time samples taken under different conditions a *functional* analysis may be made (i.e., what are the effects of the presence or absence of, or changes in the frequency of certain events). Time sampling (i.e., describing *when* events happen) must be differentiated from event sampling (i.e., describing *what* the events are). See also **Event Sampling.**

Time Out (TO)
1. As an operation: Removing the organism (usually for a short period of time) from a situation where reinforcement or punishment is available, or noticeably withholding or suspending the reinforcement or punishment contingencies for a short period of time. Usually the withdrawal is made contingent upon responding, but not necessarily so.
2. As a process: If TO is made contingent upon responding, or follows a response closely, it will result in an increase or decrease in probability or rate of responding, or maintenance of probability or rate of responding at a point higher or lower than operant level (dependent upon whether TO is from a reinforcing or punishing situation). It is important to realize that the situation into which the organism is put during time out is essentially considered "neutral"; and that the effect of the TO is determined mainly by the situation from which the organism is removed. For example: If a child were sent to his room for misbehaving during his own birthday party, the result would be quite different from sending him to his room during the parent's bridge party. In the former case (the birthday party) he would be removed from a situation in which positive consequences are available; and in the latter case he would be removed from a situation in which the frequency of positive consequences would be considerably less; and yet in both cases the time out situation (i.e., his room) is the same.

Times
A statement, originating in Precision Teaching, in reference to a change or difference between any two values (e.g., rates) in which the amount of change is expressed in terms of that number by which one value must be multiplied in order to achieve the other value. Given the values of 2 and 8, for example, the difference between them might be expressed as "times four" (i.e., 2 x 4 = 8).

In cases of lines-of-progress and steps, a "times" statement also implies that acceleration has occurred (i.e., the two values in question occur sequentially in time and the second is greater than the first).

The use of "times" statements as description of change or difference is limited to cases in which the data or values are presented on log or semilog graphs or charts. On such charts all equal "times" changes will appear to be the same size (e.g., a change from 2 to 4 and a change from 100 to 200 are both "x2"; and will both appear as being the same size on a log or semilog chart). For this reason log or semilog charts are often called "equal ratio" charts. See also **Dividby** and **Change, Amount of.**

TO
Abbreviation for "time out." See **Time Out.**

Token
A representation or symbol. A token in operant terminology is usually any physical object (such as a poker chip or check on a sheet) that may be exchanged at a later date for other reinforcers. Money is an excellent example of a token.

Token Economy
A system of reinforcement in which tokens are administered as the immediate reinforcer and "backed up" later by allowing the tokens to be exchanged for more substantial reinforcers. Also see **Token.**

Trainer
A member of the project team in Precision Teaching. See **Project Team.**

Training Program
The step-by-step outline of recommended training procedures, which results from the experimental analysis of task reformulation. Included in the program are order of introduction for the job components (based on observed difficulty level), recommended training procedures (e.g., modeling, molding, shaping, etc.), recommended stimulus alterations, suggested schedules of reinforcement, data collection procedures, and techniques for analyzing trainee progress.

Transfer, Negative
Where the cues or relevant dimensions of the S^Ds for problem solution in one situation do not apply in a second situation. Results in slower problem solution in the second situation.

Transfer, Positive
Where the cues or relevant stimulus dimensions in the S^Ds for problem solution in one instance remain constant in another instance. Results in more rapid problem solution in the second instance.

Tree
A behavior chain in which one of the components is an option. See **Findley Diagrams,** Figure 38. See also **Option** and **Grove.**

U - V

UCR

Abbreviation for "unconditioned response." See **Response, Unconditioned**.

UCS

Abbreviation for "unconditioned stimulus." See **Stimulus, Unconditioned**.

Up the Left

A term, originating in Precision Teaching, in reference to the scale along the left side of the standard Precision Teaching behavior chart which describes the movements per minute. Also called the y-axis, the ordinate, or vertical axis. See Figure 83. See also **Chart** and **Across the Bottom**.

UR

Abbreviation for "unconditioned response." See **Response, Unconditioned**.

US

Abbreviation for "unconditioned stimulus." See **Stimulus, Unconditioned**.

Figure 83. Up the Left: The vertical or Y-axis of the Standard Precision Teaching "6—16" Behavior Chart.

Variable
Any condition in the environment or organism, whether manipulated or merely observed, which changes or can be changed. See **Variable, Dependent**; and **Variable, Independent**.

Variable, Dependent
A variable which changes as a function of a change in another variable. In operant research the dependent variable is usually rate of responding, probability of responding, or some other measurable aspect of behavior.

Variable, Endogenous
A variable which interacts with another variable or system in a mutually dependent manner. E.g., if a schedule of reinforcement (which effects response rate) is altered as a function of that response rate, then the schedule and response rate would be endogenous variables. See also **Variable, Exogenous; Variable, Dependent**; and **Variable, Independent**.

Variable, Exogenous
A variable which, while affecting another variable or system, is not in turn affected. Analogous to the dependent variable in experimental design. See also **Variable, Endogenous; Variable, Dependent**; and **Variable, Independent**.

Variable, Independent
A variable which is altered or changed by the experimenter or observed by (but not manipulated by) the experimenter as it changes (naturally) to determine the effects it has on changes in the dependent variable. E.g., an experimenter might alter the independent variable of hunger (food deprived for 15, 20, and 25 hours) to determine its effect on the dependent variable of response rate when food is used as a reinforcer.

Variable, Prosthetic
Any variable which obtains in a prosthetic environment, a change in which is reversible, and which *does* reverse (return to its original value) when the prosthetic environment is discontinued. This does not mean that other variables (i.e., non-prosthetic) may not also occur in a generally prosthetic environment.

Variable, Therapeutic
Any variable which obtains in a therapeutic environment; and which is irreversible (i.e., cannot attain a previously enjoyed value). This does not mean that other variables (i.e., non-therapeutic) cannot occur in a generally therapeutic environment.

VI
Abbreviation for "variable interval schedule of reinforcement." See **Schedule, Variable Interval.**

VR
Abbreviation for "variable ratio schedule." See **Schedule, Variable Ratio.**

Week
Any seven successive calendar days. Since lines-of-progress are usually calculated on a "per week" basis (e.g., as in Precision Teaching), it is important that time-spans (e.g., the length of a phase, the duration of a vacation) are always reported in terms of weeks (as opposed to days). In cases where the time to be reported cannot be expressed in "whole weeks" (e.g., 15 days is two weeks, one day), then decimal fractions of weeks are used (e.g., two weeks, one day = 2.1428 weeks). The advantages in using decimal fractions become apparent when calculations (e.g., of lines-of-progress slopes) are made. Following is a list of the decimal portions of a week:

> one day = .1428
> two days = .2857
> three days = .4285
> four days = .5714
> five days = .7142
> six days = .8571
> seven days = one week

NOTE: These fractional parts of a week are also noted at the bottom of the Oregon Rate/Acceleration Finder. See **Acceleration Finder.**

Week(s), Effective
A term, originating in Precision Teaching, in reference to any week(s) in which the slope of the line-of-progress is different from the predicted acceleration line for that phase. Any week(s) in which the change in rate which occurs is different than that which would have occurred if the preceding phase

had been continued. The only exceptions are limiting week(s) in which the slope of the line-of-progress is flat, and lies on either the record floor or record ceiling. Of course, where other time bases are used, one might also make reference to effective "hours," "days," "minutes," or any other unit of time. See Figure 84. See also **Week(s), Limiting**.

Week(s), Limiting
A term, originating in Precision Teaching, in reference to any week or weeks in which the line-of-progress lies on the record floor or record ceiling. Called "limited" because it is a week in which the behaver has reached the lowest or highest "limit" of rate. Since both the record floor and record ceiling should be horizontal lines, the slope of the line-of-progress of a limited week would also be flat. Of course, if another time base is used, one might speak of limiting "days," "hours," "minutes," or any other unit of time. See Figure 84.

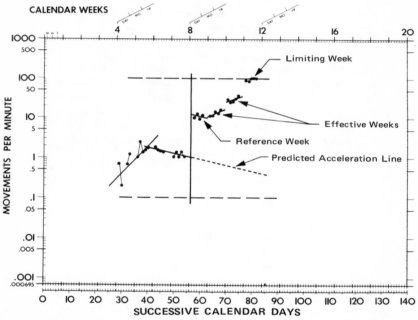

Figure 84. Week Types: This figure represents the three types of weeks which may be observed to occur in the course of a project. Reference weeks are weeks which have lines-of-progress parallel to the predicted acceleration line (i.e., the slope of that week is no different than the slope of the data in the previous phase). Note that a reference week may be higher or lower than the predicted acceleration line—only the slopes need be the same. Effective weeks are any weeks in which the line-of-progress is different than that which would be predicted (i.e., the predicted acceleration line), and which are not limiting weeks. Limiting weeks are weeks in which the rate of responding has reached the record floor or record ceiling, and cannot progress any further in that direction.

Week(s), Reference

A term, originating in Precision Teaching, in reference to any week or weeks during which the slope of the line-of-progress is the same as the slope of the predicted acceleration line. A reference week is any week in which the gain or loss in rate is not different than the gain or loss which would have been predicted from the acceleration in the previous phase. This does not mean that the two lines are at the same place on the chart, since there might have been a step between or in either of the two phases. Of course, if another time base is used, one might make reference to reference "days," "hours," "minutes," or any other unit of time. See Figure 84.

X-Axis

The horizontal axis or abscissa of a chart. The independent variable (e.g., time) is usually represented on the x-axis. Also called "across the bottom" in Precision Teaching. See Figure 1, Abscissa and Ordinate.

$\overline{X}$ ("X-Bar")

An abbreviation for the sample mean (i.e., a mean calculated from a sample of all possible values in a population—as opposed to a mean calculated from all values in the population). See **Mean**.

Y-Axis

The vertical axis or ordinate of a chart. The dependent variable (e.g., rate) is usually represented on the y-axis. Also called "up the left" in Precision Teaching. See Figure 1, Abscissa and Ordinate.

appendix:

functional and descriptive terminology

It is generally accepted that the ultimate purpose of a science of behavior is to reach a point at which the behavioral "product" of any given set of environmental conditions may be predicted (and, perhaps, controlled). It would be impossible, however, to examine and test literally *all* possible environmental conditions for the effect they produce in behaviors. Fortunately, while it may be true that each specific set of conditions may produce a slightly different behavioral product, it is *also* true that certain general characteristics found in large classes of phenomena have *roughly* the same behavioral effect in a wide variety of contexts. Classification of phenomena in terms of shared characteristics can, therefore, lead to the determination of "class effects"; and later, to the prediction of those effects which will be produced by phenomena classified in that manner at some later date. The class of all "reinforcers," for example, is comprised of all stimuli which increase the rate or probability of behavior which just precedes their occurrence. In order for any stimulus to be classified as a reinforcer it must still be tested for the function described above; but since the *class* of reinforcers has already been well investigated in the past, one is also in a position to predict (without actual test) certain other uses of that stimulus (e.g., in conditioning other reinforcers, and in cost-contingencies).

The level of classification may be quite broad (e.g., "event") or quite discrete (e.g., "third-order conditioned-reinforcing-stimulus-event, conditioned under a CRF schedule of reinforcement"). The more detailed the classification, the greater the amount of precision in prediction of effect. In addition to limits of practicality, however, movement up the continuum of classification is not in all cases possible. Take, for example, the following case where a simple "event" is continually reclassified until it is called a "conditioned positive reinforcer."

Classification	What the analyst must know before the classification may be made
Event	The phenomenon in question represents a *change* from one set of environmental conditions to another set of environmental conditions.
Event-After	The event (i.e., change in conditions) must occur *after* the behavior in question.
Stimulus-Event-After	The event must *alter* the rate or probability of the behavior preceding it.
Positive Reinforcer	The stimulus event after must *increase* the rate or probability of the behavior just preceding it.
Conditioned Positive Reinforcer	The positive reinforcer must have gained its ability to reinforce via the process of respondent conditioning.

The question is not "how detailed does one wish to be?" but rather, "how much does one *know* about the phenomenon?" More may certainly be predicted about the effects and uses of a "conditioned positive reinforcer" than a simple "event," but if the information necessary for the classification of a conditioned positive reinforcer is not available, then some "lower-level" classification must suffice—until, that is, additional information *is* obtained.

An important dichotomy may be formed between the "descriptive" and "functional" levels of classification. In the former, only the temporal and/or physical characteristics of the phenomenon are considered; and in the latter, emphasis is placed on the *affect* of the phenomena (i.e., how it changes *other* phenomena). In the list above, for example, the classifications "event" and "event-after" only require knowledge of physical change and temporal relation to the behavior. From the "stimulus-event-after" level on, however, the analyst must know not only the temporal and physical characteristics of the phenomena, but also *how it affects behavior*.

Since it seems reasonable that one would classify phenomena at the descriptive level before testing for function, it would also seem reasonable that the development of a descriptive terminology precede or at least be concurrent with the development of a functional terminology. The reverse has actually obtained. Description in the behavioral science has remained at a relatively clumsy and nonstandard level until just recently, while functional counterparts have been relatively *well* defined and standardized for some time. There are many possible reasons why this may be the case: First, description *can* occur at a colloquial level; that is, if an investigator wishes to describe some event that occurs following the emission of behavior, he can *call* it an "event after the emission of the behavior." Secondly, the majority of communication in the field regarding the results of observations and intervention procedures occurs *after* the project has been completed and the appropriate functional labels have been determined. Third, since it is the ultimate purpose of the science to predict, and since prediction requires knowledge of functional relationship, it only seems reasonable that emphasis should be placed on functional terminology. Unfortunately, even the best of rationales can prove faulty at the practical level.

First, although it is the case that "common usage" terms exist which could be used whenever simple description is required, the fact remains that several words *may* apply; and each bears certain colloquial connotations which might distort the intended meaning. It is not unusual, for example, for the word "consequence" to occur in the literature in reference to the conditions which obtain following the emission of a response, where the effects of those conditions are as yet undetermined. The simple "consequences of behavior" in other words, may or may not be reinforcing or punishing. In fact, however, to at least *one* group of people the term consequence bears definite functional connotations. In Precision Teaching, "consequence" is defined as any event which occurs as a result of the behavior, and which *alters the rate of that behavior*! Note that because contingency is a necessary condition in the Precision Teacher's use of the word "consequence" that it is not directly equivalent to the term "reinforcer." Nevertheless, it *is* a *functionally* defined term. Until standardization of descriptive terminology is achieved, conflict between various "regional" connotations of the terms employed is unavoidable.

Secondly, although it would be *hoped* that the procedures and environmental events studied in any given project could be functionally defined once the appropriate data were collected, that simply *isn't* always the case. There are several reasons why phenomena may not be functionally classifiable at the termination of a project. First, it could be that preliminary data collected early in a project require certain delays or extensions in one or more phases and result in a simple lack of time for the complete analysis originally envisioned. Second, variables may be identified after a project is under way which *appear* to bear a functional relationship to the dependent variable, but which cannot be investigated due to lack of time or the complexity of the experimental situation. It is rarely possible, for example, to completely analyze the function of seating arrangement, peer absences, and peer interactions in an applied study of math fact performances in a regular classroom. Because of a lack of standard descriptive classifications, however, it is not at all unusual for an investigator to simply omit any detailed discussion of these untested phenomena even though they represent important considerations for future investigation.

Third, of course, it could be that the tested variable simply *isn't* functionally related to the behavior. Although reporting the *absence* of a relationship could certainly help other researchers avoid wasted effort of their own, the lack of a descriptive terminology often leads to the omission of this information from final project reports.

Lastly, the emphasis placed on the desirability of functional classification and the absence of a descriptive classification system has frequently resulted in the misuse of the functional terms available. For example, "I *reinforced* that behavior, but it did not increase in rate or probability" is not at all an infrequent statement; and yet it violates the very meaning of the term "reinforcement." Functionally defined terms like "reinforcement" are not *"questions"* of function, they are functional *"facts"* which must already be established through the collection and analysis of data *before* the term is applied.

In view of the foregoing, it would appear that there is a good case for the specification of a purely descriptive system of classification. The purpose of this appendix, therefore, will be to briefly investigate previous attempts to accomplish that end and to extend and integrate those efforts into a comprehensive and workable system for use in all areas of behavioral investigation. Since all terms used in the following text have been completely defined in the main body of the Glossary, only brief definitions will be given here. Only the manner in which the functional and descriptive terms relate to each other in the sequence of classification will be discussed in detail.

the "is" equation -- descriptive analysis in Precision Teaching

One of the first widely accepted attempts to construct a separate descriptive classification system for the analysis of behavioral and environmental events appeared in a 1964 article by O. R. Lindsley entitled "The Direct Measurement and Prosthesis of Retarded Behavior" (*Journal of Education).* The analytic system, called COLAB (common language analysis of behavior) was comprised of two separate "equations" denoting the most common temporal and contingent relationships that environmental events may have with behavior. One equation was for use in description only, and the second for the classification of events with known functions.

In the descriptive equation, events were classified as occurring antecedent or subsequent to the behavior and labeled accordingly. The behavior itself was renamed a "movement" (to avoid the implication that data were available to demonstrate that the behavior was "responsive" to the environment described by the equation); and any relationship which existed between the movement and the subsequent event was labeled the "arrangement." An example of the use of this original equation follows:

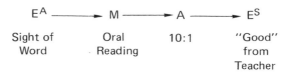

E^A	M	A	E^S
Sight of Word	Oral Reading	10:1	"Good" from Teacher

The functional equation followed the same basic format that one finds in the more traditional terminology. Once data were collected to determine the functions of events in the descriptive equation, a "translation" was performed. The "antecedent event" became a "stimulus" (i.e., it could then be said that the antecedent event "stimulated" the behavior); the "movement" became a "response" (i.e., it was then known that the movement was "responsive" to changes in elements of the equation); the "arrangement" became a "contingency" (implying basically the same thing as "schedule of reinforcement"); and the "subsequent event" became a "consequence." Figure 1 describes the one-to-one relationship between the two equations. Remember, however, that "translation" from one to the other was performed only when data were available to define the specific function of the element or elements in question.

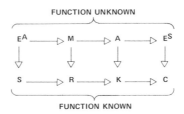

Figure 1.

The original COLAB equations soon became known as the "Is" and "Does" (or "Did") equations (i.e., one describes what *is* in the environment; and the other defines which of those elements *does* change behavior). Eventually "COLAB" was dropped altogether, and today the system is known simply as "Is-Does." At about the same time that the name of the equation was changed, "movement" became "movement-*cycle*" to indicate that "repeatable" behaviors were more amenable to change and description in these equations.

The major purpose of "Is-Does" was to provide the teacher and other applied-level persons with a method of classifying and analyzing behavioral and environmental events in a systematic manner *without* having to learn the relatively complex language of behaviorism *per se*. In this it succeeded immediately. Eventually, however, it was determined that the terms "antecedent" and "subsequent" were too restrictive. A subsequent event, because of the term "arrangement," was automatically limited to the description of events contingent upon the movement. What about events occurring after the movement but *not* dependent upon that behavior? Similarly, what about environmental constants that are not really environmental *events*? The language was changed, therefore, to allow greater flexibility. The term "program" was added to "Is" equation to refer to any environmental constant (e.g., place, time of day, number of peers present); and the term "disposition" was added as its functional corollary in the "Does" equation. The term antecedent event was replaced by "program event" which could refer to events occurring at *any* time (before, during, or after the movement); and the term "subsequent event" was replaced by the term "arranged event" to make its relationship to the behavior even more explicit. The revised equations, those presently in use in Precision Teaching, appear in Figure 2.

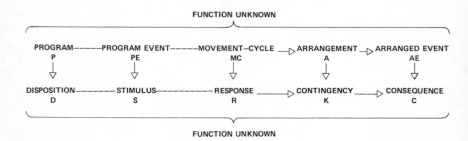

Figure 2.

The actual function which each member of the equation performs is noted by a series of modifiers. A complete list may be found under "Plan Functions or Aims" in the main Glossary; but briefly they include "acceleration," "deceleration," "maintain," "stabilize," and "fluctuate." A consequence that serves the function of accelerating behavior, for example, would be called simply an "accelerating consequence." The means by which the event served the specified function is noted by the adjective "presented" or "withdrawn" (roughly equivalent to "negative" and "positive" in reinforcement). One could have, therefore, a "withdrawn accelerating consequence" (negative reinforcer) or a "presented accelerating consequence" (positive reinforcer).

an expansion

Despite the fact that the standard Precision Teaching "Is" equation is considerably more flexible with the inclusion of the terms "program" and "program event," this increase in analytic "power" was not gained without cost. Most persons were able to immediately comprehend the meaning of "antecedent event" (if, of course, they understood the usual meaning of the terms "antecedent" and "event"); but the connotations ascribed to the word "program" reintroduced a discrepancy between "common sense" and "actual meaning." Almost any dictionary will define a program as a list of items or a plan; and since, in Precision Teaching, the "Is" equation is used for both the description of what *is* going on and what is *planned* as a change, there is little or no discrepancy in formal definition. Actual usage, however, indicates that a good proportion of the people introduced to the equation infer the latter definition only (i.e., plan); and exclude from analysis simple description of events in the environment which were not actually *planned*.

A second problem in the actual usage of the term "program event" arises simply as a function of its position in the equation. Since it occurs *on paper* before the movement-cycle, it is sometimes inferred that it must occur *temporally* before the movement-cycle—defeating the only real advantage that term has over "antecedent event."

In order to alleviate some of the problems arising from the use of the term "program event" but still retain the same flexibility in analysis, Martin Waechter, Program Director of Pearl Buck Center in Eugene, Oregon, devised a similar, but expanded system of analysis. In this system the possible temporal relationships which a program event may have to the movement-cycle are explicitly defined. If a program event may occur

197

before, during, or after the movement-cycle, why not *call* those events "before," "during," and "after"? In addition to simple "events before," Waechter also includes a classification called "events until"—one occurring only once sometime *before* the movement-cycle; and the other occurring repeatedly or continuously *until* the movement-cycle. Having disposed of the term "program event" it became advisable to find a substitute for "program." "Situation" was finally chosen. The terms "movement-cycle," "arrangement," and "arranged event" were retained from the original "Is" equation.

With a variety of discrete temporal classifications it was now possible to construct a planning sheet that regained a correlation between its physical appearance on paper and the temporal relationships it was to describe. Copies of Waechter's description and planning sheets appear in Figures 3 and 4.

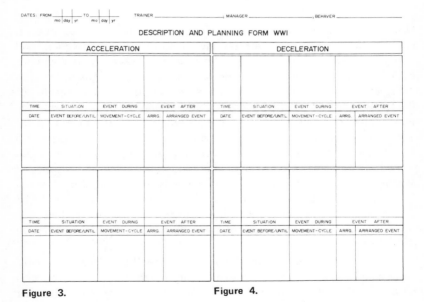

Figure 3.   Figure 4.

common criteria in descriptive classification

The two preceding sections on Lindsley's "Is-Does" and Waechter's expanded analyses represent two of the most formalized and widely used descriptive classification systems available today. Despite the fact that they each approach certain problems in slightly different manners, they share many traits in common.

First, in each approach there is a definite attempt to avoid "technical" terms which, although they may be precisely defined, are not immediately understandable to "lay people." In Lindsley's 1964 article he emphatically states that the development of "jargon" in each of the various sciences is unnecessary and a hindrance to communication. The terms "arranged event" and "event after" may not sound *impressive*, but at least they *communicate* the necessary meaning in a clear and comprehensive manner.

Second, in both sets of analyses (and, for that matter, in the "traditional" functional operant terminology) the focus of analytic attention is always the behavior. The terms "before," "during," "after," and "arranged" all refer to temporal or contingent relationships *to the behavior*. Given this one simple rule, it is almost impossible to misinterpret the meaning of the descriptive statements used in these analyses.

Based on these two criteria of simplicity and orientation toward behavior, the basic elements of these analyses will be further expanded and revised in the following sections to form a more complete system of analysis amenable to even the most detailed of descriptive purposes.

behavior

Since behavior will be the focus of analytic attention, it would probably be advisable to review some of the fundamental rules of behavior identification and definition.

The classification of events as "before" and "after" will require that the initiation and termination of each instance of behavior be readily observable. In the traditional sense this requires that the behavior involve *movement*, that is, that some part or all of the organism be transported through space. As long as some movement occurs, then it is likely that *some* means of observing the behavior is available. Albeit, if the movement is *too* small (e.g., a small muscle spasm in the heart) special equipment will be necessary. More recently, certain behaviorists have become interested in "internal" or "covert" behaviors—thought, feeling, emotion, and other "private" behaviors. Whether or not these behaviors involve movement is a moot point, but if the person emitting those behaviors is confident that he is aware of their initiation and termination, then it is conceivable that "self-analyses" of events controlling those behaviors could be achieved; and alteration plans based on those analyses success-fully employed. It should be pointed out, however, that inasmuch as the adequacy of the analysis and the reliability of any data collected cannot be verified by any other person, the results of such "self-projects" may *not* be generalized to *other* persons—except, perhaps, in the form of "sugges-tions."

Additional suggestions for the identification of behaviors most amenable to analysis and alteration may be found in the definition of "movement-cycle" and "behavior" in the main Glossary. For immediate purposes, however, the criteria of observable or identifiable initiation and termination will suffice.

constant or change?

Given any environmental phenomena (and remember, the "environment" for any given behavior may include the behavior of other organisms or even different instances of behavior for the same organism) the first analytic consideration to be made is whether or not the phenomenon in question represents a *change* in the environment, or a *constant* (unchang-ing) set of conditions. Bearing in mind that the behavior is the center of attention, the classification of "constant" or "change" is solely with respect to that behavior. A "constant," then, is defined as any environ-mental condition which remains unchanged throughout the period during which the behavior is observed. The denotation of a "constant" does *not* imply that the condition described *cannot* change, only that it *does* not change during the observation. Examples would include the place of observation, the number of people present, the time of day, and the general activity in which the behavior occurs. Constants may be further delineated in terms of the duration of their consistency. By the nature of a constant's definition, it cannot change during the course of any *single* observation; but it may be possible for it to change from day-to-day (i.e., observation-to-observation). The number of students in a class, for example, would generally be considered a constant, and yet *can* change on any single day with one or more students absent. This type of constant could be called a "session" or "daily" constant. If the constant is deliberately altered from experimental phase to experimental phase, then it could be termed a "phase" or "treatment" constant (i.e., during any one phase or treatment it remains constant, but changes *between* phases or treatments). Other adjectives may be used as deemed appropriate to the situation at hand. The specific functional and descriptive terms used to denote constants will be discussed in a later section.

"Change" will be defined as any environmental condition which *does* change (at least once) during the course of the time in which the behavior is observed. In other words, anything that cannot be classified as a constant must represent a change. Sometimes, however, the distinction between a constant and a change is relative. A principal in a school, for example, interested in a child's behavior during the entire school day, would consider each classroom that a child enters during the day a *change*. The teacher in each class, on the other hand, only sees the child in that one location, and would most likely classify her classroom as a *constant*. Therefore, the distinction between constant and change is really a matter of "perspective"—who's looking, when, and for how long.

temporal and/or contingent relationship to the behavior

If the phenomena to be classified has already been identified as a constant, then the temporal relationship it has to the behavior is already determined—it exists "throughout" the behavior continuously. It exists before, during, and after the behavior without change. If the phenomena has been classified as a *change*, then there are *several* relationships it may have to the behavior. Those possible relationships are described briefly below.

Antecedents: Any change in conditions which occurs *prior* to any given emission of the behavior in question. This does not mean that the change must occur before *every* instance of the behavior; only that when it *does* occur, it is prior to the occurrence of the behavior. There are several possible types of antecedents; and if at all possible, the change should be classified more discretely as one of the following:

> **Before**: A change in conditions which occurs antecedent to the behavior, but which generally occurs only *once* (or at most, only a

few times) prior to the emission of any given response. A change classified as "before" will *not* be repeated, even if the behavior fails to occur.

Until: A change in conditions which occurs antecedent to the emission of a response and *continues* to occur (either repeatedly or continuously) *until* the behavior occurs. A change "until" will not stop until the behavior starts.

During: Any change in conditions which occurs at the same time as the behavior. This does not mean that it must happen *every* time the behavior occurs; only that when it *does* occur, it is generally at the same time that the behavior is occurring. Changes "during" may be classified at a more discrete level through the use of one of the following modifiers:

During-all: Any change in conditions which occurs during the entire time in which the behavior is emitted. A change during-all, therefore, would start when the behavior started, and stop when the behavior stopped.

During-part: Any change in conditions which occurs at the same time as the behavior, but occurs during only *part* of the time that the behavior occurs.

Note: Alternatives to the term "during" are "concurrent" and "conjugate." Both bear certain functional connotations from their use in schedules of reinforcement, however; and the latter especially implies a "during-all" relationship to the behavior.

Subsequent: Any change in conditions which occurs *after* the emission of the behavior. Note that the subsequent change need not be *caused* by the behavior, only occur *after* it. This allows for the description of environmental conditions which may result in superstitious conditioning. If it is not known whether or not the event occurring after the behavior is caused by or contingent upon the emission of that behavior, then the term "subsequent" is most appropriate. If, however, it *is* known if the subsequent event is or is not contingent upon the behavior, then one of the following terms should be used:

After: Any change in conditions which occurs following the emission of a behavior, but which is *not* caused or dependent upon that behavior (i.e., even if the behavior does *not* occur, the change *will* occur).

Arranged: Any change in conditions which occurs following the emission of a behavior and which is *caused by or contingent*

202

upon that behavior. If the behavior does not occur, the arranged change will not occur.

Note: Additional detail may be gained in the classification of subsequent changes if the terms "immediate" and "delayed" are employed appropriately to denote how *soon* after the behavior the change occurs.

Anytime: Any change in conditions which does not bear any special or consistent relationship to the emission of the behavior. A change "anytime" may occur before, during, or after the behavior. Some of the previous classifications (e.g., change before, change after) may not bear any *necessary* relationship to the behavior, and so could be classified as changes anytime. The fact that they are *not* so classified, however, implies that they occur most often in the position described; and whether by accident or plan, have a relatively consistent relationship to the behavior. Differentiations may be made between *regular* changes anytime and *irregular* changes anytime. Examples would include the ticking of a clock (regular) and the sounds produced by a television in the background where dialogue is broken and inconsistent (irregular). Alternatively, reference could be made to changes "anytime" as irregular, and changes "always" as regular. The degree of regularity has implications in the processes of adaptation and accidental reinforcement.

Figure 5 presents the constants and changes just defined in diagrammatic form. Notice that the "constant" box encompasses all other

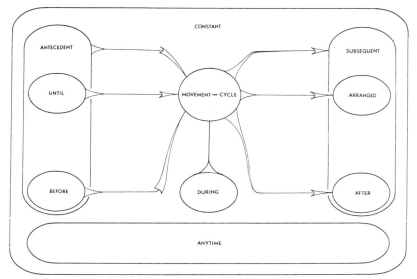

Figure 5.

elements of the equation—denoting that it is the context in which all others occur. Movement from left-to-right in the diagram is equivalent to movement through time. Antecedents, therefore, occur first, followed by the movement-cycle and changes during the movement-cycle; and finally the various subsequents are listed. Changes which may occur at any time, on the other hand, are represented in a box which extends from the extreme left to the extreme right—all through "time."

While time is represented in *horizontal* movement on the diagram, the *consistency* of relationship between each of the events and the movement-cycle is represented in the vertical. Changes which occur *until* the movement-cycle or are *arranged* by it demonstrate *necessarily* consistent relationships to the movement-cycle, and are represented in the same vertical plane. The constants, undifferentiated antecedents and subsequents, and changes which simply occur before, during, or after the movement-cycle are *not* necessarily consistent in their relationship to the movement-cycle (although, in any given analysis, they *may*), and are, therefore, represented in vertical planes just above or below the movement-cycle. Finally, changes which may occur at anytime are the least consistent in their relationship, and are described in a vertical plane *furthest* away from the movement-cycle. Notice that in both dimensions, in time and consistency of relationship, the center of analytic attention is always the behavior.

occurrence ratios

To classify an environmental change in terms of the temporal relationship it holds to the behavior does not necessarily mean that the change in question *must* occur in that position for *all* instances of behavior. It would be possible, for example, that a single occurrence of a change "before" be followed by *several* instances of the behavior. Similarly, any given instance of the behavior may be followed by several changes "after." Simply, the ratio of occurrence which obtains between the behavior and environmental changes need not be one-to-one.

The most rudimentary of ratio classifications could employ the modifiers "each" (or "one"), "many," and "all." If a modifier appeared *before* the word "change" in any change classification, then it would modify *that* term. If, on the other hand, the modifier appeared *following* the word "change," then it would modify the *referent* of that term— *behavior*. A change classified as "one change before each," therefore, would classify an environmental condition which always occurred once before each instance of the behavior. "One change after all" would denote a change in the environment which occurs once following the emission of all instances of the behavior. "Many changes until all" would classify an environmental change that occurs repeatedly until all instances of the behavior have been emitted. Alternatives, of course, could be found for the modifiers. The term "several" could be used, for example, instead of the term "many." The *position* of the modifiers, on the other hand, is governed by proper sentence construction.

The use of these simple modifiers preceding and following the temporal classification of changes increases the potential detail of a descriptive analysis immensely. Given that "changes always" are not amenable to this type of modification, there are eleven *simple* temporal classifications which may be made. With four options available in the use of modifiers (i.e., three modifiers plus the option *not* to use any) both before and after the temporal classification, the number of potential classifications increases to 144. Figure 6 demonstrates how this number is achieved.

Despite the added detail these modifiers afford, there is still a considerable amount of latitude in the specific meaning of the term "many," and, to a lesser extent, in the term "all." There will certainly be times when the exact ratio of occurrences is known, or at least may be estimated with a reasonable degree of accuracy. In these cases, the analyst should note that *specific* ratio in his description. The notational system employed may vary in accordance with the analyst's preferences, but the most common include use of a "slash" or a "colon." Take, for example, a case in which a factory worker is required to sort items according to "acceptable" or "unacceptable" quality. Each time an acceptable item is presented he is required to place it in a shipping crate; each time an unacceptable item is presented he is required to throw it in a bin marked "return." These conditions might be called simply "one change before

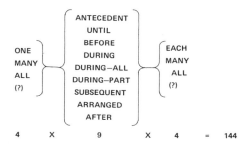

Figure 6.

205

each behavior." If, on the other hand, after every ten acceptable items the shipping crate is full and he is required to push it on to another worker, then the relationship between the circumstance of "acceptable item presented" and "crate pushing behavior" is ten items presented to each crate pushed. Using the colon, the ratios between changes and behaviors could be noted as follows:

change before	ratio	behavior	description
acceptable item presented	(1:1)	item placed in crate	one change before each behavior
item placed in crate	(10:1)	crate pushed on	many changes before each behavior

Note that in this example the necessary "change before" pushing the crate on was the behavior previously analyzed—putting the item in the crate. This is an excellent example of how one instance of behavior may function as a condition change for another instance of behavior. Note also that the "change before" pushing the crate on *could* have been defined as simply "crate full." Had this been the case, then the ratio between the change before and behavior would have been one-to-one. By specifying the components which comprise the condition of "crate full," however, greater detail is achieved in the analysis; and in most cases increased detail in description will result in a higher probability of an adequate functional analysis later. What would happen, for example, if the ratio were changed by increasing or decreasing the number of items which must be placed in the box (and, of course, altering the size of the box)? Had the conditions simply been called "crate full," then the possibility of altering that condition and specifying the nature of alteration in units of behavior might have been overlooked.

Any given ratio between changes in the environment and the behavior may occur purely accidentally or reflect an actual contingency. In the example of the factory worker, the changes in the environment and behavior were *necessarily* related—the behavior of putting an item in the crate could not occur until the "change before" of item presentation; and the behavior of pushing the crate away could not occur until ten "placing item in box" behaviors had occurred. There may be other events, however, that are not as easily classified as "necessary."

It could be the case, for example, that the factory foreman comes around to the worker after every ten or twelve crates have been filled and comments on the work. Unless it is certain that the foreman will *not* come around *unless* ten or twelve crates are full, however, the analyst could not classify that ratio as a *necessary* condition. The reader will remember that an "arranged change" was one that occurred after the behavior was emitted and was *caused* by the behavior (i.e., contingent upon it).

Therefore, whenever the ratio of occurrence between an environmental change and behavior is a necessary relationship reflecting causation or contingency, "arrangement" would appear to be an appropriate substitute for the word "ratio." An analysis of the factory worker's behavior would then be modified as follows:

One change before (item presentation) *arranges* one behavior (item in box); Ten changes before (item in box) *arranges* one behavior (push box on); Behavior (push box on) has a *ratio* of 10–12 to 1 with the change after (foreman).

(or)

item presentation	A(1:1)	place item in box
place item in box	A(10:1)	push box on
push box on	R(10–12:1)	foreman comes

It should be pointed out that *temporal* relationships may enter into ratios or arrangements. It could be, for example, that the foreman comes around once every thirty minutes—regardless of the worker's behavior. Such an arrangement could be noted in the "change anytime" box as "foreman comes regularly every thirty minutes." Similarly, it could be that the movement-cycle is "running the 100-yard dash" and the arranged event is contingent upon running it faster than before. This arrangement could be specified as:

$$A \ (TIME \quad LAST: 1)$$

In another case a researcher might want to investigate a fixed-interval schedule of reinforcement and specify the untested arrangement as:

$$A \ (1' + 1:1)$$

Since the minute is specified first, then that condition must be met first; and then the first response to follow will result in the arranged event.

In another case the arrangement may be progressive. Each time the arrangement is delivered, for example, one more movement is required than the time before:

$$A \ (\#_{t-1} + 1:1)$$

The specification of "t-1" is in reference to the last *time* that the arrangement was completed, and "#(t-1)+1" indicates that the number of movement-cycles required is the same as the number required last *plus one*.

Of course, where doubt exists that the notational system might be misinterpreted, then the actual requirements should be written out. In any event, one can see that the specification of an arrangement or ratio may take many forms.

basic analytic procedure

Earlier in this paper it was stated that the ultimate purpose of a science was to predict and/or control the phenomenon with which it was concerned. It was also noted, however, that in order to reliably and efficiently achieve this end, the phenomena in question should first be grouped and classified on the basis of common characteristics. Then, as more and more information is gained about the classified phenomena, the classification becomes more and more detailed until a functional level is attained. Even then, of course, functional levels may continue to become more and more refined—each step adding to the precision and certainty with which the prediction of outcome may be made. There are basically three procedural steps requisite to movement up the scale of classification—observation, alteration, and recording.

In the "observation" step the analyst observes the behavior in which he is interested and classifies the surrounding environmental events into their appropriate descriptive (i.e., physical and temporal) categories. Alternatively, in the purely experimental setting, the researcher would specify those conditions which would be allowed or made to happen in the first phase of research. Data are then collected to establish the value of the dependent variable under these conditions (e.g., rate of response). Generally this phase of operations is called a "reference phase"; and indeed, it will serve the function of providing a reference against which the affect of future alterations in conditions may be compared.[1]

In the "alteration" step the analyst changes some small part of the environment that is believed to control the behavior.[2] The change employed must be noted in a second descriptive analysis in order to completely document the nature of that change. The continuation of measuring the value of the dependent variable will then reflect the effect that change produced in the behavior—if any.

In the "recording" step the analyst records, in functional terminology, any of the environmental conditions which, when altered, affected the behavior. The procedures may then be repeated with several

---

[1] The first phase in an experiment is often called a "baseline." The use of that term denotes stability and/or predictability in the data, however, and should be used with some caution. See "baseline" and "phase, reference" in the main body of this Glossary for a fuller description of the differences between the two.

[2] Only small changes in the equation are made in each phase to avoid confusion as to which of several changes might have produced any given alteration in performances. If both the time of day and the material read in a reading project were changed at once, for example, then the alteration in performance might be ascribed to *either* change or the *combination* of the changes. Therefore, in order to separate the possible effects, the project would have to be repeated with each change made separately.

alterations, each providing more and more information and allowing, therefore, greater and greater detail to be achieved at the functional level of classification.

In fact, the actual procedures usually undertaken in formal experimentation are considerably more sophisticated and complicated than presented here. The confidence that one may have in the affect of a change made only once is relatively small. Nevertheless, in virtually all experimental procedures the steps of observation, alteration, and recording are followed in some multiple or context of other events. The interested reader is encouraged to read "methods of confirmation" in the main Glossary for a brief overview of the standard experimental paradigms employed in behavioral research.

The first descriptive classification, that which is done in the "observation" step, is generally called the "descriptive *analysis*" or "reference description." It is, simply, an analysis of what is already occurring in the environment. The second descriptive classification, performed in the "alteration" step, is generally called a "descriptive *plan*" or "change description." Here one does not analyze what *is* going on, but, rather, plans or describes what *will* happen. Finally, the translation of descriptive statements into functional terminology is called the "functional analysis"—since it involves the analysis of data for the determination of function. Other titles could, of course, be employed. For example, "observation analysis," "alteration plan," and "functional record" would serve just as well as the more formal titles given above. Regardless of the names one ascribes to them, however, it should be clear that *two* descriptive statements (one before and one after change) are required for each final functional statement—if one wishes to note procedure as opposed to simple result.

events and stimulus events

The purpose of this appendix was to present a system of classification which would enable the analyst to separate simple descriptive statements from those with functional denotations and still maintain a high degree of "detail." The relationships described up to this point could, however, apply equally well to both descriptive *and* functional classifications. While the analyst would normally resort to "traditional" classifications (e.g., "reinforcer") after function had been determined, it *would* be possible to simply retain the descriptive statements already constructed and add functional modifiers.

Up until now all changes in the environment have simply been called "changes." In most usages of behavioral terminology, however, distinctions are made between classes of changes called "events" and "stimulus events." An event is simply *any* change in the environment; whereas a *stimulus* event is any change in the environment that *alters the rate or probability of behavior* (i.e., it is an event that "stimulates" the organism in some manner). One *could* denote function, therefore, simply by the addition of the term "stimulus" to the appropriate descriptive classification. In general, this procedure of modification via the use of the term "stimulus" is in accord with accepted practice in basic behavioral terminology. The original term for an event which increases the rate or probability of the behavior which just precedes it, for example, was "reinforcing *stimulus* event." The original use of the term "stimulus" as the primary functional descriptor can probably be most easily seen in the abbreviations still used for the various elements of functional behavioral classifications:

discriminative stimulus = S^D or S^Δ ⎫
positive stimulus = S^+ ⎬ occur prior to the behavior
aversive stimulus = S^- ⎭

positive reinforcer = S^{R+} ⎫
⎬ occur after the behavior
negative reinforcer = S^{R-} ⎭

Note that in all cases, the basis for the abbreviation is "S" (for "stimulus"). Today, however, it is common to refer to the class of all functional *antecedents* as "stimuli"; and the class of all functional *subsequents* as "reinforcers."[3] This shortening of terms, while desirable from the standpoint of creating a "cleaner" and less clumsy language system, has at least one undesirable side-effect. Because the term "stimulus event" has been shortened to "stimulus" and connotes an *antecedent* condition, it would be ill-advised to refer to a "stimulus-constant." The former would connote change, and the latter consistency. To avoid this conflict of meanings, alternative descriptive and functional terms for the general and unchanging context in which the behavior occurs must be found. Borrowing once again from Waechter's system of descriptive analysis, the term "situation" would appear to be a reasonable choice for

---

[3] Although "reinforcer" is used to denote all effective stimulus events occurring after the emission of a behavior, there is one case in which that usage will lead to some confusion. A "reinforcer" is generally defined as any stimulus occurring after the response that increases the rate or probability of that response. A "negative" reinforcer (S^{R-}), on the other hand, will *decrease* the rate or probability of the behavior just preceding it. Despite its abbreviation, therefore, it is more properly called a "punisher" when used in that context. This is an excellent example of how two conventions may sometimes conflict with one another (e.g., classifying all functional subsequents as "reinforcers"; and defining all stimuli which increase the rate or probability of preceding behavior as "reinforcers" also).

the descriptive side of the equation, and "setting" for its functional counterpart. Both the formal denotations and usual connotations of those terms apply quite well to their intended uses.

Now the basic systems of descriptive and functional classifications are virtually identical with the exception of "constant" specification and the modifier "stimulus." Figures 7 and 8 show these two analyses in similar format for comparison.

The obvious advantage in having both functional and descriptive classifications based on the same construction lies in the reduction of terms the new behaviorist must learn. Considering the "investment" in time and literature spent on the development of the presently used system of functional classification, however, it is highly unlikely that the field as a whole will shift to this relatively new approach; and it cannot be denied that statements in this alternative functional classification system will be longer and generally more clumsy than before. Instead of "positive reinforcer," for example, the writer would have to say "accelerating stimulus event after." Nevertheless, there are potential uses for this system in the instruction of "applied behaviorists" like teachers, counselors, and therapists. This population of practitioners is generally not in a position to devote great amounts of their time in the development of sophisticated behavioral language skills; and *any* reduction or simplification in the material to be consumed would be of assistance.

how much to use and when?

An extremely flexible and detailed system of descriptive classification has been presented in this appendix in an effort to at least begin a trend toward more explicit and unambiguous differentiation between descriptive and functional statements. The correlation between this system and the previously developed systems of Lindsley and Waechter is easily determined, but beyond a shadow of a doubt this latest attempt is far more complex than either of its predecessors. Certainly the flexibility of this new system will be a delight to researchers and the most detailed of applied-situation investigators; but similarly, it could be rather superfluous for the teacher or counselor. In the sections which follow, therefore, an attempt will be made to outline a *series* of equations ranging from simplex to complex.

By presenting several descriptive classification systems with varying degrees of detail and complexity it is hoped that one may be found which

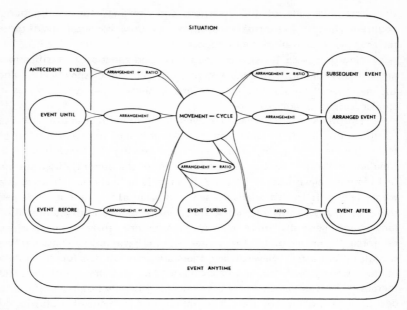

Figure 7.

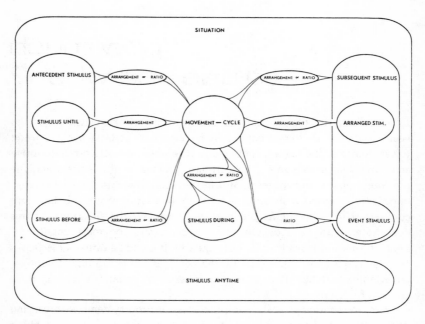

Figure 8.

meets exactly the needs of any given person. Since each level represents an expansion of the previous level, as opposed to an entirely different equation, it should also be relatively simple for the reader to "move up" to more complex descriptive classifications as the need arises.

Level One: The basic temporal relationships described by "antecedent" and "subsequent" event classifications, while not particularly detailed in terms of contingency and consistency of relationship to the behavior, nevertheless *do* represent the two most easily made classifications in event analysis. If care is taken to make the descriptions of the events in question as detailed and complete as possible, then most forms of behavior/environment interactions may be adequately classified with these two categories. See Figure 9.

Level Two: Other than the simple classification of events occurring antecedent and subsequent to the behavior, the single most important distinction which may be made in the classification of events is between "arranged events" and simple "events after." The importance of this distinction behaviorally is essentially the same as that which may be made between contingent and noncontingent reinforcement—the former has a much higher probability of generating and maintaining the behavior in question. See Figure 10.

Figure 9.

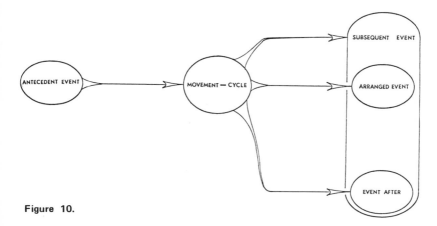

Figure 10.

213

Level Three: Having distinguished between arranged events and simple events after, the next logical expansion of the equation would be the addition of actual arrangement and/or ratio specification. One could start with the simple modifiers of "one or each," "many," and "all"; and then work up to numerical ratios when possible. See Figure 11.

Level Four: The addition of "situation" to the analysis would bring the equation up to a level of detail equivalent to the equations devised by Lindsley. See Figure 12.

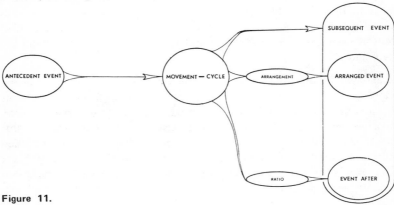

Figure 11.

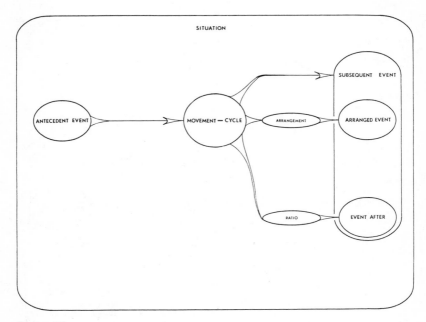

Figure 12.

Note: From here on the addition of terms to the equation is less easily sequenced. Rather than following any *specific* sequence, it would probably be wise for the trainer to choose those terms which are most immediately needed to obtain useful distinctions in the descriptive analyses desired. The following sequence of levels represents, therefore, only one of literally twenty-four possible sequences of equation expansion.

Level Five: Expanding the classification of antecedent events into events "until" and events "before" would in most cases represent the next most needed improvement. See Figure 13.

Level Six: The addition of "event during" to the classification system would permit the analyst to note instances of potential conjugate reinforcement or response-dependent discriminative stimulation. See Figure 14.

Level Seven: The addition of a specific provision for noting ratios or arrangements between each of the events and the movement-cycle, while less often required than the specification of the events themselves, will add considerable detail to the analysis. As in the case with the arranged event, the ratios and arrangements may be first specified as "one or each," "many," and "all"; and eventually stated numerically. See Figure 15.

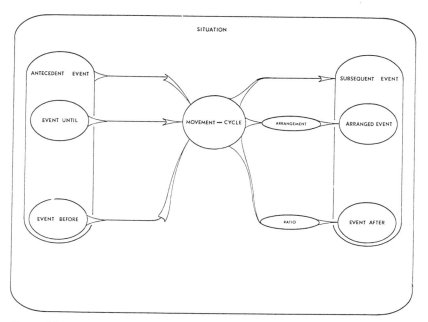

Figure 13.

Level Eight: Although rarely needed, the classification of "event any-time" can finally be added to allow the classification of those regular or irregular events which are entirely independent of the occurrence of the movement-cycle, but which may, in fact, affect it. See Figure 16.

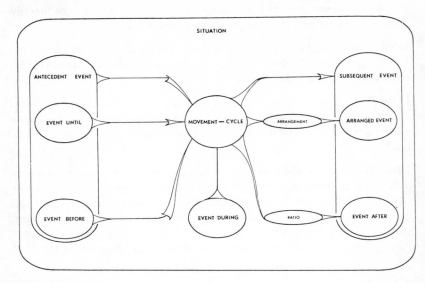

Figure 14.

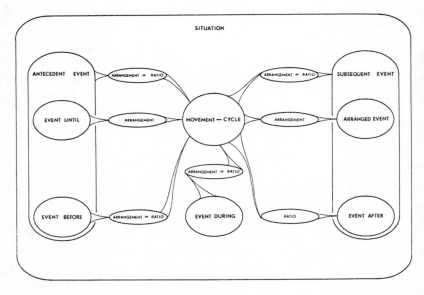

Figure 15.

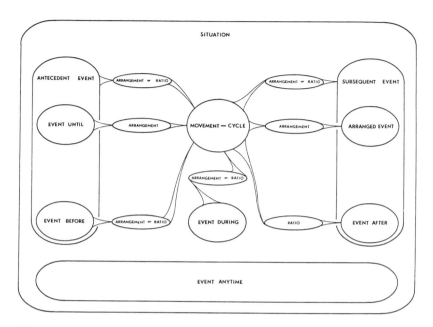

Figure 16.

the final analysis

Following is a flow-chart of sorts which illustrates the procedures one might employ in the classification of environmental phenomena in descriptive and functional categories. Since the choice at any level may be made by simply checking the appropriate term, a similar list could be constructed on a computer sheet to facilitate information storage and collation. See Figure 17.

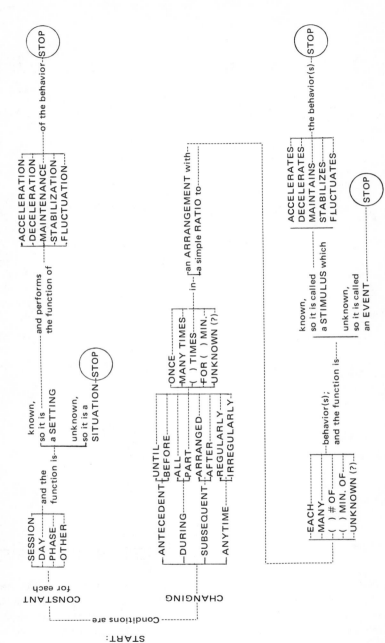

Figure 17.

in conclusion

This appendix represents an attempt to examine and collate the information and thought known to this writer regarding the need and possible construction of a system of descriptive classification. It represents only a small portion of the problems facing the continued development of behavioral terminology; but certainly not an *insignificant* portion. If the content of this appendix has been adequately prepared, then the reader should now be aware of three things: *why* a descriptive classification system is needed; *when* such a system should be used; and *how* such a system might be constructed.

Ultimately a system of descriptive classification *must* be standardized and recognized as such by the field as a whole. Without such recognition, communication will suffer immensely. Inasmuch as the specific needs of individuals will vary in accordance with the area in which they work and bias their preference for one system over another, it would be foolish to assume that the system presented here will satisfy everyone equally. Only use and publication will eventually lead to the emergence of a system of demonstrated appeal and applicability. It is hoped, however, that certain aims in construction will be noted—simplicity, orientation toward behavior, and flexibility.

Without a commitment to simplicity, the behavioral language as we know it will continue to divide into phrases and terms limited in application to those who originate them. The terms should be *understandable*—immediately and fully—to anyone with minimal comprehension of basic analytic considerations.

Orientation toward the behavior will insure that a certain correlation exists between the already established system of functional analysis and any new attempt at description. It will further allow certain reductions to be made in the number of words necessary for classification. It is not necessary to call an event an "event after the behavior," for example, if it is understood that all modifiers like "after" are *always* in reference to the behavior. "Event after" will suffice.

Assuming that not all possible phenomena have been investigated and labeled as yet, flexibility in classification is essential. Instead of having to derive a completely new term to classify a new set of conditions and changes, one should only have to rearrange descriptors presently available. For this purpose the distinctions between "constants" and "changes," and "stimuli" and "events" are particularly useful. When used in conjunction with temporal, contingent, and functional modifiers, they allow an almost unlimited number of classifications to be formed. The specification of additional parameters (e.g., intensity, and locus) could, of course, be added to the system of existing modifiers for even greater flexibility.

Lastly, the choice of term or system of classification should not be based on a desire to sound "impressive," to create a new "jargon," or to immortalize one's name. Too many language systems have been developed already just for the sake of being different. Before creating a new system of classification or employing a new set of modifiers, therefore, the reader is encouraged to carefully determine whether or not it represents a *contribution* or merely another *alternative* to some existing system or term. If it is really more understandable, more flexible, and simpler, then *use* it; if not, then use what's already available.

DATE DUE